WALKING
POINT

WALKING
POINT

CHIEF JAMES WATSON
with KEVIN DOCKERY

WALKING POINT

THE EXPERIENCES OF A
FOUNDING MEMBER OF
THE ELITE NAVY
SEALs

WILLIAM MORROW AND COMPANY, INC.

NEW YORK

Library of Congress Cataloging-in-Publication Data

Watson, James, Chief.
    Walking point : the experiences of a founding member of the elite Navy SEALs / James Watson with Kevin Dockery. — 1st ed.
      p.   cm.
    ISBN 0-688-14302-4
    1. Watson, James, Chief. 2. United States. Navy. SEALs—History. 3. United States. Navy—Biography. I. Dockery, Kevin. II. Title
VG87.W38   1997
359.9—dc20   96-31032
                                                     CIP

THIS BOOK IS DEDICATED TO MY DAUGHTER
SAMANTHA WATSON VANDEVOORD
—WELCOME BACK—
AND
IN MEMORY OF MY MOTHER,
ANNA WATSON,
AND MY SON JOE,
WHO NEVER HAD A CHANCE TO ENJOY LIFE

Contents

WALKING POINT

CHAPTER 1

Training, Travel, and MTTs

T RAINING WAS SOMETHING WE DID on almost a constant basis at the SEAL Teams, or to us just "the Teams." Learning the wide variety of skills and knowledge needed by the SEALs in order to complete their missions was something that was never ending. Team members would constantly be attending different classes, developing skills that had never officially been part of the Navy before, and then bringing their new knowledge back to the Teams for testing and evaluation. If a class was determined to be valuable enough, it was officially incorporated into the Team's schedule. Other skills would be considered either not useful enough to be worth the time, or better able to be taught to the Team by teammates rather than by sending men to a formal school or course.

It has long been known that the best way to learn a skill completely is to have to teach it to others. SEALs who attended a particular school would share what they knew with the rest of the Team, so that additional men didn't have to be sent to the regular school. This worked very well in some situations, especially those where the knowledge could be taught in the field in a hands-on way, which was called OJT or "on-the-job training" in military parlance. After attending Army Ranger School, I felt that this was an example of a course that had valuable information of use to the SEALs, but something that could be better taught within the Teams by a number of SEALs who were well trained in the subject.

The Teams would sometimes send groups of SEALs and UDT men to other countries in order to teach their naval forces how to operate in, and under, the water. After the SEALs were commissioned, this became an important part of the overall SEAL mission. All of the services' Special Forces units had been ordered by President John Kennedy to be able to fight in a guerrilla-style war, as demanded by the cold war. They were also to be able to teach indigenous (native) forces how to conduct their own antiguerrilla campaigns.

The Army Special Forces were the premiere military unit tasked with the instruction of foreign services. A basic Green Beret A-Team is officially a twelve-man unit trained and equipped to raise an eighteen-hundred-man guerrilla organization behind enemy lines during time of war. In actual operations at firebases in Vietnam, I never met an A-Team that had more than six guys, only one being an officer—an example of the difference between "the book" and the real world.

In spite of the strong protestations from the Army that we were "encroaching on their territory," the SEALs' part in this type of training was spelled out in Naval Warfare Information Publication (NWIP) 29–1, published in December 1962. NWIP 29–1 stated what our mission was during "direct conflict with an enemy" (read that as during a flat-out war); it also described what the SEALs' antiguerrilla mission was going to be in the dirtier world of the cold war.

Only recently declassified, a condensed version of what NWIP 29–1 stated as part of the SEAL mission is as follows:

> To accomplish limited counterinsurgency civic action tasks that are normally incidental to counterguerrilla operations. Possibilities include medical aid, elementary civil engineering activities, boat operations and maintenance and basic education of the indigenous population.
>
> To organize, train, assist, and advise the United States, Allied, and other friendly military or paramilitary forces in the conduct of any of the above tasks.

To follow these directives of NWIP 29–1, the SEALs assigned MTTs, or Mobile Training Teams, to undertake the training of foreign forces in their own countries. The SEAL Teams had MTTs in Vietnam within a few months of their commissioning, teaching the South Vietnamese clandestine maritime operations. Both SEAL Team One and Team Two had people operating in Vietnam, and the Teams also sent MTTs to other parts of the world to conduct training with our allies.

On January 8, 1963, a year to the day after the formation of SEAL Team Two, a group of us left for Ankara, Turkey, as MTT 1–63. As part of the Joint U.S. Military Mission for Aid to Turkey (JUSMMAT), we would be training a group of Turkish naval ratings in UDT and SEAL operations. After we helped establish a solid cadre of trained Turkish naval personnel, the Turks would run their own UDT training program and operate as part of the NATO forces in the eastern Mediterranean. This was going to be my first major opportunity to act as a UDT/SEAL instructor and I was looking forward to it.

The whole mission was a supersecret one, and none of us knew where exactly we were heading before we took off on the trip. Bob "the Eagle" Gallagher, who was the leading petty officer of the MTT, had already left for Turkey some time before the rest of us. Bob acted as the advance party to set up transportation, pick training sites, and generally make everything ready for us to begin training as soon as we arrived incountry.

The whole UDT/SEAL training idea for the Turkish mission was under the control of a mustang lieutenant (an officer who had come up from the enlisted ranks) in Ankara, Turkey, but none of us plain workingmen knew anything about that. What we did know was that we couldn't tell anyone about where we were going on our mission, not our families or even our teammates. We found out later on that another MTT had gone over to Greece at about the same time and was training Greek Special Forces soldiers in roughly the same skills we were teaching the Turks—all of this shortly before Cyprus exploded in civil war between the Greek and Turkish Cypriots in December 1963. This explained the need for secrecy.

Along with Jose Taylor, as the officer in charge (OIC), five of us—Don Wayne "Wayno" Boles, Doc "Leg" Martin, Bob Stamey,

John Tegg, and myself—all left on a civilian aircraft to begin our trip to Turkey. Jose was an officer but had come up through the ranks as a mustang and was just one of the guys. Our gear had been shipped to Bob Gallagher at JUSMMAT and we were taking our personal clothes and materials. We were traveling under a Class II priority, which made it easy for us to get whatever seats might be available, and our orders allowed us sixty-five pounds of baggage each and authorized an additional two hundred pounds of excess baggage if we needed it. However, as sailors and SEALs, we knew how to travel light and fast. Our orders really started making the trip worthwhile right at the start.

The travel orders we had were pretty open, to say the least. "On or about 10 January, 1963 [we were to] proceed to Ankara, Turkey . . . and such other places as may be necessary in the execution of these orders in connection with naval matters. . . . You are authorized to vary the order of any visit, or re-visit such places as may be necessary in the execution of these orders." The orders were signed by J. F. Callahan, Jr. (the first commanding officer of SEAL Team Two).

In addition to what was a free ticket to the world in the form of our orders, we were also authorized to draw an advance per diem of thirty days at fifteen dollars per day for expenses. This was traveling SEAL style, a privilege that we never abused, though we did take advantage of it.

It did take us a while to get to Ankara, at least a few days, maybe a week. Stopovers in London and Frankfurt were made in accordance with our orders, solely for us to get the lay of the land and understand the natives better. Later on we learned that some Navy captain in Ankara was getting just a little nervous about our taking so long to get to Turkey.

"Where are the men?" he asked Bob Gallagher. "Just where are the men? They were supposed to be here yesterday! You and your detachment are supposed to be getting down to Arzuz and setting up your training program. Do you have their itinerary? Do you have any idea when they're getting here?"

Bob wasn't quite as worried about our taking so long as the

Navy officer: he'd seen the orders and noticed the plush European locations that were on our list of stopovers. "Shit, sir," he said, "you'll see those guys when they run out of per diem."

We were just about out of money when we finally arrived in Ankara. Bob met us and gathered his wandering flock about him at a hotel in Ankara. He was pretty well whipped when we saw him; he had just driven over from our base in Arzuz. The trip was about an eight- to ten-hour drive over the Taurus Mountains on a road that was first laid down by Alexander the Great.

Driving that distance was quite a chore. First off, it was a dirt road, improved over what Alexander had left but still not very comfortable. Drivers' behavior on bridges demonstrated part of the attitude of the Turks and where it came from. When you came to a bridge, you usually found it was a single-lane affair. If two vehicles approached the bridge from opposite ends at the same time, the driver who turned his headlights on first had the right-of-way. It was an officially recognized game of chicken, on a bridge over a whole lot of nothing. We learned that game real fast. This was going to be a fun country to operate in.

We arrived at the hotel we were going to stay at during the short time we were in Ankara. Bob Gallagher turned in early and left us to our own devices after telling us the lay of the land. We were ready to party again. *Merhaba* is hello in Turkish and we didn't need much more than that, so off we went to the bar in the hotel.

We were all authorized to pack weapons while in Turkey, but we hadn't been able to reach our gear yet. Bob had been carrying a .45 in his belt at the small of his back when he picked us up and moved us to the hotel. There was dissension in the population of Turkey at the time and a good deal of the trouble could be found in Ankara. Since we were at a hotel and Bob had turned in, none of us thought anything more about the dangers of the situation.

In the bar, we started buying Turkish booze, and I bought it pretty heavy for this one chick I had my eye on. For myself, I did well with the local beer. The local favorite tipple was Raki, fairly deadly stuff that came in a container about the size of a Coke bottle. The clear liquid that came out of the Raki bottle would be mixed with a glass of water for drinking. To the Turks, this stuff was called Aslan Sūt, "Lion's Milk," and God bless the man who could go through a whole bottle of the stuff. Lion's Milk tasted a bit like licorice and would turn your eyeballs into a red road map with just a few drinks.

While learning about Turkey and the native habits, I was putting the moves on this lady and apparently wasn't doing a bad job. She wanted to know my room number, and I started borrowing money from Jose and anybody else who hadn't gone through the per diem yet.

When it came time for the bar to close up, my local honey was gone. She had done her job—she'd taken the Amerikanim for all the money she could get—and split. I was disappointed, and Jose, who had been drinking right along with us, just plain got pissed.

"We're going to take this place apart, Jim," Jose said. "Nobody screws over one of us. We'll teach these Turks a lesson."

The next thing we knew, about a dozen Turks had us backed up into a corner. One or more of them obviously understood English and they wanted to make us eat our words. I believe it was Doc Martin who got to a hotel phone and called Bob Gallagher.

"Get down here now!" Doc said. "We're backed into a corner."

True to form, Bob showed up before things got completely out of hand and we had to beat up those poor ignorant Turks. After all, they didn't know they were messing with the Navy SEALs. But Bob showed up with his .45 in hand, hollering something in Turkish. The locals suddenly decided somewhere else was the place to be and vacated the area. That was my first experience in Turkey.

Afterward, we all went up to our rooms and turned in. The next day, we went over to JUSMMAT and finally checked in with the lieutenant who had been bugging Gallagher about where we were. On top of meeting the lieutenant, we had to go through a whole program of meeting all of the high-ranking U.S. Navy officials and Turkish officers before we could draw our vehicles and some equipment, and finally get on the road out of town.

To travel along this road, JUSMMAT gave us several three-quarter-ton weapons carriers. These vehicles, a cross between a jeep and a small truck, looked like they had been around since World War II. Simply put, they were big, ugly, uncomfortable pieces of shit. But the powers that were letting us draw them insisted that they were "mechanically sound." So off we went, to the southeast from Ankara.

Most of our gear came in at Iskenderun, way the-hell-and-gone over the Taurus Mountains from Ankara, and that still wasn't our final destination. Another forty miles south of Iskenderun was our base camp, just outside the small village of Arzuz, right on the Syrian border.

Arzuz was about as far from anywhere as I had ever been. It seemed that there had been more people in Greenland, north of the Arctic Circle, when I was on deployment in UDT 21 than there were around here. Most of the native population around the compound consisted of sheep and goats. The Syrians weren't exactly our best friends at the time, and not eighty miles offshore was Cyprus, where the Turks and the Greeks had been butting heads for the last couple of thousand years.

Nice neighborhood, but at least in Iskenderun we were able to pick up our personal weapons. Along with our weapons, we picked up the rest of our gear, such as the large pyramid tents, cots, sleeping gear, rubber boats, and all of the other things we were going to need to set up a training program.

The area we would be training in was right in the bay of Iskenderun, the most eastern point of the Mediterranean Sea. The village of Arzuz was at the base of a mountain range that rose up almost right from the shore of the Mediterranean. The scrub brush and grass grew down to the shore and the rocky beach was flat—not exactly the kind of place you'd expect to see used as a backdrop for a California beach movie. Little streams and creeks led from the hills into the water. And that water was cold.

The first thing we thought about when we saw the area was the temperature of the water. No wet suits or thermal protection of any kind was available for our students, or ourselves for that matter.

So much for the sunny Mediterranean. On top of the general problems we were expecting to have with foreign students, now we looked forward to just trying to get the guys into the water.

Setting up our camp was a quick chore. We lived in a sixteen-by-thirty-four-foot tent and the Turks lived in a number of tents they had brought with them. Our corpsman, Doc Martin, had brought a load of medical supplies with him, enough to support 200 men for eight months, according to the manuals. Grabbing one of the Turkish tents, Doc quickly set up a small infirmary for the students. We had been told to expect from 100 to 150 students in the first class. Doc was not going to get caught short.

The first few days were mostly spent getting our own house in order. A couple of steel CONEX boxes (lockable shipping containers) acted as our supply sheds and arms room. We had brought a number of weapons with us and spent some time checking them out. Along with Smith & Wesson Combat Masterpiece revolvers as sidearms, we had a number of M3A1 .45-caliber greaseguns and several new AR-15 rifles. Along with our M3A1 greaseguns, we had a couple of suppressed models with OSS silencers from World War II. Not exactly an impressive arsenal, but one that managed to make us feel much more comfortable.

Soon after we had set up, along came our Turkish students. A lot of time was spent during those first days running back and forth between town and our base, getting everything lined up for our students and ironing out the inevitable last-minute problems. The senior student in charge was a young officer named Tanguch. From what I understand, Tanguch is still an officer in the Soualty Commandos and is presently a captain or admiral.

Along with Tanguch, we had a number of Turkish Navy chiefs to help ride herd on the remainder of the students. The number of high-ranking and quality personnel sent to us by the Turks reflected the importance of our mission. We were to do more than just set up a Turkish UDT school; our tasking included teaching the men how to dive and parachute and, above all, how to teach what we were teaching them. These men would be responsible for instructing future Turkish UDT classes, and we were going to make sure that they measured up right from the beginning.

Not speaking Turkish, we had a few interpreters available. One interpreter was assigned to us from higher command and one of the Turkish officer/students also spoke English. This was enough to get us started in training, and we began with physical training, good old PT. The same thing we'd started every day with at the SEAL base back at Little Creek, Virginia.

Rudy Boesch, chief of SEAL Team Two, would have been proud. We ran the Turks ragged, and they loved it for the most part. These guys absolutely wanted to be like the American frogmen they had heard so much about. They wanted everything we planned to dish out to them and more.

Within our first week, we were running PT in Turkish. None of us could speak the language very well—Bob Gallagher spoke it the best of any of us—but we soon learned how to say, "The next exercise will be . . ." And our students followed along. We rotated leading PT among ourselves, and quickly got past using the three instructors at a time that we started out with.

Along with the PT and light swimming we were doing in our Phase One training, we also ran some hand-to-hand combat classes. Nothing fancy, just some basic judo throws, how to defend against a knife, how to take a weapon from a man, things like that. Some of the pictures we have of the mission show Turkish students demonstrating what we had shown them to a bunch of high-ranking Turkish officers, and this was within just a few weeks of our beginning instruction.

One thing that the Turks stayed right with the Americans on was the cutting down of class size during UDT training. We started with about 120 Turkish students and winnowed them down to about 20 to 25 students before we even started Hell Week. All of this nonsense you hear about how big and bad the Turks are, how you have to kill them in order to make them quit, is just stories. The Turks are just as human as you or I, and can get just as tired or cold as any of us.

What we did learn about early on was how the Turkish military was run at that time, and may still be, for all I know. The basic leadership technique in the Turkish military is to control the men through fear. A Turkish *asker* (pronounced ah-SKAYER) or trooper, what we would call a seaman, can never better himself in the military. The *asker* is drafted for four years and is at the very bottom of the ladder; serving as cannon fodder and doing grunt work are the most he can expect from his military career.

The Turkish high school graduate is in a much better position; he's petty officer material and he will be ranked as such when he enters the military. A Turkish officer has some education beyond high school and probably more than a few family connections.

For an *asker* in the Turkish military, life is hard. If he screws up—and we all do at one time or another—and if the mistake is serious enough, a petty officer can kill the *asker* on the spot, as long as he has a witness to the original mistake. An officer in the same situation doesn't even need the witness.

When we caught an *asker* stealing cigarettes from our instructors' tent, we learned just how rough Turkish military justice could be. After the students were done working the *asker* over, he was turned over to the authorities for some jail time. And believe me, you never want to spend time in a Turkish jail. When an imprisoned *asker* finally got out of jail, his enlistment time began again from day one and he would have four years to go. The *asker* we caught was within a couple of months of the end of his enlistment, and as soon as he got out of jail, his tour started all over again.

Our life wasn't quite as rough as that lived by the *askers* in the Turkish military. In fact, our camp was reasonably comfortable. The Turks lived in their tents; our cadre had a large tent set up for our use. And we even had a small cookshed with a roofed-over open-sided area attached to it for eating under cover. There were some portable generators included in our equipment, so we had refrigeration available for the cookshed.

For chow, we were eating Turkish food right alongside our students. In a little village nearby, there was a *cay* (CHA-ee) or tea shop where we could get some local chow that we didn't have to cook ourselves. There were a few chickens walking about, but the Turkish menu in the shop didn't have anything like fried chicken on it. The local Turkish diet seemed to consist mostly of grease and beans, with very little meat. If a local got a piece of meat the size of a McDonald's hamburger—and I'm not talking about a quarter-pounder here—a couple of times a week, he was at the top of the local food chain.

For ourselves, we were eating a lot of *yurmurta* (yoo-moor-TA)—that's eggs and *ekmek* (ek-MEK) bread—on the local economy. There were rations being sent to us, for both ourselves and the students, but these were rationed rations. Supposedly, we were receiving double rations, but you couldn't tell that by the amount we had to eat. The locals were practically wringing the eggs out of their chickens to supply the demand we were putting on the menu at the tea shop. The little local bakery was working overtime turning out bread for us, and I must say that it was damned good bread.

As far as the Turks were concerned, American bread just wasn't any good. You could take a whole loaf of it and just squash it in your hand down to the size of a bun. The local flatbread was substantial and made good eating. The funny thing is that now people are talking about getting away from the white bread we've been eating for so long and returning to a more basic bread with better nutrition. The Turks knew that and were telling us over thirty years ago. Besides that, you could take a loaf of Turkish bread and use it as a five-inch projectile. Hit somebody with that sucker at velocity and you'd kill him for sure.

We had a few support personnel, mostly *askers,* running things at the cookshed and around the camp. One incident at the cookshed illustrated life for the *askers* in the Turkish military better than anything else we saw while in Turkey. The refrigerators we had in the cookshed weren't grounded properly, but they didn't belong to us and we weren't supposed to mess with anything belonging to the Turks. Bob Gallagher warned the *askers* about the danger of working with the refrigerators, but the warning just didn't take hold. One young kid grabbed the refrigerator door while he was standing in a pool of water and just fried himself. The juice flowed right through that kid and killed him on the spot.

As far as the Turks were concerned, this event was no big deal. They buried the kid and just wanted to continue training. No notification to his family or anything. It was the Turkish way; when a kid left his family after he got drafted, they never expected to see him again. But this wasn't the way we operated, and we notified the family.

By this time, training was going pretty well. Doc Martin had set up sick call, opening up his tent to the locals, starting a couple of days each week. It wasn't long before the local demand had Doc running sick call for the Turks almost every day. One time, we had a guy walk in with a kid who couldn't have been more than five years old. The kid had his arm all wrapped up in rags and was badly hurt. We found out later that this pair had walked to our camp for four days, coming down from the mountains, because the guy had heard that there was an American doctor available.

Doc unwrapped the kid's arm and found he had a compound fracture of the forearm. The bone was sticking out of the skin and infection had set in big time. A mess isn't the word for what we found underneath that bundle of rags.

We took the kid into the little sick bay Doc had set up. There were bunks in the tent so that some patients could lay up and recuperate. And Doc Martin cured that kid's infection and saved his life. Trouble was, the infection was only part of the problem; the break still had to be dealt with, and Doc just wasn't set up for that sort of operation. We had to get the kid into a real hospital, and soon, or he could lose the arm.

In Turkey, the military owned the hospitals, and the military didn't have a lot of use for the local civilians—especially not some goat-herding kid down from the mountains. Bob Gallagher and Jose Taylor sent Wayne Boles and me, along with one of our student interpreters, to the local hospital along with the kid. We literally shamed those people at the hospital into taking in that Turkish kid and treating his arm. He needed surgery and we were going to see that he got it.

We finally had to get back to camp and continue our classes. But years later we found out that the kid had made it, which was no small surprise. That hospital hadn't been like one of ours back in the States. In the Navy, we have sculleries, where the garbage from the chow halls is put, that is cleaner than that hospital. Join the Navy and see the world, and learn to appreciate what we have back here at home.

Now we were going to start jump-training our students. We went up to Incirlik, a thirty-five-hundred-acre U.S. air base ten miles east of Adana, taking with us the free-fall jump rigs we had brought from the States. Jose Taylor was a real balls-to-the-wall type of officer and he was going to see to it that we could jump from the first plane available. Our orders read that we could jump from basically anything that could fly, so whatever was available was fine with him.

At the time I went to Turkey, I was not free-fall qualified. The only two men in the detachment who were free-fall qualified were Bob Gallagher and Wayne Boles. But when we came back to the States, we were all free-fall qualified. All we had to jump with was free-fall rigs, so the detachment became free-fall qualified, no problem.

We did have some slight problem with the Air Force in Turkey. Seems the fly-boys didn't feel we had the proper authorization to use one of their planes. Jose got pissed fairly quickly at this chicken-shit attitude. "You want clearance?" Jose asked. "I'll get you clearance." And he picked up the phone and called NAVEUROPE. NAVEUROPE was the European Navy Command and was as high as you could go in the chain of command we were in without calling the Pentagon itself.

Whom Jose talked to, I just don't know. But before we left the air base, some colonel was all over Jose telling him, "You just let us know whenever you want this Gooney Bird [DC-3] and we'll jump you." Big change in attitude when the orders come down from the top.

Things got funnier even later in our training period. We were driving around in black jeeps with JUSMMAT in big white letters all over them, so we were visible a mile away. When we came onto the air base, it didn't matter where we went or how we parked, it wasn't very long before some Air Force guy would show up and ask us, "Are you ready to jump today? Do you want us to fly you now?"

Jose may not have had the authority to do what he did, but once you start with something like that, you can't back down. Whatever it was that he stirred up, it sure shook up the fly-boys.

Back at Arzuz, class work continued while the rest of us set up the planes and whatever else we would need for the later phases of training. Swimming went along pretty well, but we literally had to throw our students into the water to get them started. And I'm not saying that as a joke. The water was cold and those Turks were not keen on getting wet in it. Once they were in, everything was fine. But to get them into the water took the old heave-ho from the instructors—not exactly our usual insertion technique.

As training progressed, it finally became time to give our Turks Hell Week. Back in Underwater Demolition Team Replacement (UDTR) training at Little Creek and in Coronado, California, Hell Week was the biggest single hurdle that had to be overcome by future UDT or SEAL operators. Six days straight of maximum physical output and minimum sleep. Twenty-three-hour days were the norm during Hell Week back in the States, but to make sure the trainees were kept safe, the instructors worked only eight-hour shifts to keep themselves sharp.

We couldn't do the whole of Hell Week like we did back at the Creek, so we did what was possible. From sunup to sundown, we ran our Turks' asses ragged, set off half-pound TNT charges, and really made them work. Our students got one hell of a lot more sleep than we did during our Hell Week. The simple fact was that there were just too few instructors, and we needed to get some sleep in order to stay sharp enough to keep things safe. The Turks may have had a slightly different attitude toward training losses, but we were the ones who would have had to explain any loss to our own bosses back at Little Creek.

Every once in a while, a couple of us would get up in the middle of the night, wake up the students, and put them through their paces. Altogether, things were going pretty well. The men were shaping up from the PT, swimming was improving, and the classes in hand-to-hand were coming along. We tried to get some extra swim fins for our students, but that proved to be a problem with the higher-ups in Supply. Finally, the fins showed up, but as far as wet suits went, forget it. There just weren't any to be had in Turkey. Our students were going to be cold in the water and stay that way.

We had brought an IBS (Inflatable Boat, Small) or two with us from the States. Now we were going to start teaching the men cast and recovery, the traditional way a UDT man exited a boat by slipping over the side, and was later picked up at speed by sticking his arm through a sling and being pulled back aboard. To do that, first we had to get hold of a good, reliable boat to attach the IBS to. What they sent us floated, but I would hardly describe it as a boat. And the rig they had set up was really hard to use for cast and recoveries. From where the coxswain sat in the boat, you would lose sight of the swimmers in the water while they were still twenty yards away from the pickup point. The bow of the boat was just too high, but there was nothing we could do about the basic design of the craft.

Bob Gallagher turned to me and asked, "Jim, can we play games with this, and can you run that boat?"

The fact was that we were not about to let a Turk run the pickup boat. If we plowed over and killed a student, that would be all she wrote for us. I told Bob that we could do the job with what we had, but that some serious cooperation was going to be needed.

Wayne Boles, John Tegg, Bob Stamey, Doc Martin, and Bob Gallagher were all involved with our cast and recovery training. Gallagher acted as the snare man while I ran the boat. We set up a marker so that I would know just where the student was and could steer the boat to where Gallagher could reach the swimmer with his snare. I wasn't able to see the swimmer for the last twenty yards of the run, and that was hairy.

We did not use a student for a pickup until we had the system down pat. All the instructors got into the water on this one, much to everyone's joy. But when we finally got everything together, the system worked out fine. The golden rule was that we would not attempt a training evolution with our students until we had worked out everything for ourselves, including all the details that could go wrong.

The students really got a charge out of cast and recovery. After we taught the Turkish snare man how to operate, things went even more smoothly, as Bob Gallagher could now help make sure the boat stayed lined up with the swimmers in the water. Our students were happy, and now Hell Week was over, which might have been what they were really happy about.

The next phase of training was demolitions, but there was no equipment problem with that. The explosives we had been using for Hell Week were part of a supply Bob had sent me to get earlier. Now we had plenty to use in teaching the students how to make their own charges. Bob had put me in charge of obtaining the necessary supplies on one of our trips to the air base at Incirlik.

We had a permit from JUSMMAT for what could only be described as a limited amount of explosives. The list allowed us one case—fifty pounds—of half-pound TNT blocks, one twenty-pound haversack, a handful of blasting caps, one roll each of time fuzes and primacord, a couple of fuze igniters, enough powder to maybe go fishing, and not much more than that.

The air base we were being supplied from was the same one that Francis Gary Powers had flown out of when his U-2 was shot down over Russia in 1960. Security at such a place is tight, and that didn't make my orders from Gallagher any easier to carry out.

"All right," Bob said to me, "you leave early in the morning and take the weapons carrier." Now the carrier had a cover over the back end to protect any cargo, and to hide it from view as well. "I don't care how you do it, Jim," he continued, "beg, borrow, or steal, but I want the springs on that carrier bottomed out from the weight of everything you bring back from the base. And screw the list. You're a UDT man [we still didn't call ourselves SEALs very often] and you get the job done."

What could I say? The Eagle had spoken. Off to the air base I went. Arriving at the base, I showed my authorization to the sergeant in charge of the ammunition bunkers. The paperwork was in order—after all, we were authorized to get some explosives—and the sergeant assigned a young airman to assist me.

Driving out to the bunker area, I talked to the kid, who was riding in the truck with me. After only a few questions, I realized that this kid was so green you could mow him like a lawn. He didn't know shit from shinola as far as explosives went, and this was my chance to fill Bob's shopping list. *Wahoo, it's payday!*

"You know what you're supposed to get, don't you" the kid asked trustingly.

Putting on my best understanding tone, I answered, "Of course I do, son, no problem. First, we have to go to the bunker where the TNT is." And off we went to the different magazines.

As we traveled along, I just threw cases into the truck and hoped my luck didn't run out. Boxes of TNT, primacord, time fuzes, haversacks, even a couple of shaped charges all went into the back of the truck. It was a three-quarter-ton truck that I was loading but I think I got about two tons into it. Once the tarp was tied down and everything was secured, however, I still needed to pick up one more item.

"All right," I asked the airman, "where do we get the caps?"

"What?" he asked incredulously.

"Blasting caps," I said. "I need to have some blasting caps to go with all of this stuff. At least a couple of boxes of them."

"But you'll have to have another vehicle for them," the kid said.

Actually, the boy wasn't all that stupid. You do not normally transport blasting caps along with the main explosives the caps are meant to set off. That helps avoid accidents and having to fill in big holes in the roads. But I wasn't going to be able to do things like that. If I came back for another load, I would probably get caught for what I took the first time. Being ballsy can get the job done; being greedy can get you caught.

"Look, son," I said, "we have to treat this situation like a combat mission. We're operating under a different set of rules here and this is the only truck I've got."

The kid folded, and off we went to the magazine where the caps were stored. Grabbing several boxes of caps, fifty caps to the box, I turned to the truck. "Where are you going to put the caps?" the kid asked.

"In the glove compartment," I answered. "That way they're not in back with the rest of the stuff, are they?"

Now we were headed back to the main gate that secured the magazine area from the rest of the base. "Pull in over there by the gate," the kid said, "and I'll go in and get you your red flags and Turkish 'Explosives' signs."

"Bullshit," I said. "I'm not traveling all the way back to my base right away. I don't know what it's like for you based here, but I don't get a chance to eat American food very often. It's about four-thirty now and I'm going over to the NCO club and getting myself a steak."

"But what are you going to do with the truck?" he asked.

"Park it in the fucking parking lot," I answered. "What the hell do you think I'm going to do with it? And if you tell anyone about it, I'll tear your head off!"

The poor kid turned white as a sheet and could only say "Yes, sir!" to my little tirade.

Once at the NCO club, I just walked in, sat down, and ordered some food and a beer. The airman came in and sat down with me. Leaning forward, he said in a conspiratorial whisper, "You weren't kidding, were you!"

We had parked the truck out in the lot, just like I had said. "No," I growled quietly, "and if you say anything, you'll find out I wasn't kidding about tearing your head off either."

But there wasn't any untoward incident, and, after buying some booze and other necessities, I headed back over the Taurus Mountains to our little training camp. We traveled armed at the time—not anything fancy like a web holster and a .45, just a .38 lying on the seat next to you. And I had secured the .38 in the glove compartment, on top of the blasting caps, when I'd gone into the NCO club. That was a pretty good trip. I showed up with everything that Gallagher wanted and more. I really think he was proud of me that time.

The only thing was that it wasn't much of a challenge getting over on the Air Force. There was another example when John got tired of our primitive bathroom facilities. All we had to start with was a hole in the ground with two spots you put your feet in and leaned back from. This wasn't very comfortable for us Westerners, so we took a wooden chair and knocked the seat out of it. The only trouble with that arrangement was that you kept getting splinters in your butt. John went into one of the Air Force latrines and just unbolted the seat from the toilet. Now we had some civilized comfort.

Funny thing about the Air Force: It can keep track of some of the most serious things in the world, atomic weapons, and it does a good job of it. But in everything else, the Air Force is just easy. For a SEAL, an air base was like walking into a commissary with a credit card. Anything we wanted was ours. We could bullshit those guys out of anything.

And Rick Marcinko proved that years later big time when he ran Red Cell in the mid-1980s. The Red Cell guys would act like terrorists and completely take over a base, testing out the security and giving the SPs (Shore Patrol) a run for their money. Red Cell stole a pallet of bombs once and planted them near Air Force One. The bombs were practice ones, but they could have been real enough. Years earlier, I had proved that you could get explosives from the military if you knew what you were doing. The Air Force still probably doesn't know what was missing after my little shopping trip.

But once we had the explosives, a whole new problem arose with just the basic instruction portion of the training. I found out from one of the interpreters that the Turkish officer who was leading the class was not telling the students what I was instructing him to say. For example, I would say the object I was holding up was a Mark 51 fragmentation grenade. But the officer would tell the students that I was holding a Mark 26 smoke grenade. This was a problem, and not a little one. When training with demolitions and grenades, communications are not something that you want a problem with.

The Turkish officer's logic was that the enlisted men, which included me, always needed to be corrected in what they did. So, of course, I could not be correct in what I was telling the officer to say. This kind of leadership was going to get somebody killed fast, and it might be me.

"All right," I said at one of the instructors' meetings, "now we have to come up with a way to make these officers realize that we know what we're talking about." A little brainstorming and we had a plan laid out.

Up till then, we had been having some problems with all of the Turkish officers save Tanguch, who was the senior officer. We had about four Turkish officers in our training class and all of these guys had the "better than you" attitude that seems to come with some men as soon as they receive their commissions. And now one of them was getting things so messed up that it could result in one of us getting killed. This problem was far from a unique one and would happen again with another officer during my first combat tour in Vietnam.

The wake-up call we had decided on for the Turkish officer was not a pleasant one. We had been using half-pound TNT blocks for most of our explosive charges up till then. TNT comes in a rectangular cardboard container with metal ends. One of the ends is threaded and has a hole in it to accept the blasting cap. One night, we took one of the metal ends off a TNT block, removed the solid explosive, and crimped the metal end back on as best we could. Now we had an empty container that looked just like a live charge. Making up a complete firing assembly, minus the cap, and attaching it to our dummy block made up a very realistic-looking explosive charge that had no real explosive components. Only by holding the charge and feeling that there was no weight in the assembly could you tell that the charge was a dummy.

The next day, I gathered the class in a circle, making sure that the particular officer I wanted to make an example of was there. We called the students "my soldiers" all the time, and this was how I addressed them: "Gather around, my soldiers. Now we must review what we have learned so far. What is this I have in my hand?" I asked, holding up the dummy charge.

"That is a firing assembly, Instructor!" my students answered through the interpreter.

And on we went through the class, naming the different components of the assembly and how many there were. Nothing new, just a standard review. Needless to say, my students all knew what I was holding, or at least they thought they did. The eyes of my students got large indeed when I pulled the fuse lighter and ignited the time delay.

Setting the charge down by my feet, I continued addressing my students, from the center of the circle. "My soldiers," I said, "that will not explode. And your instructor would not lie to you. When your instructor tells you something, he's telling you the truth and is telling you correctly. You have to believe in your instructor."

At this point, the fuse was burning merrily along as I reached the edge of the circle. The students watched the fuse burn as I stepped over them. "You must believe me," I said. "That charge is not going to blow up."

But I was walking away from where the explosion would take place. Much to their credit, my students sat and watched that fuse burn. All except one. The one officer I had been having the most trouble with attempted to move, but he wasn't able to get past the ring of students.

When the fuse reached the end of its delay, there was a final spit of flame as it burned out. With that *spifft* of sound, I walked back into the circle and tore the charge apart. "See, my soldiers," I said, "I would not lie to you or hurt you. This was a lesson in trust. None of us are here to hurt you. We are only here to teach you, and you have got to listen to us, because your ass is going to depend on it someday."

My little lesson worked. The officer in question didn't make it through the whole course anyway, and we didn't have any more trouble with any of the other officers either. But we still had problems with the higher command in the Turkish military.

After demolitions, we wanted to give the men some weapons training. To teach the men weapons, we first had to get the ordnance they would use in the Turkish military. The primary weapon the Turks used at the time was the British Mark III Sten gun from World War II. The Sten was a good enough weapon for its time, which was around 1945, but this was 1963. Anyway, that was what our guys would be using, so that was what we needed to have.

We thought we would have no problem getting the guns we needed; the Turks had warehouses full of Stens. Wrong. Gallagher went to see about getting thirty guns and ammunition, and was given a stone wall even he had trouble getting through. The problem was that the Turks didn't want to let go of any weapons at all. They were saving them all for the upcoming war, they told Bob Gallagher.

"Well, how the hell are you going to train for that war if you don't give the men the weapons today?" Bob asked.

But the Eagle's logic didn't matter. The Turks finally agreed to let us have the weapons we needed, but no ammunition. This made for some real quiet weapons drills until we managed to get a limited amount of ammunition for firing practice. Our kids proved pretty good, though. We taught them instinctive firing, where you aim the weapon from the pit of your stomach, pointing your entire body to aim the gun. Instinctive firing is a fast and accurate technique, once you're taught it correctly. We had learned it from the British SAS some time earlier at Fort Bragg, North Carolina.

The weapons training, which I had been put in charge of, went well. We created night problems for our students: infiltration and movement, how to spot the enemy, how not to be spotted by the enemy. These drills went on without much incident, except for one night.

During one of our little scenarios, we suddenly heard Du Pont lures going off in the distance. For those of you in the outside (civilian) world, a Du Pont lure is a small explosive charge set off in the water to stun fish. The fish float to the surface and you can pick and choose what you want—not that I would ever consider using such a nonsporting fishing tactic.

That night, we heard a whole number of what sounded like small underwater explosions. And all of the explosions originated near a small fishing boat out in the Gulf of Alexandretta (Iskenderun). This was a great big no-no. None of the Turkish people were supposed to have any kind of explosives.

Our Turkish officer in charge of the students explained to Jose Taylor and Bob Gallagher that he and the students were effectively the police in the local area. He was going to take care of the situation with this little fishing boat, but he needed loaded weapons. Who were we to argue? We gave him some loaded magazines for the Stens and off he went with some of the students.

We took the Turks out to the fishing boat in the craft we used for cast and recoveries. Boarding the fishing boat, the Turks confiscated everything there was, including the boat. It turned out to be a Syrian fishing craft from across the boarder, not twenty-five miles away. After snatching up everything the fishermen had, the Turks left them stranded on the beach to make their own way home. It was during this incident that we learned that there was very little love lost between the Turks and the Syrians, a situation that still hasn't changed to this day.

We didn't get into the middle of any of this, other than carrying the Turks out to the boat. What happened to the fish and all of the other stuff from the boat we never did find out. I suppose that the fish may have been sold in the local marketplace. What I do know is that none of it ended up in our mess shed.

To add to our own messing—meals to you non-Navy readers— every time we had the chance, we went into a little hotel in Iskenderun and ate from the local economy. Our technique for ordering was simple. We would start at the top of the menu and work our way completely through the list. Turkish food portions were nothing like what we were used to back in the States, so we could easily stay there eating for four or five hours. Sometimes we would pay in American money, when the owners felt like accepting it. But most often we used local currency. The local denominations were the kurus (koo-ROOSH) and the lira. A kurus was a hundredth of a lira, and a lira worked out to be about sixty cents American.

Training was going well now. We had the class pared down to about twenty-five guys and they were coming together. Bob decided that the Turks needed some liberty and gave them time off to loosen them up a little bit and let them know that we were on their side. In return, the Turks took us to a Turkish wedding, and that was quite an affair.

The wedding was in a little town outside of Adana, maybe one hundred miles northwest from where our camp was. For some reason, we were accepted at the wedding, but our Turkish students were not made welcome. This was a weird situation. There was no love lost between the average Turk from back in the boonies and the Americans, but we were made more welcome than the Turks who had brought us. Maybe the students were considered too close to us. Whatever it was, it sure put a dent in the party.

It quickly became time for us to get away from the wedding before something happened. We went into a small restaurant/bar in Adana, right on the river. Out the back door of the restaurant was a forty- or fifty-foot drop down to the river, which was about two feet deep but ran along at something like Mach 2.

A local civilian at the bar made some nasty comment about Americans while we were there. Considering we didn't speak Turkish all that well, we could more or less ignore the insult. But our brand-new Turkish UDT men could sure as hell understand the local language, and they didn't like what was said at all. Before Bob Gallagher and I realized what was going on, students grabbed that loudmouthed Turk and threw him out the back door and into the river.

Even if that guy survived the long drop, the rapid water would have torn him apart within seconds. Our students had just killed that man. Bob and I figured out what had happened, as the level of excitement picked up fast in the little bar. "Get together," we told the students, "because something is going to happen now."

We tried to get organized and get the hell out of Dodge. Liberty was over as of that moment. The students had told us everything that had happened and we knew there was going to be trouble. And trouble soon showed up in the form of the Turkish Policia.

I don't know how many Turkish cops finally showed up; I lost count. Motioning to me and Wayne Boles, Bob told us to stay out of things and watch what happened. The police, actually men from a local army unit, gathered up a bunch of our students; our senior Turkish officer, Tanguch; and a few of our Turkish chiefs, Ishmael, Imingen, and Tin. The cops packed them into a paddy wagon and drove off with them.

Bob grabbed me and said, "Where's the jeep? Our men just got locked up, and if we don't follow them, we'll lose them for sure. I have no idea where the local jail is."

That was all it took—within seconds we were in the jeep and tearing off after that Turkish paddy wagon. Following the wagon, we soon spotted the stockade that had to be where they were going to put our men. The stockade was a big affair, maximum security and definitely not the place I most wanted to be while in Turkey. It had big walls with big doors, and the whole thing was topped off with coils of barbed wire.

Once we got to the stockade, our first step was to get to the person in charge and find out what was going on. But none of the Turks we were trying to communicate with spoke any English at all, and Bob was struggling with his limited command of Turkish. Tanguch spoke English well, but he was inside the stockade somewhere and we couldn't get to him.

Finally, we got the guards to take us to the *yūzbasi* (YOOZ-ba-shih), an army captain who was apparently in charge. The captain called in another Turk who spoke English a little bit better than Bob spoke Turkish; he would try to translate for us. By this time, only Bob and I were left; we had sent the rest of the SEALs back to the camp. If anyone ended up in jail, it would be Bob and me.

And with that thought through my head, we went on to the next step. What that involved was answering a lot of questions from the Turkish captain. He wanted to know who we were and what were we doing in his country. We answered him as best we could and told him about the Turkish UDT school that was being started.

Now Bob turned to me and said, "Jimbo, do you realize just what is going on here?"

"Yeah," I answered, "I think so."

"Well, you're right," he said. "We're under arrest too, for being with them. Just cool it and don't get excited. Let's see how we can handle it."

If I had to be in trouble, Bob Gallagher was the guy I wanted to be in trouble with. He can be diplomatic and calm a situation down, spreading oil on troubled waters, when he wants to. He can also kick in the door and hose a room down just as well.

Bob continued his conversation with the Turkish captain and I was satisfied just to sit back and watch. But now the conversation started to get a little weird. The captain was asking us what we thought of the leathernecks, the U.S. Marine Corps.

"Marines," we said, "they're number one, boy." A SEAL can say anything when he has to. Besides, it was becoming obvious that this captain had been involved with the U.S. Marines at one time or another. This was no time to tell the captain that the Marines landed only after the UDTs had opened up the beach for them.

Then the captain started asking Bob whether he had ever been in Korea with the leathernecks. Now Bob started laying it on pretty thick. He had been in Korea, the Marines were great, and anyone who worked with them also had to be great.

The situation began to change in our favor. This captain was coming over to our side. Before I knew what was happening, the captain had pulled in two other people to join us. Now these guys were signing affidavits that neither we nor our students had even been in the town that night. Nobody had seen any sign of any Americans or Turkish commandos. When they finally turned our students over to us, we knew it was time to beat a hasty retreat out of town.

We didn't need a lot of encouragement. We hit the road in one big cloud of dust. As we were leaving, Tanguch turned to Bob and said, "Mr. Instructor, you don't just walk out of a Turkish jail!"

Putting his arm around Tanguch, Bob answered, "Well, Tanguch, you just pulled a good UDT liberty. Let's get the fuck out of here and go home."

We had gotten out of Adana and were on our way back to
Arzuz. Everything was cool and things were going to be fine. But
there was something we had to teach the Turks about how we ran
things in the UDTs and SEAL Teams. The students had been out
with the instructors on liberty the day before, but now liberty was
over and it was time to go back to work.

At 5:30 in the morning, it was time for PT, and tough shit if
you had a hangover. We held reveille the next morning after our
little adventure in Adana. Normally, the Turks held their own
wake-up call and reported to us that they were ready for PT, but
that morning we were out there busting the Turks' balls, shaking
tents, and cutting guy lines. We were generally making pests of ourselves and letting the Turks know just who was in charge.

This was what we wanted to instill in our students—that when
it was party time, you could party hard; but when it was work time,
the work had to get done, no matter what. A simple rule in the
Teams was, if you could not party and get up for work the next
morning, you just didn't party the night before. Things have always
been that way, and it didn't take very long for the Turks to get the
message and things to get back on an even keel.

Later on, our Team caught a plane ride back to camp from one
of our trips to the air base. We jumped into the camp area. The
only trouble was that on one of the jumps, Jose Taylor, our officer
in charge, managed to land badly and break his leg. Bob Gallagher
was still in the airplane when the accident occurred, and the pilot
called back to him all excited and reported Jose's injury. Bob's answer must have shaken up that pilot a little bit: "Well, shit. Fuck
him. Now we're going to have to send back to the States for a
new officer."

So much for sympathy within the SEAL Teams.

Jose was something else though. Whether Bob had meant what
he said or not, Jose was a good leader. During the nights when we
were in our tents, drinking rum and playing hearts, he would be
there right alongside us. As a matter of fact, Jose would get so drunk
that he just took a gainer backward off his stool and ended up

splayed out on the floor. It got so bad that we finally started making him wear a football helmet when he started drinking so he wouldn't hit his head so much.

Jose didn't want to go home, but there wasn't any question that his leg was broken. The way the damned thing was bent, it was obvious to us all that he had screwed up. But finally, we got him into the hospital at Incirlik. He was eventually sent back to the States.

There wasn't any problem with our ops after Jose left—Bob Gallagher was an excellent leader and things were moving along smoothly—but the Navy back at the Creek, and maybe the Turks for all I know, wanted us to have an officer in charge. So the Navy and the Teams sent us a brand-new ensign, fresh out of UDTR.

Ensign William Painter had been one of the listed plankowners (the original commissioning crew) of SEAL Team Two, but had still been in training when the Team was formed. A number of guys were like this; they had been on the roster but for one reason or another didn't make that very first formation at one in the afternoon on January 8, 1962. But none of the other guys, whether they were in the UDTs or SEALs, were quite like Ensign Painter.

The word came to us that Mr. Painter would be arriving at Incirlik at such-and-such a time. I don't know what I'd done to piss Bob Gallagher off, but I was assigned to go pick up Mr. Painter. In the meantime, the class was preparing to break camp and move out to the Taurus Mountains to start the ground training phase of its airborne schooling.

Something fairly odd had happened to the detachment while we were in Turkey, prior to Mr. Painter's arrival. Out of a six-man detachment, five of us had advanced in rate (rank) while taking the standard rate test. Gallagher made Chief, and Wayne Boles, Doe Martin, and I made First Class in all of our respective rates. Even John Tegg made Third-Class Journalist, a rating not practiced much at the Teams. The only reason Bob Stamey didn't take the exam was that he didn't have enough time in rate to qualify.

I don't want to give the impression that we didn't follow the rules when we took the test. We had a Navy proctor, timed exams, all that good stuff. It just happened that we all were good enough in our respective rates to pass the exams easily. We played by the rules, ahem.

When I went to pick up Mr. Painter, we had no idea just who it was we were getting. Word had come to us from the Creek that Mr. Painter had left a seminary because of a problem with cheating on exams. Here was a guy who had been studying to be a priest, and the only reason he had quit his calling was that when he turned in a number of fellow students for cheating, the higher-ups didn't do anything about it. After quitting the seminary, Mr. Painter had joined the Navy and volunteered for UDTR. It was quite a change from trying to be a priest to qualifying as a frogman, and then being picked to be a SEAL.

But Mr. Painter had qualified and was one of the brotherhood; that made him okay in my book until he screwed up. And doing that didn't take him very long.

When the plane arrived, I went up and introduced myself to Mr. Painter, who was really hot to get going. "Let's just get in the jeep," he said. "I have to get down there and take control of the situation."

Take control of the situation? "Whoa, whoa, whoa, hoss," I said, "I've got more time underwater than you have in the Navy. What are you talking about?"

Then Mr. Painter went on to explain how he was the officer in charge and that he had heard all these things about the detachment before leaving the Creek and—

"Wait a minute," I said interrupting his tirade. "What things are you talking about, sir?"

Mr. Painter went on about how the detachment had been screwed up from the start. How we'd had a mustang leader in charge and that he had obviously not kept a tight rein on things. He said having five men out of six advancing on their exams was unheard of; there must have been some hanky-panky going on, and he was here to get to the bottom of things.

When Mr. Painter finally slowed down, I spoke up. "Well, sir, that's pretty good. Tell you what, I haven't had any American food in a while, and where you're going, you are not going to get any for a while either. What we're going to do is stop at the NCO club and get a few beers and a steak. If you have trouble with that, sir, you find another fucking ride to Arzuz, because that's what I'm going to do and I've got the jeep."

His reaction to my little speech was something like dumbfounded amazement. Here he was, the OFFICER IN CHARGE, and a lowly first class was ignoring his authority. What he didn't know was that I had learned something from Bob Gallagher: Once you start pushing your weight around, don't stop. If you do, things will probably back up on you and squash you into the ground.

Off we went to the NCO club. I don't even remember if Mr. Painter wanted to go to the officers' club. Not that it mattered much; *I* was going to the NCO club. After dinner and a few drinks, I learned something else about our stalwart leader: He didn't drink. *Uh-huh,* I said to myself, *Problem Number One, never trust a man who doesn't drink—especially an officer.*

Finally, we were on our way to Iskenderun and Arzuz. There were just the two of us in the JUSMMAT jeep, a road, and a whole lot of nothing else, especially no witnesses. I was going to mess with Mr. Painter's head.

I began to tell Mr. Painter exactly what he wanted to hear, satisfying all of his suspicions about us. And as we drove along that deserted mountain road, in a land that was old before Jesus walked, I turned to him and said, "Now prove it, because it's just you and me here."

That definitely tightened his sphincter a little bit. He couldn't believe what I had said. People just didn't act like I did in his orderly little world. Certainly people didn't admit to what I had admitted. I had really blown his mind, which was exactly what I had set out to do.

The rest of the trip passed without incident and it was a much subdued Ensign Painter whom I delivered to Bob Gallagher's tender keeping. Not that Bob couldn't handle the situation easily.

Wayne Boles and I were supposed to head back into the mountains to the Turkish Army Ranger camp. We were going to use the camp's facilities to conduct airborne ground and tower training.

The Turks had a jump tower at the Ranger camp, although it wasn't anything like the thirty-four-foot towers everybody was familiar with back in the States. But the Turkish tower was close to what we wanted; we would just have to work on it a little bit to bring it up to our specifications. Boles and I would also have to build up some swing landing trainers, which a student could use to practice his parachute landing fall and learn about his parachute control lines under safer conditions than being airborne.

Now Mr. Painter wanted to get into the act, review our training plans and make his own arrangements. After all, he was our "official" leader. Bullshit; Bob Gallagher was in charge, and he wasted no time in letting Mr. Painter known where things stood.

"Look, sir," Bob said, "this has all been laid on for some time. Yes, you're here to take charge. But we are not changing plans in the middle of the fucking training schedule just to make you happy. Now, if you want to be the head of this MTT, you go right ahead. But this is the training schedule; these are the people and who's teaching what. And this is the way it's going to be, sir."

Each of us had a different job according to the individual's strengths. I was teaching swimming, demolitions, and weapons with Gallagher. For jumping, it was Gallagher, Stamey, and me. We doubled up with each other over the length of the course, but different people were in charge of different phases as they came up.

Boles and I were to set up the physical materials for the ground phase of airborne training and Gallagher and I would be in charge of the training itself. So off Boles and I went to the Ranger camp with Mr. Painter's blessing—not that he really had much choice in the matter.

Showing up at the camp, we immediately had a little problem to deal with. We didn't have an interpreter with us and Boles and I didn't speak all that much Turkish. The problem was quickly solved as the Turks had an interpreter they could assign to us, so Boles and I went in to meet with the Turkish colonel in charge of the camp.

That meeting with the colonel was one of those lessons in life that I never forgot. And I am very glad that Wayne Boles and I remained cool-headed. The colonel sat behind his desk, staying quiet and listening to what the interpreter said, all the time watching Boles and me. The colonel knew we were enlisted men, but unlike some other Turkish officers, this man made no outward sign as to what he thought of us. The meeting went on like this for two hours.

The colonel wanted to know how could he assist us. He had been told by his higher command to support us in any way, shape, or form that we required, that our mission was a new thing for the Turkish military, and that we were considered top-drawer instructors.

We became involved in some pretty technical discussions. We wanted to know if we could run cables from the existing jump tower to a secure position down a hill. This would let our students get a feel for what the initial opening shock would be like when they jumped, and it would allow them to practice the proper way to exit a plane. We wanted to use some wooden racks we had seen as training devices and wanted to know if we could we get some pulleys. Boles and I got down to the nuts and bolts of the training we wanted to conduct.

The meeting went well. It was constructive and we knew when it was over, after two hours, that we could get our mission done. Now it came time for the lesson. Standing up behind his desk, the colonel spoke, in perfect English: "Gentlemen, I hope you enjoy your stay with us. It was nice talking to you."

That floored me. He had been sitting there, listening to our interpreter, and he had understood every word we said. He had been setting us up and trying to see if one of us would say something derogatory about the Turks, or the colonel himself.

That was one of the biggest lessons I ever learned as a young first class in the Teams. When you are working through an interpreter, you don't really know if the person you are talking to understands you or not. So watch what you say. That was a lesson that has stuck with me through Vietnam and to this day. If a guy says he doesn't speak English, don't trust the prick; he may be setting you up.

Thinking about a situation like this, you can actually work it to your advantage. If you didn't need to listen to what the interpreter was saying to you, you could tune out the interpreter and spend that time composing your answers. That would make it look like you were coming back with a snap answer when you actually had all the time you needed.

After my little lesson with the colonel, we got down to work setting up the training facilities for our class and modifying the jump tower to meet our needs. To practice moving in, hooking up, and exiting the plane, we had an old Gooney Bird (DC-3) fuselage available. But the Turks didn't like where the fuselage was in relationship to the rest of our training facilities. What they wanted was for all of our needs to be met in one area. The plane body, however, was well outside of this area, and we couldn't see any way to move the big cow. The Turks said, "No problem," and we left it up to them.

Sometimes, those of us in the industrialized nations forget that there are other ways to do things rather than use heavy equipment. Turkey is in that part of the world where major construction can be done with little more than muscle power. And that was exactly how the Turks moved that plane body.

It seemed that there must have been a thousand Turks swarming around that airplane. In the Teams, we practice "up boat" when we lift and carry an IBS during training, and that's exactly what the Turks did. Like a bunch of ants around a picnic hotdog, the Turks did an "up airplane." They physically lifted the body of the DC-3, carried it up a hill, and put it down alongside our thirty-four-foot tower. Never underestimate the abilities of a large bunch of Turkish *askers*.

Our tower was ready. We rigged up some cables to create a slide down from the tower. We had pulleys on the cables so the students could hang from a regular parachute harness attached to a pulley. By jumping out and up from the top of the tower, the student felt what it was like to exit the plane and, when he reached the end of the cable and slid down the wire, he felt the opening shock of his "parachute."

We attached the harnesses to the pulleys by connecting the risers from the harnesses (the long straps, attached to the shroud lines, that run down from the canopies) to the pulleys with snap-links. The risers we were using were quick-release Capewells from sport rigs, not like the standard military system that we used back in the States for the same training. Using this system, we could simply hook up the students to the risers using the attachments on their parachute harnesses, rather than trying to rig up each student as he came up the tower.

Before we let the Turks try this system, we were going to do it ourselves. By this time, everybody from the camp had shown up and ground training was ready to begin. Rating the instructors by size, Tegg was our lightest man, then Stamey, Boles, myself, on up to Gallagher, who was the biggest guy in our detachment.

That afternoon, we would jump the tower rigs starting with our lightest man, working our way up in weight. By the time we got to Boles, myself, and Gallagher, we would be jumping hard to put as much strain on the system as possible. By doing this, we could be sure that none of our students would overstrain the system and drop like a rock to the ground.

On the morning we were going to test the tower rig, we started giving PT to our students as usual. While we were leading our class, we could see all this activity going on over at the tower. A whole bunch of *askers* were going up the ladder with sandbags on their shoulders.

What the hell are they doing? we wondered. But we couldn't question them; this was their home and we were invited guests. Ignoring what was going on, we continued with our training. After lunch, we started out to the tower to try the rigs. Since we had to do this exercise, we thought we'd have some fun while we were at it. Tegg jumped, Stamey jumped, and then it came time for Boles, me, and Gallagher. We really tried out the system, jumping way up into the air rather than just up and out from the tower as our students would.

Nothing went wrong, and Gallagher was even talking about two of us jumping in tandem, just to make absolutely sure the system would hold. But things were satisfactory without our having to jump two guys on one rig. After we finished our testing, up the ladder came another *asker*. This guy reached out with a knife and started cutting open the sandbags and dumping them off the tower.

Just what the hell was going on? Those poor sons of bitches had spent the morning climbing that tower and piling sandbags. Now another guy just dumps them out? All we could think was that it must have been punishment or something like that. Then up came this Turkish sergeant, or whatever he was, laughing his ass off.

Bob Gallagher went up to the guy and asked him just what was going on. Still laughing, the Turk said, "Well, sir, we were going to test that rig for you using the sandbags for dummies. Now we don't have to, since you dummies checked it out pretty well."

The Turks hadn't wanted us to take any risks checking out the system. They were going to use sandbags but hadn't told us about it. By testing the system, however, we did increase the amount of respect the Turks had for us. All we ever showed our allies was the utmost in respect and military discipline (which was a bit more than we showed our own officer).

By this time in our training, Mr. Painter had a real yen to go out and do something. Up till now, we hadn't allowed him to affect the training schedule much. But he wanted to be actively involved and there wasn't much we could say. Except of course for what Bob Gallagher would say.

Bob reminded Mr. Painter that one of the reasons Wayne Boles and I had been sent up ahead of the group was so that we could adjust to the altitude of the camp. The Ranger camp was thousands of feet higher up than our little camp in Arzuz, which was basically at sea level. With our Turkish students now in as good physical shape as we were, or maybe even better, we needed every advantage to be sure we could keep up with them. High altitude can sap your energy faster than anything if you're not used to it.

But Mr. Painter wasn't buying any of this. He wanted to lead PT, feeling that he was new to the Teams and still needed to set an example. That was fine with us, so the next morning, he was out running the students up the hills. Hills my ass, those things were mountains. Mr. Painter hadn't gone five hundred yards before he started sounding like a badly tuned and leaking steam engine.

Mr. Painter was still game; I have to give him that. By that afternoon, he came up to Bob again. "Everything is going good," Painter said. "What do you want me to do now?"

"See that mountain behind the barracks?" Bob asked. "Go climb the son of a bitch and stay out of our way."

The next afternoon, all the Turks were facing the mountain with binoculars held up to their eyes. He had done it. Mr. Painter had taken Bob at his word and, by God, that man was climbing the mountain. He got up the mountain and down again, just like his chief told him to.

While Mr. Painter was learning how to run at high altitudes, we continued with the Turks' jump training. Because you couldn't clearly see from the door how a student was jumping and handling himself during his tower training, we had set up a small school-type desk at the bottom of the tower. Gallagher, Boles, or I would sit at the desk and grade the students on their performance. The students had to jump up and out of the tower to get a passing grade. Another man at the top of the tower acted like a jump master, smacking the jumper who was standing in the "door" on the ass and telling him to "Go!"

At one time, I was up in the tower, smacking the students on the ass, while Bob Gallagher was down on the ground at the desk, grading them. This one big Turk jumped out and really hit the line hard. Bob saw how the student had jumped and bent down over his desk, writing up the man's performance. What Bob didn't see was that the railroad iron we had supporting the cable had twisted like a pretzel. This one last student was not coming down where all of the others had landed.

While Gallagher had his head bent, the student floated down and landed right in front of him. Though this sudden thud startled the hell out of Bob, he wasn't about to show it. "What are you doing here?" he barked, as the student scrambled to get back to the relative safety of his fellow Turks.

Finally we completed all the tower training we wanted our students to have before actually jumping. Things had gone very well and nobody had a bad feeling about anything that had gone on. The Turkish Rangers respected the commandos and vice versa. Now it was off to Ankara and some real jumping with T-10 parachutes.

The only thing was, when we got to Ankara, there was another U.S. military unit there to try to take over our training. An Army Special Forces (or "blankethead," as we SEALs called the Green Berets) colonel got all over Bob's ass about what was going to be done with our Turkish allies. The colonel was going to pull in two Army A-Teams, riggers, the whole nine yards, in order to do the training with properly qualified people. Bob just straight out told that colonel that there wasn't any problem with the training schedule as it stood. He explained that every man of the MTT was a qualified rigger and instructor and that our detachment was the equivalent of the Army's A-Team. In his usual graceful manner, Bob just bullshitted his way through the problem and the Army backed off.

The Turkish airborne was operating from a base near Ankara and gave us the use of a couple of Gooney Birds. It also took care of our chutes and everything else we needed. Bob briefed the pilots, stressing that he wanted them to pay serious attention and keep a tight formation.

Our drop zone (DZ), across a highway, was about a mile wide and four or five miles long. At the end of that zone was a bunch of high-tension electric wires, and we obviously did not want our students getting anywhere near them. So for our purposes, the DZ was a mile wide and three miles long, not too large an area when you're dealing with student jumpers.

Piling on board the planes, Gallagher and Boles took one stick (group of jumpers) while Stamey and I took the other stick in the next plane. We had about fourteen men on board each plane, twelve of whom were jumpers. As the jump masters, we were all wearing free-fall rigs, while the students were jumping with T-10s and static lines.

Coming over the road on the first jump, we set the number one Turk in the stick in the door. When I hit the man on the ass and told him to go, he was out the door. The next student was a little hesitant about going out the door, but he exited the plane. The third student wasn't going out the door no matter what I said. He froze in the door and I couldn't move the guy.

We still had most of the stick still inside the plane and those Turks just were not moving. They had seen that their buddies really didn't want to jump. Screaming to be heard over the sound of the plane's engines coming in the open door, we tried to find out just what the hell was wrong.

I realized that the Turks needed a leader. The students knew I wasn't wearing a reserve parachute, just the free-fall rig on my back. "Okay," I asked them, "will you follow me if I lead?"

"Yeah, yeah!" was their answer.

"Stamey," I said, "keep pumping them up." And I went up to the front of the aircraft, where we had some reserve chute packs. Strapping a rig on my chest, I told the pilots to make another run. I didn't really think the reserve chute was going to do me much good. At the altitude where we were jumping, there wouldn't be time to deploy the damned thing if my main canopy malfunctioned. But now wasn't the time for such thoughts.

Going back to Stamey, I told him to get in back of the stick, behind the last student. "And when I clear this door," I said, "you put your shoulder into that last man and you push these guys out."

According to Stamey, once I jumped there wasn't anything he had to do to get those students out of the plane. When they saw their instructor going out the door, each one of those Turks piled out by the numbers. We never had any more trouble with them for the remaining five jumps we did. The problem had all been because the students didn't want to do something that their instructor wasn't going to do. Once I jumped, Turkish pride wasn't going to let one of those men even hesitate to exit the plane.

After jump training, we had a little ceremony for our students. Bob Gallagher had some American jump wings made up locally and we passed them out to our students. In turn, the men gave us some Turkish jump wings to take back with us.

Now it was time to go on to Chubuklu, near Istanbul, to do dive training near the Black Sea. Istanbul, the place people think of when they think of Turkey, is at the end of the Bosporus, a short strait that flows south from the Black Sea. Near Istanbul was the Turkish diving center at Chubuklu, right on the Borporus. Martin, Boles, and Stamey were responsible for running the diving part of training. Gallagher and I were not going to have much to do with it, and Tegg was just going to hang around and help out a little bit. Mr. Painter was the OIC, so he was in overall charge of the whole operation, but he really didn't have a hell of a lot to do with the day-to-day stuff.

Our whole detachment went to Istanbul after the class had completed parachute training. The Turks were given some time off and the rest of us worked on coordinating the details on the dive training with the Turks at Chubuklu. But not all the time we spent in Istanbul went to setting up the diving school.

We found the U.S. Air Force NCO club facility in Istanbul. It was stashed up a little side street on the third floor of a small building. Since we were traditional Navy men, and the Air Force was a sister service, we had a few disagreements with some of the service personnel who frequented the club. In fact the bar manager threatened to throw us out after we got into one too many "little hassles" at the club.

Bob Gallagher responded to the manager in his usual diplomatic manner: he told the manager to kiss his ass. Bob said that the only difference between the booze that they served in the club and what we had been drinking over the last several months was that the club had ice. The manager said he was thinking about putting up a sign that the club didn't offer TV but now had the "Friday Night Fights" thanks to the Navy and SEAL Team Two.

We had just spent several months in the boonies and really weren't in the mood to take much in the way of shit from anyone. One night, however, the Air Force personnel demonstrated just how good they were at giving out hassles to their sister servicemen. This one night, I remember that there was a frog on the bar—

just this little baby green frog that had somehow ended up there. We hadn't brought it and nobody else knew how the little sucker had gotten in.

While we were drinking rum-and-Cokes, Bob decided to start playing with this damned frog. Wanting to show the fleet sailors who were in the bar with us just how a UDT man could do anything, he put the little frog into his drink, where it promptly sank to the bottom. With his audience looking on, Bob drained his glass, leaving the frog at the bottom. Then he turned to me like it was my turn and put the little frog into my glass.

I wasn't going to let him down, so I finished my drink. There were twelve or fourteen other servicemen in the club at the time. I couldn't tell who was in what service; just about everyone was in civilian clothes. But the onlookers decided to make some derogatory comments about our drinking habits. Turning to the crowd, Bob said, "You sons of bitches better keep your comments to yourselves or you'll all get what you're asking for."

Boles, Stamey, Tegg, and I were all in the bar and we were not going to have any trouble backing Gallagher up. But the other servicemen just kept making their little jokes, until Bob finally said, "That's enough! Come on, Jim."

Okay, it was time for the party to begin. Bob yanked me off the stool I was sitting on and we started down this spiral staircase that led out of the club. The remainder of the club's customers decided that they could take the two of us, so they started toward the staircase.

Of course, Bob and I weren't worried. We had our teammates in the club with us and they would back up our play. The only thing was that when the fight actually started, our teammates weren't anywhere to be seen. I kept looking over my shoulder and finally spoke up. "Bob," I said, "there's six steps behind us full of people and I don't see any friendly faces."

"No problem," Bob answered. "Wait till we get to the door to the outside. It's only wide enough for two people. I'll step right and you step left. We can nail these guys two at a time as they come out."

When you exited the club, there was a stone wall just about ten feet in front of the door. You had to turn left to reach the street itself. As we hit the door, Bob went right, I went left, and we proceeded to ambush each of the men who came out the door after us.

Bob treated the last man a little differently. Grabbing the man by the collar and the seat of his pants, he drove that guy flat into the wall like something straight out of a cartoon. Bob and I were the only two guys standing in the middle of a mess of bodies, blood, and general rubble. As I looked around to see who might be getting up, the one guy I didn't want to see standing was the first person getting to his feet.

This guy had to be six feet six and looked as big as a barn. *Oh, shit,* I thought as I looked up at this big sucker. Deciding to move fast, I front snap-kicked him solid, and he just looked at me. *Oh, damn, I must have missed,* I thought, and I hauled back and nailed him again. And this time I was sure I didn't miss. Only thing was, he just stood there looking at me and smiling.

Enough of this shit. Grabbing the guy by his arms, I used a judo throw to drop him to the ground, driving my knee into him in the process. This time, my big partner wasn't smiling, or getting up either. The fight was effectively over, and nobody had laid a hand on me.

I had come out of this fight clean, not a mark on me. Not that I could say the same for Bob. When he had run that one guy into the wall, some blood had splashed all over the front of his sweater. As we were standing there, we could hear the sound of police sirens off in the distance. "You've got it," Bob called out as he went sailing over the wall and out of sight.

Like all good frogmen, I greeted the police with open arms.

"Am I glad you guys have finally gotten here," I said to the arriving APs (Air Police). "A whole bunch of guys just went over the wall there. They beat the shit out of these guys! They all just went that way."

The man I had just finished dropping in a big way was starting to get up. Speaking in what was probably an unnaturally high voice for him, he started to agree with my story! "He's telling it straight," the man said. "A whole bunch of them just went over the wall!"

A whole bunch, my ass; it had just been Bob and me. But I wasn't about to argue the point. Later on, at Air Police headquarters, I ended up being a witness to the incident. Filling out a witness form, I stated that a whole bunch of those "other guys" had beaten the hell out of these poor Air Force fly-boys. Back at the hotel, I met up with Bob and learned about what else had happened.

During our fight down in the street, Wayne Boles had been having his own little party on the second floor. He had grabbed some guy who had been coming down after us and held the guy out over the banister. The only thing between the floor and the hanging airman was the strength of Boles's arm. Whatever it was that happened, I don't think the guy apologized correctly, and Boles just dropped the man to the pavement below.

Only thing was, Boles didn't get away clean like Bob and me. Later that evening, I had to go down to AP headquarters again. This time I had to get Boles out of jail. Pretending to be the officer in charge of SEAL Detachment MTT 1–63–1, I said I needed to have my man released to me immediately. Just take the bull by the horns and kill the guys with numbers.

At any rate, I managed to sucker the APs. No, we weren't in uniform. No, I couldn't tell them just who we were. We were operating out of JUSMMAT under a need-to-know classification. Now I had these guys convinced that I was the officer in charge and that these SEALs ("No, I can't tell you who we are") were under my command. Only trouble was, Boles wasn't cooperating.

"Where's the chief [Gallagher]?" Boles asked. "When are you going to get the chief?"

"The chief works for me too," I told the APs, trying to get Boles to play along. I was ready to kill him for giving me additional problems while I was getting him out of jail. The trick worked, and I got Boles free of the APs and back to the hotel. Sitting around the hotel the rest of the night, we entertained ourselves just telling war stories.

I never did find out where Mr. Painter, our actual OIC, was that night. He had gotten mad at us, for getting into fights I believe, and just went out on his own. It was something about our not acting sufficiently respectable, given our ranking as senior petty officers in the U.S. Navy and official guests of the Turkish government. We mostly just ignored him.

When we started indoctrinating our Turks in dive training, they couldn't have been in much better hands. Doc Martin was a very good diving corpsman and Boles was an excellent diver. Out of the group of us, those two were the best men underwater.

The underwater equipment we used to teach the Turks was just regular open-circuit scuba gear, much the same thing used by sport divers all over the world today. The students were taught the safe operation of scuba gear and how to work underwater without getting killed. The underwater environment is a hostile one and it isn't very forgiving of mistakes.

On our first day of open-water work, we were all at Chubuklu to help handle the class. The students had completed their pool training with no problems and it was time to get wet in the Bosporus. We started with sixty-foot free ascents in open water.

The sixty-foot free ascent requires a diver to rise from a depth of sixty feet without breathing in any air from his scuba rig. Since the air in a diver's lungs is compressed from the pressure of the water at sixty feet, he must constantly exhale on his way up, or his lungs will quickly burst from the expanding air. This is not the safest operation to conduct underwater with beginning divers, so a careful watch is constantly kept on the students while they are submerged.

To help keep things under control, Doc Martin had rigged a stage at the sixty-foot level. The students dove down from the surface and followed a buoy line to the stage. Right off the edge of the shore was a sheer underwater cliff. The water beyond immediately dropped down four or five hundred feet, so the stage was an absolute necessity to run the class safely.

Bob Gallagher and I rubbed elbows with the Turkish commercial divers at Chubuklu that morning. After having breakfast with the men, we both planned to go back to the hotel. Mr. Painter was in a happy mood that day. He had just gotten the word that he had made Lieutenant, Junior Grade (j.g.), so at least he wasn't an ensign anymore. After congratulating Mr. Painter, we proceeded with another Navy tradition: We picked up the new j.g. and threw him into the Bosporus. He climbed out, and with that, Bob and I went back to the hotel.

We couldn't have been back at the hotel more than fifteen minutes before Bob was banging on my door. "Jim," he said, "let's go. Grab your shit and come on; we have to go."

"Bob," I said, slightly confused, "just what the hell is going on?"

"No time for that now," Bob said. "I'll tell you on the way."

One thing that isn't done in the Teams is arguing with Bob Gallagher, especially not when he's serious. We were out the door and into a cab within a minute or two.

"One of the guys is missing," said Bob when we had settled into the cab.

"What!" I said incredulously. "Who?"

"They wouldn't tell me," he answered. "All they said was that one of our guys is missing. They went down on a dive and now they can't find him."

This was probably the worst thing imaginable. All we could do on the way to the dive site was attempt to figure what might have happened. We knew it couldn't be Doc Martin who was missing; he was just too good underwater. Boles was an expert as well. All we could come up with was that it had to be Tegg or Stamey. Neither of us were even thinking about Mr. Painter at the time. When we had left, he hadn't even been in the water.

Once we reached the seawall along the Bosporus, we had to wait for the boat to come and pick us up. While we waited impatiently, somebody started shouting in Turkish, "Body in the water! Body in the water!"

Bob, who understood what was being shouted, grabbed my arm and hollered, "Look!"

Floating along in the water below us was the body of a woman, and she was facedown. Both of us jumped over the seawall and into the water. With the help of the Turks who were milling around, we managed to get the woman out of the water and onto dry land. Bob and I both worked on her, giving her mouth-to-mouth and getting her breathing on her own.

Then we were approached by a U.S. Navy officer—either a commander or lieutenant commander, I don't remember which—and he had the word as to which of our men was lost in the water. "I don't understand this," he said. "You two guys have just saved someone else's life, while you're waiting for a boat to go find one of you own who's lost in the water."

"Well," Bob said, "if we lost one, at least we saved one, so now we're even."

That didn't go over too well with this black-shoe officer. Now wasn't the time for our normal joking around—not that Bob really gave a damn about what this officer might think, but perhaps that was one time we should have been more concerned with an officer's opinion.

The officer told us who was missing. It was Mr. Painter. Looking at each other, all Bob and I could think was that we had sent our first officer home with a broken leg, and now one had drowned. What the hell were our teammates back at the Creek going to think of us? As the boat arrived, Bob and I tried to figure out what Mr. Painter had been doing in the water in the first place. He had nothing to do with the actual dive training except as the officer in charge.

When we got to the site, Mr. Painter had been missing for well over an hour. Everyone was a little excited and most of the divers were in the water searching. Bob grabbed Doc Martin and asked him what had happened.

"Bob," Doc said, "the son of a bitch started to put on gear to get into the water while I was briefing everyone about the operation. I turned to him and said, 'Mr. Painter, don't get in the water by yourself. You wait for one of the guys to go with you.' You know what he said? 'Don't you tell me what to do. I'm an officer and I can take care of myself.' How are you going to argue with something like that?"

Doc went on to say that Mr. Painter had made a dive, then surfaced and called over to ask Doc what decompression stops he had to make on the way up from a depth of 180 or 200 feet. Mr. Painter didn't believe that free ascents could be made right there at pierside and he had gone down to try to reach the bottom. It was very deep for scuba diving; there were World War II submarines that would have been crushed if they had tried to reach the bottom right there.

Mr. Painter might not have reached the bottom on his first dive, but he might have reached it later. After he surfaced, Doc Martin told him to get out of the water. With that, Doc turned back to his class and continued with his students. That was the last time anyone saw Lieutenant William Painter alive. He became the first SEAL loss from either Team, and his body was never found.

We were accused of killing Mr. Painter. Now, we may not have liked the man very much, but that is a long way from killing a teammate. Some Navy captain had it in his head that we weren't getting along with Mr. Painter. The officer came right out and stated that he thought Bob and I had something to do with Mr. Painter's disappearance. And with that he asked us to turn our weapons over to him, which we did.

We didn't know what to do. A Navy officer had relieved us of our weapons and practically come right out and accused us of killing our officer. That same Navy officer would not let Bob send a message to Little Creek. If we wanted to notify Little Creek about anything, the communications had to go through his office.

There wasn't anything for us to do, so we went back to the hotel and tried to figure something out. The big question was how we could cover our collective asses, because we hadn't done anything wrong but this Navy officer wanted to hang us. The general opinion was that Mr. Painter had been killed by his own stupidity, only we were going to have to pay for his mistake as well.

Bob was going over our orders, trying to find a way out, and he did. "I've got it," he said.

"Got what?"

"A way for us to get out of this mess. The way the orders are written states, 'You are authorized to vary the order of any visit, or revisit such places as may be necessary in the execution of these orders.' Jim, pack your stuff. You're going home. I'll call and get you an airline ticket. You and I are the only two guys that are not involved in the diving here. I have to get this mess squared away, so that leaves you to get back to the Creek and get us some help here."

All of the necessary financial data, charge numbers and so on, was in our orders, so it wasn't any big deal for Bob to get me a plane ticket. Within a few days, I was back on my way to Little Creek. As soon as I hit the States, Joe DiMartino, one of the Team's officers, picked me up at the Norfolk, Virginia, airport and took me straight to Tom Tarbox's house.

I finally settled down at about two o'clock in the morning. Mr. Tarbox (Team Two, executive officer) wanted to know what had been happening back in Turkey. I told him that an officer back there was accusing us of causing Mr. Painter's disappearance. Because Mr. Painter was a young officer and we hadn't been getting along with him, the officer thought that we must have killed our own leader. What Bob and the rest of the guys needed more than anything was for a very sharp administrative officer to go over to Turkey and straighten the whole thing out.

Within thirty-six hours of my arriving in Norfolk, the Team sent Dante (Stephensen) Shapiro over to Turkey. They would have been hard pressed to come up with a better man for the mission. Dante was a sharp officer and one hell of an administrator. Within a relatively short time, he got everything straightened out and operating smoothly again. He took over training as the new OIC and cleared all of the other mess away. Thanks to his timely help, the SEAL Team Two MTT to Turkey was a complete success.

Not to say that we didn't bend more than a few rules in getting the mission done. But that's how we did things in the Teams. None of us were qualified, on paper, to run an airborne school, but we did. We weren't supposed to be authorized weapons or the quantities of explosives we needed to complete the training, but we got them.

The bottom line on our training showed up some years later. When the Turks invaded Cyprus, Bob Gallagher, myself, and a few of the other guys received letters from the men in our first class.

The letters said that our commandos had done very well, that they had completed every mission assigned to them, and that they had never lost a man. Everything we had taught them had come in handy, and they hadn't forgotten our lessons.

One of the weird things that came out of that situation was that, as I mentioned earlier, Team Two had sent another MTT over to train the Greeks at the same time we were in Turkey. The Greeks were the Turks' opponents in Cyprus. The joke was that when Cyprus started, we would find out which MTT had taught its students the best. It was obvious that we had, since the Turks won.

Dante left the Teams soon after the Turkish operation. But he still kept a Team attitude and stayed a sharp administrator. Do you know how to make a small fortune in the restaurant business? You start out with a large fortune. Well, that old joke doesn't hold for Dante. He owns Dante's Down the Hatch in downtown Atlanta, and you'd have a hard time finding a better place.

CHAPTER 2

Team Losses

L IEUTENANT (J.G.) WILLIAM PAINTER was the first loss we had in the SEAL Teams, but he was far from the last man who would give his life while in service with the Teams. Duty in the Teams, whether in the SEALs or the UDTs, was hazardous just from exposure to our regular training. Man isn't built to stay underwater for long periods of time or to fly through the air after jumping out of a perfectly good airplane. But we did all of these things, and the Navy even gave us some extra pay because some of our duties were so dangerous.

The hazards of being in the UDTs had been shown to me before I had even graduated from training. While I was still a trainee with UDTR Class 23 down in Puerto Rico in 1960, the rest of the UDT crew from Little Creek was conducting underwater training over at St. Thomas in the Virgin Islands. Word came back to us that there had been a diving accident at St. Thomas, one that cost the Teams two men.

Exactly what happened was never fully know, since the only two witnesses were both dead. Cunningham and McCallister had been swim buddies on a dive, one of the men operating with a closed-circuit rig, the other with a regular open-circuit scuba rig. It is very possible that the man using the closed-circuit rig had come down with oxygen poisoning, something that can easily sneak up on you. He may have caused the accident that resulted in the drowning of both divers.

One thing I do know is that you never leave your swim buddy. Both men stuck together, and both men drowned. Lethal diving accidents were very rare in the Teams; I think this may have been

49

the very first one. But it was not the last and it was my introduction to the fact that frogmen can die. The incident was taken very hard in the Teams. We could see this on our instructors' faces.

Mr. Painter was an underwater loss. The next man we lost from SEAL Team Two was killed in a parachuting accident. Melvin Melochick was a young kid, kind of a frisky little loudmouth sometimes, who was a hell of a good jumper. Starting out as an up-and-coming operator, Melochick would have become a good hunter in Vietnam if he had been given the chance. He was a little wild at times, but we all could be that way.

Mel and I had done a lot of work together in early 1965, mostly centering on parachute jumping. There was an Armed Forces Day demonstration in May 1965 that SEAL Team Two was going to participate in. Both Mel and I were on the Jump Team and we were going to conduct a water jump at Naval Air Station (NAS) Norfolk as our part of the demonstration. The Jump Team went out to do a practice jump at the NAS a few days before the public demonstration. Other duties kept me from going on the practice jump, so I had already seen Melochick for the last time.

Jerry Todd took my place on the practice jump that day. Since it was a water jump, where the parachutists would land in a branch of the Chesapeake Bay rather than on dry land, the jump uniform was mostly just bare skin, bathing suits, and no helmets. That was how we did a water jump back then, with very little material that might tangle up a jumper after he hit the water.

A photographer was along on the practice jump, staying aboard the plane and taking pictures as the jumpers exited from the rear ramp. One of the pictures made the cover of the New York *Daily News*. As Mel left the tailgate of the plane, he turned around and waved to the photographer. The caption on the news photo read, "Jumper waves goodbye." It was Mel's last jump. He was killed before he hit the water.

The report on the jump told me most of the story about what went wrong. Todd said later that he had never made direct physical contact with Mel during the jump. As the team was free falling to its twenty-two-hundred-foot opening altitude, Jerry saw that he was right above Mel. Mel waved his arms, telling Jerry that he was about to open his parachute. It was standard operating procedure to wave off before you pulled, just in case somebody was above you. Although his arms were waving, Mel probably never even knew Jerry was there; but Jerry, right above him, would tangle with Mel's canopy if he didn't get out of the way. This wasn't considered a big problem, so Jerry turned and started to maneuver away from above Mel.

The trouble was that the team was jumping in bare skin, which does not offer much wind resistance as you're dropping through the air. Jerry just didn't have enough drag against the air for his turn to work before Mel opened his canopy. The next thing Jerry knew, he had a face full of parachute and was still falling at well over a hundred miles per hour. Striking Melochick, the hard case of the altimeter on Jerry's reserve chute tore open the back of Mel's head.

Melochick was killed instantly. Jerry was able to break free and open his own chute before he hit the water.

On May 15, 1965, I traveled to St. Clair, Pennsylvania, with Bob Stamey as one of the escorts on Melochick's last trip home. The whole Team flew up to St. Clair the day of Mel's funeral. His parents were very hospitable to us and appreciated how we treated one of our own.

One small part of the funeral ceremony centered on the fact that Mel had never liked to wear a uniform. That young SEAL received full military honors while resting in his casket wearing civilian clothes. Once we had done that, there wasn't any way for someone to make us undo it, and I think Mel would have appreciated the gesture. Full military honors may have required Mel to be buried in uniform, but we of his Team wanted him to have things his way.

After we left the cemetery, the family invited us all to a banquet hall for something akin to an Irish wake. Mel's parents even gave me Mel's Paracommander sport parachute before I left Pennsylvania. The Paracommander was a hot rig on the civilian sport jumping circuit then, better than what we had even in the Teams, and a very expensive piece of equipment. As a first class with a young family at the time, I could never have afforded such a luxury for myself. It's been a long time now, but I wish I could reach his folks somehow today if they are still around.

That trip to Pennsylvania was one of the toughest things I've ever had to do in my life. Mel was a good kid and I think he really would have made a name for himself in the Teams. After the accident, procedures were changed for water jumps so that what had happened to Mel wouldn't happen again.

Losses in the Teams were something that just came with the territory, and losses weren't restricted to the SEALs. We lost Jim Fox of UDT 22 to an accident while testing the Fulton Skyhook recovery system on June 24, 1964. The Fulton Skyhook could extract a man from a very small area, even as small as a rubber raft, by means of a harness attached to a nylon line raised by a balloon. Once the line was grabbed by a special rig on a plane, the aircraft crew could winch up the man wearing the harness. While Fox was demonstrating the rig, his nylon line snapped as he was being pulled into the pickup plane, and he fell into the Chesapeake.

The biggest number of SEAL losses, however, happened on a little soggy chunk of real estate half a world away from Little Creek. A dinky little part of Southeast Asia called Vietnam.

One thing the SEALs have been accused of—and I have heard some historians really bitch about this—is being lousy record keepers. We were operators, not clerks. We did the minimum amount of paperwork we could, and even that only when we were told to. The SEAL Team Two official Command and Control Histories were not even started until around 1967, and then we backlogged them to 1962.

Some people use those official Command and Control Histories as their only available unclassified source of SEAL Vietnam history. And, though nobody tried to hide the facts, the lack of details in the official documents sometimes causes mistakes by writers who misinterpret what they do have available. Two very conscientious SEAL historians, Kevin Dockery, who wrote *Walking Point* with me, and Commander T. L. Bosiljevac, both made the same mistake in their respective books. And that mistake centers on one of the early SEAL Team Two losses in Vietnam—specifically, my swim buddy Arthur "One-Lump" Williams.

The official SEAL records read like this:

```
SEAL TEAM TWO—COMMAND AND CONTROL HISTORY, 1968
CONFIDENTIAL
ENCLOSURE (2)
CHRONOLOGICAL OUTLINE
. . . . . . . . . . . . . . . . . . . . . . . . . . . . . . . . . . . . . . . . . . . . . . . . . .
18 Jan 1968—A. WILLIAMS (Sixth Platoon) fatally wounded
. . . . . . . . . . . . . . . . . . . . . . . . . . . . . . . . . . . . . . . . . . . . . . . . . .
ENCLOSURE (1)
CONFIDENTIAL
SEAL TEAM TWO HISTORY FOR 1968
I. Introduction
. . . . . . . . . . . . . . . . . . . . . . . . . . . . . . . . . . . . . . . . . . . . . . . . . .
```

The month of January dealt a severe blow to SEAL Team TWO as three of its members lost their lives. On 18 January, while conducting an emergency extraction under fire, GMG1 Arthur G. WILLIAMS of the Sixth Platoon was fatally wounded after receiving a round under his arm which lodged in his spine. . . .

What the two writers took this to mean, they both put in their books as follows. From *Seals in Action* by Kevin Dockery (New York: Avon Books, 1991, p. 141):

> On January 18, while conducting an emergency extraction under fire, GMG1 Arthur G. Williams of the Sixth Platoon was killed. A round entered under William's arm and lodged in his spine, killing him almost instantly.

From *SEALs: UDT/SEAL Operations in Vietnam* by Commander T. L. Bosiljevac (New York: Ivy Books, 1990, p. 82):

> Gunner's Mate First Class Arthur Williams was mortally wounded on 18 January as his platoon was making an

emergency extraction under fire. The SEAL Team Two 6th platoon member received a gunshot wound under his arm and the round lodged in his spine. He died shortly after, becoming the first SEAL Team Two fatality of the war.

What really happened was a lot different than what was reported by these two men, even though they are both honorable and exacting researchers. They just made a mistake. The fact that it was a mistake is obvious in part because Commander Bosiljevac—Bo to his friends (I consider myself privileged to be one)—is an active-duty SEAL officer and he would never intentionally say something wrong about a teammate. Bo had to use only unclassified material for his book, which was really his college master's thesis. Kevin "Doc" Dockery is a very conscientious historian who is held in high regard by many in the Special Warfare community for his knowledge and integrity, a level of acceptance given to very few non-SEALs. Doc has wanted to take this opportunity to set the record straight about my friend One-Lump.

In the last few years, new SEAL records have become available to the public. The SEAL Barndance cards, a record of each operation we did in Vietnam, and the official Spotrep reports, which were sent up to higher command, list the action where One-Lump was hit. Those documents are reproduced in part here.

PAGE TWO C O N F I D E N T I A L
GAME WARDEN SPOTREP 1/18/116.2.0/1 (U)
1. SEAL SQUADS 6A, 6B, MST LCPL, STAB, 2 LDNN, SEAWOLFS 43, 47, LT. KOCHEY.
2. 6A INSERTED XS 303 212 AT 180430H BY STAB. PATROLLED XS 308 214. CAPTURED ONE VC, 2 GRENADES (1 MK 26, 1 VC), 2 CLIPS AMMO. CONTINUED TO PATROL NORTH. HEARD NUMEROUS SIGNAL SHOTS AND MUCH MOVEMENT IN AREA. EXTRACTED BY STAB XS 310 214 AT 180930H. RECEIVED HEAVY S/A WEAPONS FIRE FROM BOTH BANKS DURING EXTRACTION AND PASSAGE DOWN CANAL. 1 US WIA. VC CAS (UNK). SEAWOLFS PROVIDED COVER DURING EXTRACTION AND MEDEVACED 1 US WIA. 6B INSERTED XS 311 201 BY STAB AT 180430H. PATROLLED NE TO XS 315 204,

THEN SE TO XS 318 195, THEN NW TO XS 309 212. HEARD NUMER-
OUS SIGNAL SHOTS AND PREVIOUSLY MENTIONED FIREFIGHT.
SET AMBUSH. NO CONTACT EXTRACTED BY STAB AT XS 310 202
AT 181015H.

3. 180400H TO 181015H.

4. AREA SEARCH VIC XS 31 21

5. CAPTURED 1 VC, 2 GRENADES, 2 CLIPS AMMO. 1 US WIA. BARN-
   DANCE 6-35A

6. CONSIDER CLOSED

   GP-4

   BT

. . . .

BARNDANCE: 6-35A   COORD: XS 308 213

DATES: 18 JANUARY, 1968   TIMES: 0440-1000 H

1. UNITS INVOLVED: SEAL SQUADS 6A, 6B, 2 LDNN, MST-2
   UNITS, SEALWOLVES HAL 3 DET 4

2. TASK: AREA SEARCH

3. METHOD OF INSERTION: STAB   EXTRACTION: STAB

4. TERRAIN: VERY SWAMPY; NUMEROUS CANALS AND STREAMS

5. TIDE: HIGH   WEATHER: HOT, DRY

6. MOON: FULL

7. ENEMY ENCOUNTERED: UNKNOWN, POSSIBLY 5 TO 6 V.C.

8. CASUALTIES: 1 U.S. WIA (WILLIAMS); 1 V.C. PRISONER

9. NAMES OF SEALS INVOLVED: KOCHEY, YEAW, TIPTON, SUTHER-
   LAND, FALLON, MACLEAN, FRADENBURGH, JOHNSTON, COZART,
   SILVA, GRAYSON, WILLIAMS, NAM, THUAN

10. RESULTS: 6A INSERTED AT 0440H AND MOVED TO DRY LAND AND
    SET A PERIMETER TILL FIRST LIGHT. THEN PATROLLED NE BUT
    UNSURE AS TO POSITION CALLED FOR EXTRACTION. WHEN EX-
    TRACTING BY STAB UNKNOWN NUMBER OF VC OPENED FIRE. IN THE
    ENSUING FIRE FIGHT WILLIAMS WAS WOUNDED AND MEDEVAC WAS
    PROVIDED BY SEAWOLVES. 6B INSERTED 1000 METERS DOWN
    RIVER AND SET PERIMETER TILL FIRST LIGHT. PATROLLED NW
    TOWARD 6A AND SET AMBUSH 200 FROM 6A WHEN FIRE FIGHT COM-
    MENCED. AFTER FIRING CEASED 6B EXTRACTED.

    AGENT LATER REPORTED ONE (1) V.C. KIA; FOUR (4) V.C.

WIA. THE STAB RECEIVED SEVEN (7) HITS IN ENGINE ARMOR
AND UPPER ENGINE COVER AND ONE (1) IN HULL. ALL DAMAGE
REPAIRABLE

. . . .

Bob "Archie" Grayson was on the op when One-Lump was hit and helped fill out some details about what happened. It was January 18, 1968, and One-Lump's squad was pulling out of a hostile area with a VC prisoner it had just captured. While getting on board the extraction boat, the squad was ambushed by an unknown number of heavily armed VC. As the boat was extracting, one of the Mercury outboards crapped out. With an engine down and heavy fire coming in, things were more than a little confusing. It may have been one of the first rounds fired that hit One-Lump, but it only took one to do the job.

The bullet went in under One-Lump's arm and stopped near his spinal cord. The wound was very serious, but One-Lump was not killed instantly. In fact, he recovered enough that they medevaced him back to the States, where he was in Portsmouth Naval Hospital for some time.

I think it was something like nine months that One-Lump hung on in the hospital. We took up a collection for him at the Team to buy him something to make his stay at the hospital a little easier. Remote-control televisions were still pretty new back then and, since One-Lump's wound kept him in bed, we decided to buy him one. As his good friend, I was going to take the TV to him at the hospital.

The seriousness of One-Lump's wound wasn't in question. But it did appear to us that he was recovering, even though he looked terrible and was in pain much of the time. As usual, Rudy Boesch was the most practical one among us, and he suggested that we wait to give One-Lump the TV until the doctors said it was okay. The doctors had even given us the word that One-Lump was going to be okay, which made what happened next even harder.

Because of what Rudy had said, I went to the hospital and spoke directly to the doctors who were treating One-Lump. He was doing fairly well. The doctors told me, "He has one more major operation. If he gets through that one, he will be home free."

"Home free" wasn't quite what One-Lump would actually be; he would still be half paralyzed from the injury, but at least he would be alive. The doctors told me to hold off on delivering the TV until after One-Lump recovered from his last operation.

So we waited back at the Team. After about a week, I went back to the hospital and spoke to the doctors again. Their news sounded pretty good to me. One-Lump was over the hump and recovering. With the situation looking pretty good, we went out and bought the TV.

It was never delivered. Doctors can't know everything. Shortly after my last visit, One-Lump took a sudden turn for the worse and died.

That was hard on all of us, especially since it had looked like One-Lump was going to make it. We took the TV over to his wife, and she said to leave it at the hospital for any SEAL who was WIA (wounded in action) from Vietnam.

Art Williams was not the first combat loss for SEAL Team Two in the Vietnam War; Eugene Fraley was. On January 21, 1968, Fraley was killed instantly when a boobytrap he was working on exploded prematurely. Within ten days of Fraley's being killed, we also lost Clarence Risher in the close house-to-house fighting in Chau Doc as part of the Tet Offensive.

Navy Special Warfare lost forty-nine men in Southeast Asia in the years between 1965 and 1972. Thirty-five SEALs were lost from SEAL Team One, nine from SEAL Team Two, and five from the UDTs. Losses were a part of war and you just had to shut that part of life out of your head. At least that's what I did. During all of the military funerals I've attended, I tried not to think about the real reason that we were there, to say good-bye to a teammate. Dwelling on the possibility of being killed while in the SEALs was an almost sure way of becoming the next statistic. When you walked away from a SEAL's funeral, a small part of you would think, *Hey, that could have been me!* But you soon developed your own way of dealing with losses, which kept you from thinking that way for very long.

As part of SEAL tradition, the lost teammate's friends would go out to a bar somewhere, have a few beers, and tell some stories about their missing shipmate. After that, they just went back to doing their jobs. There's a reason SEAL training is so hard; it's because the job is so hard that it takes a strong man, strong in body and mind, to get the work done.

We always paid our respects. But our lost shipmate had known the risks as well as we did. We did prepare for the possibility of being lost in action, as much as we could prepare for such a thing. The Teams and the Navy had procedures we followed to make sure that our families and anyone else we left behind were taken care of—military insurance, wills, and stuff like that. But in the Teams, privately, we had our own preparations made.

All the SEALs I knew had made arrangements that there would be a beer party—what some might call a wake—held in their honor if they paid the big bill. As I had it arranged with my wife, she would take five hundred dollars of my insurance money (that was just about the standard amount) and throw a beer party for my buddies.

I remember one SEAL's party that his wife attended. That was how we did things. We would say good-bye to one of our own, and then get on with the business of being SEALs. The one absolute rule we had was that the immediate family of the man who had been lost had the last word on what was done in the way of a funeral.

After One-Lump was gone, J. P. "Jess" Tolison was one of my closest friends in the Team, especially since we had gone to so many schools together during the formative years of SEAL Team Two. Jess had gotten a commission and was sent over to the west coast to serve as an officer with SEAL Team One. While working on setting up a training site in California, Jess was killed in a traffic accident.

Since his family was still back in Norfolk, Jess was returned to Virginia for services. The commanding officer of SEAL Team One escorted the body back to Little Creek and insisted that the services be an all-officer affair with only officers acting as pallbearers. The CO of Team One would himself give the national ensign (what we call the colors in the Navy) from the coffin to Jess's wife. The only trouble was, that was not how Jess's surviving family saw things.

Jess's wife put her foot down and said that chiefs would be the pallbearers and would conduct the ceremony. It was pointed out to her that Jess had been an officer when he was killed. "But he was a chief a lot longer than he was an officer" was all that she had to say. R. A. "Trash Mouth" Tolison, Jess's brother, and I were among the chiefs who carried the coffin and laid Jess Tolison to rest. I was the man who gave the folded ensign over to Mrs. Tolison, at her specific request and over the protests of the skipper from Team One. There have been few jobs that I ever found harder.

When R.A. had told me that Mrs. Tolison wanted me to hand the ensign over, I couldn't believe it. "You have got to be shitting me!" was all I could say. That sort of thing was more than a little out of my line and was normally reserved for the attending commanding officer. "You know he would do it for you," R.A. later said. After the services, we held our own party for Jess.

Sometimes, what we did to say good-bye to our own was not very well understood by people outside of the Team. Usually we just said "Fuck them!" about anyone who could not understand why we held a beer party. It was to celebrate a teammate's life, not his death. But that just didn't seem right to some people. One time, we had a loss at Team Two where the father of the SEAL we were honoring was a full-bird Marine colonel. There was a hell of a lot of Marine brass at the funeral at Hampton Roads, Virginia.

After the ceremony, Bob Gallagher and Rudy Boesch went over to the colonel and invited him to the beer party we were holding for his son over at RT's (Red and Tony's). The officer came completely unglued and thought the idea of a party was the worst thing he had ever heard of. I suppose you have to cut the colonel some slack; after all, it was his son's funeral. But the beer parties had become a tradition with us, one that is still carried on in the Teams today. The SEALs operate unlike anyone else in the Navy, and we say good-bye to our own the same way.

CHAPTER 3

On Deployment: A Working Party

I N JUNE 1961 I HAD AN UNUSUAL TOUR OF DUTY that took up the whole month. The Navy had cut a deal with AT&T to supply divers for a project the company was conducting. AT&T was running underwater cables from Devonshire Bay, Bermuda, to Cape May, New Jersey. Steel casings had to be placed around the cables in the surf zone around Bermuda to protect them from damage. No civilian firm would take the job. AT&T offered the Navy and the government a number of dedicated lines free in return for help. NASA was building up then and most of the phone lines were going to go to that agency. AT&T would pick up the tab for the project except for our regular Navy pay; the company would pay us a small per diem and pay for time underwater.

The Navy agreed to the project and a number of us from UDT 21 found ourselves flying down to Bermuda. The officer in charge of the detachment was nicknamed "Bull" Williams and the chief's name was Robinson. "Robby" Robinson was a real health nut, always exercising, pumping iron, and eating wheat germ. The rest of us were looking forward to a good time in Bermuda. We figured the hard work that AT&T was going to pay us for would be exercise enough.

After we arrived, we had to rent some houses near the work site. The government was convinced that the available military housing was just too far from the work site to be practical. Now we were all able to draw our per diem and locate our own housing. We ended up with two houses, one for the partygoers and the other for Robby, Bull, and a couple of the younger guys.

I was quickly placed in charge of the cooking, supplies, and household accounts. Supplies consisted mostly of booze. There were five shelves in a closet that I kept full of liquor. Instead of buying just beer by the case, I bought booze by the case from the store at the air base. Each shelf of the closet was dedicated to a type of booze—whiskey, rum, vodka, whatever the guys wanted. Food was easy because we had bummed cases of five-in-one C rations from the military. Each day I would leave the dive site about forty-five minutes before lunch and again before dinner. I would go to the house and heat up a bunch of rations and have everything ready for the guys when they got in.

The guys at the air base commented on the way we went through booze. I would show up at the base with a three-quarter-ton truck and load up several times a week. "You guys buy cases the way normal people buy bottles" was the only comment from the NCO running the store. By the end of the job, we had spent a little over $2,300 on food and booze. The most expensive bottle you could buy at the base was only about $1.75. But the guys never questioned me about the booze bill. I also bought some condiments and other things to improve the taste of the rations a bit.

At the end of the job, those bastards made me account for every penny of the $100 dollars I'd spent on food. "How could you spend that much money on food in just five weeks?" they asked. But as far as the $2,200 booze bill, there was never a question asked.

Representing the people who hired this zoo was a recently retired frogman from UDT 11 on the west coast. The cable project was the first job that this guy was doing for AT&T, and he was going to see to it that he made a name for himself with the company, at our expense if necessary. Bull and Robby wouldn't stand up to the guy no matter what he pulled. As far as they were concerned, he was in charge of the bunch of us.

None of us found the situation very agreeable. As usual, I was the loudest bitcher of the bunch. In fact Robby told me one day that if I didn't stop running off at the mouth, he would dock my per diem. I laughed in his face and asked if this was a union job. I hadn't been off the docks of Jersey and New York so long that I couldn't see a snow job.

I had been fortunate enough in the Teams and the Navy to be able to call things the way that I saw them. In a way, I defied authority when I could see it was plainly in the wrong and I knew what was right. In spite of all that, I always had friends. It seemed that my attitude was more common in the Teams than anywhere else in the Navy. That was probably why I got along.

After setting up at the houses, we went down to the site with the AT&T rep to see the job firsthand. The two cables were already in place. One of the cables was about two inches in diameter and the other about four inches. The AT&T rep figured we would have to lay fifty to sixty yards of shielding per cable, per day, to complete the job in the allotted six weeks. The shielding was a two-part casing that had to be placed under and over the wire and then bolted together. After looking at the job we just said, "No problem," and got to work.

Getting the casing parts in place was the first part of the job. Covering our rubber boat with a sheet of plywood, we used it to transport the sections of the casing from the beach to the cable. One man would run the boat and a second man would handle the sections, moving them to the edge of the boat. The rest of us were in the water putting the sections in place. When the boat had the casing where we wanted it, the man handling the sections would push it over the side. One swimmer would get a grip on the section as it hit the water and it would quickly pull him to the bottom. Once on the bottom, he would manhandle the section over to the cable and drop it.

Getting the sections in place was all done without scuba gear. Since we were just bouncing up and down off the bottom, it was easier to hold our breath for the short time we spent underwater.

In a few days we had all the pieces in place and were ready to start the assembly work. Along with our rubber boat, we had a thirteen-foot aluminum runabout with a ten-horsepower outboard motor. We soon learned that our rubber boat was handier to move the sections around with, but the thirteen-footer acted as a nice utility boat.

Chuck Newell was running the utility boat, zipping around with the outboard. Everything was going fine until Gene Fraley jumped into the boat. As soon as Fraley got in, the boat's outboard quit. Fraley was considered jinxed. Everything he touched broke. All he had to do was just get near something and it quit working. Chuck kept pulling and cursing at that outboard, but it would not start. Chuck was a pretty big man and Fraley was just a little guy. After looking at Fraley, Chuck just reached over and tossed him out of the boat and into the water. The outboard started on the next pull and Chuck motored away, leaving Fraley floundering toward the beach.

It was time for the underwater work to start. After pairing up into swim teams, we started bolting together the casing sections. Louie "Hoss" Kucinski and I were swim buddies on this job and worked on the heavy cable. Art Hammond and Rex Johnson were swim buddies working on the smaller cable. Everybody else worked in support of the divers in the water. On any diving job, 90 percent of the work is done on the surface, and the job goes no better than the support you have.

The water depth for the job ran from the surf line out to about sixty feet. The Bermuda waters are warm and clear blue. The work itself involved putting one of the casing sections under the cable, and moving that heavy cable could be a bitch. Another section of casing went on top of the first, sandwiching the cable between them. Bolting the two sections together completed a part of the cable shield. The sections interlocked, so what we were effectively doing was building a long, flexible steel pipe.

The rest of the crew made sure we had the nuts and bolts we needed. Skinning down, diving without equipment, they would put materials in place and bring us bottles of air (scuba tanks) when we needed them. The operation went on like this from sunup to sundown every day, seven days a week.

After about two or three weeks we had a small mutiny. Robby and Bull wouldn't say anything to the AT&T rep, but Louie and I jumped into his shit. "This is bullshit," we said. "We need a damn day off!" Finally, the guy relented and gave us the upcoming Sunday off. Real big of the jerk. Here we were, getting $23 a day per diem and $5.50 an hour for underwater time. There wasn't a professional diver in the States who would have worked at that job for those wages. And we were working like demons besides. Nice of the guy to give us a single day off.

The two houses we had rented were up a little hill from the Elbow Beach Surf Club. When we rented the houses, we were told that the guys would have access to the club. During the nights we hung out at the club. If you went to the club, you were supposed to be wearing a coat and tie.

One night, Rex Johnson was thrown out because he didn't have a coat or tie on. When he went back to the club, he put on the required clothes, sort of. Rex had his coat and tie, but he had changed into sneakers, the old-fashioned black high-top kind. After a short argument, it was pointed out that sneakers were not against the rules and Rex got in. That was one of our little ways of getting known real quick.

But by the second week we were down there, we finally got our Sunday off. Sam Fournier, Art Hammond, and I took our guitars down to the beach. Sam was a good guitar player and Art had taught me to play. What we had figured was to take a couple of cases of beer with us and spend the day playing guitars on the beach, usually a surefire way to attract some girls. It paid off, but not the way we figured.

While we sat on the beach, playing music and drinking beer, a young guy came over and introduced himself. He was a sailor from the Navy base at the other end of the island. He wanted to know all about us, if we were frogmen, where we were living. This kid just wanted to be a friend to a bunch of frogmen.

"Look," he said, "you guys haven't been on the island long, have you? Don't know where the women are or anything like that, right?"

We told him we didn't, and tried to figure out what he was driving at.

"If I can bring a dozen or so ladies to your house, can I come with them? We can have a regular party."

"You have got to be kidding us."

"No, no," he said, "I know a lot of nurses and I can bring them over to the house. They'd love to meet you guys."

"If you can do that, you've got a deal. You bring some women to the house and we'll wine, dine, and booze the bunch of you."

"Great. I'll see you guys tonight I'll bring at least two women for every guy."

Right.

With that the kid ran off, and we didn't think much more of it. He was all we managed to attract that day on the beach, so we finally went back to the house. Later on, the kid showed up on his brand-new BMW motorcycle. We all stood around looking at the bike and invited the kid into the house for a drink. Turning to Fraley, we told him to stay the hell away from the kid's motorcycle. "I won't touch it," he said. "Don't worry, I won't touch it." For a guy who was a walking disaster area, Fraley was always attracted to the wrong things.

Once inside, the kid told us that he would be a little late that evening, but that he and the girls were still coming over. Five minutes after we had gone into the house, Fraley entered, holding the bike's clutch assembly in his hands. "But all I did was touch it," he said.

After reassembling his bike, the kid took off. Art Hammond and I had a date later at the Surf Club with a couple of girls we had met earlier. Back then, whenever we rode on civilian aircraft, we had to wear suits. All of us were about the same size, so this increased our wardrobe opportunities. One night we would wear our own suits; the next night we might exchange jackets or trousers. Suiting up, we went off to the club.

Things were going along well at the club when Art asked, "Hey, Jim, why don't you call up to the house? See if that kid showed up." It sounded okay to me, so I went over to the phone and called in. We had a phone hooked up while we were there and everybody answered the phone, "Frog Manor, duty frog speaking." Outside the Norfolk area, frogmen were a novelty, and we played it for all it was worth.

I think it was Fraley who answered the phone. In the background I could hear all this giggling and noise. Something was going on up there. "Jimmy, get up here," Fraley said. "We need help."

"What the hell do you mean, 'We need help'? Just what's going on up there, anyway?"

"The kid showed up. There're more women here than you can shake a stick at."

Suddenly, getting back to the house sounded like a good idea. Going back to the table, I told Art what had happened. "Come on, Art, they're there."

"What's going on?" one of the ladies asked.

"There's a party at our house," I answered. "You're welcome to come along, but once we walk in the door, you're on your own." Classy repartee was never my strong point.

Going back to the house was amazing. There actually were two women for every guy. The ladies were nurses from King Edward Hospital and helped make the job an almost legendary tour.

The hospital was just around the corner from the house, about as convenient as you could get. And these were nice ladies; there was Joyce, Bobbie, Jean, Haffy, Judy, Millie, Agnes, Lorna, Red, even one we called Minnie Mouse. They were all super ladies and we got along real well. Before long, these ladies would come over every night after their shift was done. They didn't believe us when we told them that we had been diving all day.

"That's impossible," they would say. "You guys can't be diving all day and then partying all night. You guys are just down here on leave and partying, right? Where did you say this dive site was?"

The next day we were out in the water working when they showed up. We could see them up on the hill overlooking the beach, waving at us.

That night, things changed quite a bit. By about ten, the girls had paired off with us and just slowed things down gradually. They basically put us to sleep. The next day, they explained to us what happened. After the girls had seen what we were doing, they just decided that we had to get at least one night's sleep. That was the kind of rapport we had with them. As the job went on, a regular schedule started developing. As the shifts changed at the hospital, the shifts changed at the house.

We just wished things had gone as well at the job site. It wasn't that we couldn't do the work well or that the job was hard. Things went pretty smoothly and we enjoyed ourselves. It was just that the AT&T guy was a real pain in the ass. He wanted to be the Lloyd Bridges of AT&T. *Sea Hunt* was a popular television program then.

One day, just to show us what a super diver he was, the AT&T rep flipped over backward from the boat into the water. The action really did impress us, especially the way the guy flopped around after all his gear peeled off from the impact with the water. He damn near drowned.

The jerk's word just wasn't worth much. When we finally revolted a bit and said we wanted a full weekend off, he agreed. But to get the time off, we had to lay one hundred yards of cover on each cable in one day. Robby and Bull just nodded their heads. It wasn't that they were having such a great time. Every day after work, Robby would just go to the house and pump his iron for a while, eat his wheat germ, and live a "healthy" lifestyle.

Finally, I came out and said what was on my mind. I told Robby that if he did an honest day's work, when he got home he would be too tired to lift his weights. That really pissed him off. Louie finally told me to back off from telling Robby and Bull what I thought of their leadership. Since I was such a new guy to the Teams, Louie explained to me how much trouble Robby could make for me if he wanted to. I listened to Louie and quieted down a bit.

While we were working on the job, some of the guys from back at the Creek showed up. Roy Boehm, Gene Tinnin, and Harry "Lump Lump" Williams had been out on a Navy ship for some other project. Of course, since they were in Bermuda, they stayed with us. Robby and Bull tried to warn us that Roy and the gang were "just a bunch of alcoholics" and would drink all the booze. We just ignored them.

Cleaning up one night, Roy was in the shower while Lump

Lump was waiting his turn. When Lump Lump came out of the shower, Roy had already taken Lump Lump's clothes and was gone. Rule of the house: first one out, best one dressed.

Gene Tinnin was listening to us complain about Robby, "Mr. Muscle Beach." "Why don't you just take his weights and toss them off the pier?" Gene asked. Well, to tell the truth, most of us were just too new in the Team to do something like that. But Gene wasn't. He just took all of Robby's weights and tossed them into the water. The chief had to dive for two days before he found them all. To this day, Robinson thinks that I tossed his stuff into the water.

Louie had his thirty-first birthday while we were down in Bermuda. Not that we needed another excuse for a party. We needed time off. We had the AT&T man verify the mark we had placed to indicate the start. Working hard, we finished the day with 108 yards done on one cable and 110 yards on the other. But that wasn't quite good enough. That sorry bastard accused us of making a short count. "A short count?" we said. "You checked the marker yourself and swam the length when we finished." But that still wasn't good enough. But, out of the goodness of his heart and concern for our welfare, we could have one day off.

One of the nurses knew the men from the local fire brigade. One night at the house, along came a fire truck. The firemen partied with us until they got a call about a fire. They went to put out the fire, but showed up again as soon as they could. The firemen were pretty good and we got along well with them. Anytime we needed something down at the site that they could provide, the firemen were glad to be of help.

The firemen showed up with their engines down on the beach at the job site. Using the pumps and hoses from the fire trucks, we ran a water line out to the cables. With the water hose, we could jet away sand from under the cable and get the casings on without having to lift the damned thing. Getting close to the beach, we were able to sink the cable into the sand by again using the hose to move the sand out of the way.

The AT&T man had told us we would have to sink the cables

under the sand to finish up the job. If we finished early, he promised us the rest of the six weeks off to relax in Bermuda. That sounded good, so we put out a bit more and completed the job a week early. It was help from the fire department that allowed us to finish so soon and to do even more of the job than was originally asked of us.

But the two earlier warnings weren't enough for us to learn. When we finished, that miserable bastard ordered us off the island and closed up the job. Bull and Robby didn't stick up for us, so there wasn't anything to do but head for home. I hope that ex-UDT man's word stood him well at AT&T. If the company treated him as he treated us, he would have been out of a job within about six minutes. After the job was over, I never heard from the guy again. Didn't mind, either.

Eugenio Crescini ended up making a cruise chart of the Bermuda trip. On the chart were drawings of all the actions we did down there and caricatures of all the members of the detachment. At the bottom of the chart is written: "Dedicated to the top-grade nurses, King Edward Hospital, Bermuda."

The party when we left Bermuda was a real blowout. By the time we climbed onto the plane the next day, all of us had sworn off booze forever. It was time to live the good and healthy life. When we landed in New York, however, there was a footrace from the plane to the nearest bar.

That Bermuda job, for all of the personality conflicts, was the finest and most fun trip I took in the UDTs or SEALs. We worked hard and played even harder. There were enough shit jobs that we had to do. Later on in the SEALs, we had some good deployments, usually centering on training some allied forces. Those were occasionally a great time, even though they would be a lot of work. But nothing ever did quite compare to the Bermuda trip when I was in UDT 21. Every now and then, along came a trip that was one of the reasons for becoming a frogman.

CHAPTER 4

Diving

ONE OF THE THINGS I NEVER REALLY LIKED in the SEALs, or the UDTs for that matter, was diving. I worked underwater because it was part of the job and you had to get the job done, no matter what.

The kind of diving I'm talking about is not like the clear-water sport diving so many people enjoy today. We did that kind of diving down in the Florida Keys and off St. Thomas and Puerto Rico. Scuba diving among the reefs in the clear, warm waters of the Caribbean is fun, even for me. But slipping under the cold, dark waters at night, or operating in muddy, dark muck where you literally cannot see your hand in front of your mask, isn't fun to me.

My dislike of diving was noticed, and tested, by the higher-ups in the Team. Many guys found they just couldn't face going on a dive one day. It was a lot like suddenly turning claustrophobic after having been in a small space for too long. In fact, we called any kind of fear "getting clausty." But getting clausty especially applied to diving.

I have spent hundreds of hours underwater, most of them breathing through a rebreather rig that will quickly kill you if you screw up. Nobody touches my rig before a dive, and I always test a breathing rig before using it. Those practices are just common sense and the basic rules of operating underwater. Those rules were among the few that I followed almost religiously.

In the SEALs we didn't dive as much as the men in the UDTs did. We still kept up our training and had regular dive qualifications.

One time in 1961, before the SEALs were commissioned, I was in UDT 21 when a call came in for a team of divers to go on an operation. I had been to St. Thomas the year before and was diver qualified. At the time, not everyone in the UDTs was diver qualified. Everyone in the Team was a fully trained surface swimmer, but not all the men had been to diving school, where you learned all the different breathing rigs and how to operate them underwater. Being diver qualified was one of the reasons that some men, myself included, were picked to be plankowners—the original crew said to each own a plank of a ship's deck—when the SEALs were commissioned.

It was a Saturday in December, about midafternoon, when the call came in from the engineering group that was building the Chesapeake Bay Bridge-Tunnel complex. The engineers had been dredging the channel that the sections of the tunnel were going into, when a problem came up.

The tunnel was being built in sections on dry land, sealed, and towed into place over the dredged channel. When the sections were sunk, they would be connected up, made watertight, and emptied of the water.

Some of the equipment being used in the construction project was very large, and more than a little expensive. The call was about a piece of equipment that had been lost over the side of some barge in the bay. What the engineers wanted to know was if we could use some of our underwater search gear, like our hand-held sonar, to locate their lost equipment. Visibility in the Chesapeake was maybe three feet, and the hard-hat divers the company was using just couldn't find this multimillion-dollar piece of lost equipment.

Scotty Lyons was a new man in UDT 21 when the call came in. I had been in the UDT for only about a year and a half, so I was hardly a seasoned veteran. But I was the leading petty officer on duty when the call came in, and I was assigned to go out on the search dive. Since Scotty was available, I took him along as my swim buddy.

We got out the AN/PQS-1B hand-held sonar rig, which could locate objects underwater as far as 120 yards away. Along with the sonar, we broke out a couple of sets of open-circuit breathing rigs and generally got our gear together. It was colder than hell at the time, so I was already dreading the dive. But the job had to be done and we had agreed to do it.

The engineers sent in a boat to pick up Scotty and me. On the trip out to the site, they explained where the lost gear was thought to be. Once we were in the water, Scotty and I started pinging away with our sonar. We had just one false alarm on our first dive. On our second dive, we located the lost gear and marked it for recovery. Scotty was operating the sonar. Being fresh out of diving school, he was sharper on the gear than I was. I had not operated with him before and was just a bit clausty about working with a stranger, even if he was a teammate. But the dive had gone well. We had found what we came for and started surfacing to leave.

It was while we were coming up that the trouble began. Without knowing it, we had drifted underneath the barge the engineers were working from. Now the water was so dark you couldn't tell if your eyes were open or closed. Even telling up from down was a bit of a problem. If you panic underwater, you die. So we didn't panic; we just tried to feel out the situation. That's when the situation turned from bad to worse.

Underneath the big barge was a real mess. Cables, protrusions, pipes, and just plain junk stuck out all over, ready to trap an unwary diver. You couldn't see a damned thing, so avoiding the entanglements was a big problem, and we got tangled up.

I first noticed that I couldn't move at all. Reaching back for my buddy line, the line that connected me to Scotty, I could feel that it was stretched tight. The line was tangled with a mooring cable. I was stuck and I couldn't tell where my swim buddy was. Scotty could be in real trouble, drowning only a few feet from me, and I wouldn't be able to see him.

Then I felt Scotty's hands along the buddy line and at least knew where he was. Up to this point, all I had going through my mind was the situation we were in. Here I was tangled up underneath a giant barge, with a diver I had never been underwater with. Scotty had been through the Underwater Swimmers School at Key West while I had gone through the Team training at St. Thomas. Now the question was who would go spastic first, him or me.

Once our hands touched underwater, however, things calmed down. Scotty was doing exactly the same thing I was, just the way we were supposed to. Okay, we were both tangled up, but we both had air and our heads were screwed on right. Our confidence came back and neither of us panicked. We couldn't cut the line, since that would sever the only connection we had between us. We had to get out of our predicament another way.

By feel, we could tell how the buddy line was tangled with the mooring cable. Gradually, we freed ourselves, went back down a bit, and moved out from underneath the barge. After coming up from that dive, even the sharp cold of the wind felt good.

When we finally got to the surface, the engineers didn't want us to go down and connect the cable to the lost equipment. They had hard-hat divers who would do that, and our diving was done. I would have gone down again to finish the job, but not having to do that made things even better. The company men said that they wanted to be sure they had Scotty's and my names correct, and that we would be hearing from the higher officers before Christmas. That sounded pretty good; we figured on a nice company check for finding that multimillion-dollar piece of gear. But all that ever showed up was a pleasant thank-you note.

What did come out of the dive that was worthwhile was the knowledge that all the dive training at the Teams was turning out well-qualified men who could operate together. In other words, the schooling was doing just what it was supposed to. It was nice to know that so clearly. I still didn't like diving, but I knew I could trust my fellow divers in the Teams.

CHAPTER 5

Time at the Teams

A S MUCH AS DEPLOYMENTS, schools, and traveling around took us away from the Creek, it was the regular schedule of day-to-day events in the Team that gave us the abilities we needed to be really successful SEALs. As much as we abused ourselves with our drinking, carousing, and general hell-raising, it was the constant emphasis on physical fitness and maintaining what had been started at UDTR that allowed us to get away with all the damage we inflicted on ourselves.

From day one of the SEALs, a typical day at the Team began with physical training, better known as PT. PT was conducted as a Team with everyone participating. In the morning, everyone would fall out for Quarters in the same uniform, most often in a tan canvas bathing suit, blue and gold T-shirt, and sneakers. Quarters would be held, everybody accounted for, and any company-wide announcements would be made at that time.

With Rudy Boesch running the show, if you came out to Quarters not dressed for PT but in a uniform such as khakis for a chief or fatigues, you better have a chit signed by God for Rudy to let you out of PT. "Where are you going and why aren't you taking PT?" would be the first words from Rudy's mouth.

Before the SEALs were even commissioned, Rudy was running PT, first for the UDTs and then for us. If you want to see the benefits of regular exercise, take a look at retired Master Chief Rudy Boesch. There are pictures of Rudy on the 1970 Olympic bobsled team. Except for his hair color being a bit lighter, there is no difference between a picture of Rudy today and one taken way back then. Even the haircut hasn't changed.

After everything settled from Quarters, Rudy began to put us through our paces. "Okay, everybody," Rudy would say. "Right [or left] face. Forward, double time, ho!"

Leaving the Team area, we started out running around the golf course and out to Beach Seven. When we got to Beach Seven, Rudy turned left, led us up to the enlisted men's beach, turned around, ran down to the officers' beach, and touched the fence there; then he went back to the Beach Seven road and back to the Team area. Sometimes, for a change of scenery, Rudy altered the route. But in general, that was the way we ran, and we ran in a loose formation. The group started out tight and gradually spread out along the run.

After finishing the run, we did about forty-five minutes to an hour of PT, general calisthenics. Exercises would include jumping jacks, sets of twenty-five push-ups at a time adding up to maybe a hundred push-ups total. Other exercises included body twists, belly busters, "Hello, darlings," and all kinds of methods of turning, twisting, and pushing yourself that led to building up a good sweat.

Of course, not all of us liked to do PT in the morning, especially not a run. Rudy couldn't watch everybody all the time. To help each other out, we would take turns at being in the front of the formation. Those guys in the back of the group could take things a bit easier. The big gag was to skip out of runs.

Rudy would always be out in front on a run, leading the pack. When we went down the Beach Seven road, it was not a big problem to dive into the underbrush or behind a sand dune. With the Team merrily running along, you could take a break, rest behind the bushes, and smoke a cigarette, while waiting for the formation to come back. When the group came back, just falling in behind them would let you complete your "run." Since you were rested, you could demonstrate to Rudy your physical fitness by sprinting the last half mile or so, beating everyone else back to the Team.

If Rudy happened to see you slip out of the group, he would run the group back by another route. But Rudy rarely caught us. Louie Kucinski, Jess Tolison, and I did this sort of thing all the time. The young lions were all for the rah-rah SEAL shit and Rudy would be leading them mostly. Personally, I think Rudy gave us old farts a break.

It wasn't that we fell out of shape very much; we just had a lot of fun slipping out of PT. When I went over to Vietnam on my second tour, I had a number of the young lions come up to me wondering just what was going on. "Hey, Chief," they said, "you always goofed off on the runs back at the Creek. Over here, you're always up front when we have to pick them up and lay them down. Just where do you get it from?"

"Adrenaline" would be my answer. "That and fear can keep me outrunning you in this mud better than anything."

But back at Little Creek, PT was only the start of the day. After PT was over, we would go back to the Team building, shower up, and get into the uniform of the day. The remainder of the morning would be devoted to departmental work. Every man in the Team was in a department. Whether it was Ordnance, Sub Ops, Cartography, or whatever, each man would spend time doing his department's work.

At 1300 hours, we would muster again. Normally, on Tuesdays and Thursdays, we would have an ocean swim, sometimes with fins and sometimes without. Going down to Beach Seven, the whole Team would get into the water and strike out, again with Rudy in the lead. Depending on how cold it was, you could wear a wet suit. That choice was up to the individual. Swims could strike out toward the officers' beach or the enlisted men's beach, but they didn't go in the same direction all the time.

Monday, Wednesday, and Friday afternoons were devoted to our individual platoons. Each platoon had a little hole-in-the-wall where we kept our gear and other necessities. And I do mean just a hole-in-the-wall, nothing much more than a couple of double-door wall lockers. In the Teams today, each individual SEAL has more room in his equipment cage, just for his own gear, than we had for an entire platoon in the early days.

In the 1960s we didn't have as much individual gear assigned to each man as they do today. All we really had was the uniform, judo *gi,* wet suit, mask, and fins.

If you were in the Training Platoon, you would spend your afternoon getting a lesson plan together for the next class or putting together a training outline for a deployment. Platoons getting ready to deploy would take the classes or otherwise prepare to leave.

Deployments and detachments were going out all the time, before and during the Vietnam War. The majority of the time, a detachment would be announced on the bulletin board and you could just sign your name if you were qualified and wanted to go. Occasionally, a platoon would be told that it was being deployed to go somewhere. When assigned to Vietnam, the platoons had a regular rotation schedule that was closely followed.

But the platoon numbers didn't always add up. Before the Vietnam buildup, and during the war, we had a number of platoons on paper that didn't have any manpower. When these platoons were preparing to deploy, guys could enter the platoon if they wanted. There were supposed to be five full platoons in SEAL Team Two during most of my tour in the Teams, but—between training schools, injuries, and assignments—we never really had five. There were more like three full operating platoons and a few extra men.

As of November 1967, SEAL Team Two consisted of 23 officers and 115 enlisted men. This was up considerably from our original allowed complement of 10 officers and 50 enlisted men back in 1962. The Team was broken down into a headquarters group and, at the beginning of the year, platoons of 2 officers and 10 enlisted men (2/10). This was soon changed after experience in Vietnam dictated a larger operational platoon. By May 1967, our deployed platoons consisted of 2 officers and 12 enlisted men (2/12) and often had an additional 1 or 2 men along who would be assigned as advisers or to other detachments.

Let's say Second Platoon was going to France on a deployment. The number needed was a full platoon plus two. Second Platoon was where I spent the most time while in the SEALs and we almost never had a full platoon. So when a deployment came up and the numbers were low, guys in other platoons would just say they wanted to go. It would be up to the chief and platoon officers to decide whether to accept any individual to join the platoon.

Sometimes, people would abuse the system. There were guys who, after Team Two received the Vietnam commitment, suddenly transferred to all kinds of other assignments. They just didn't want to go to war. Others decided that they'd had enough of being SEALs and would literally go across the street, back to the UDTs. Our opinion of these fellows, offered by Bob Gallagher, was that they wanted to wear the name, but didn't want to play the game. Operating in time of war was what the SEALs were supposed to do.

But before you could operate, you had to get qualified. Being qualified to operate was where we got the term "operator" from. And an operator in the Teams was a man who would go out there and get the job done, no matter what it took.

In the early days of the Team, qualifications included various weapons courses, a land navigation course taught at the Creek, Jungle Warfare School, Instructors' School, and a number of other basic courses. Most of the training was from the courses we had evaluated during the first few years of the Team. Some were taught "out of house," while others would be taught by SEAL instructors.

I remember walking up to Gene Tinnin at the end of my UDTR training, sticking my hand out, and saying, "How's it going, buddy?" That son of a bitch looked me straight in the eye and said, "You haven't walked through the doors of UDT 21 yet. I'm no buddy of yours."

For encounters like that, I've got an elephant's memory. A few years later, Gene and I were good friends. He walked up to the doors of SEAL Team Two with his baggage in his hand. Gene wasn't a plankowner, but he came over to the SEAL Team early on. Sticking his hand out, Gene said, "Hey, Jimbo, how's my buddy doing?"

Now it was my turn. "*You* don't call me buddy," I growled, "until you get qualified to operate, fella." Don't get pissed, just get even.

On a regular day, liberty call usually went out by around 3:30 in the afternoon. If you had been caught pulling something, such as skipping out on a run, or just plain old had the duty for that evening, it was time to start extra duty. Other than that, it was usually time to go out to the club for a few beers. Lord help you if you started toward your locker before Rudy hollered, "Liberty!" That was almost a sure way of getting extra duty. But by around 3:30, everyone would be hanging around the general vicinity of the lockers, just to be ready when liberty was called.

Our first skipper, John Callahan, ran things just a little differently our first few months as a SEAL Team. When we got back from lunch, if there wasn't anything to do, Callahan would walk across the quarterdeck, the front area of the building where the officers' offices were, and tell Rudy to put liberty down. Sometimes, the skipper was carrying a few cases of beer that he left on the quarterdeck. The skipper then told Rudy to have the men clean up the quarterdeck and to put liberty down. This went on in the days when we were always waiting for some equipment or other gear to show up. Without something constructive for us to do, Callahan couldn't see the reason for keeping us just hanging around.

Not that the skipper could get away so easily. The commanding officers (COs) and their executive officers (XOs) of the SEAL Teams had a hard row to hoe. Sometimes they would work to midnight, and I saw almost every one of them during my tour do the same thing. The Teams were always so shorthanded in administrative personnel that the COs and XOs would often have to do admin work till the wee hours, work that in another place might be done by a yeoman or some other office personnel. But that was just part of the price of being in the Teams and being a leader of the Teams.

We had dedicated men and officers, and a closeness that just isn't found in the Teams today. That is not to say that the Teams are not tight-knit groups, but in today's politically correct Navy, the hell-raising and carrying on that actually brought us closer together back in the 1960s can't be continued. I can see in the faces of the young lions today, who are a hell of a bunch of operators in their own right, how they wish they could have been with us back then when they hear the stories told by us old war-horses.

On Fridays, things ran a little differently. No PT on Fridays. Instead we had soccer, and the games ran all morning. Playing competitive sports was a good way of blowing off steam and still getting some heavy exercise in the bargain. Soccer was chosen in part because of the tremendous workout it would give your legs. But our soccer didn't resemble the official game much.

We had two foreigners in the Team, Per Erik "Swede" Tornblum and Claudius Kratky, and those two guys were our soccer kings. Overseas, soccer is the sport, and both Swede and Kratky had grown up with the game. Some of the other guys in the Team became pretty good at soccer. Gallagher was good and so was Hook Tury, who later went on to play in a semipro soccer team that was organized in Norfolk. Pierre Birtz was also one of the good players.

Since soccer was Swede's sport, he insisted we play the game right and learn the rules. He gave regular classes on what a forward did, how a wing played, and all of the nuts and bolts. Swede was a real pain that way. This was a laugh, because none of us cared that much about the rules of the game. All we wanted to do was get out there and kick the ball around. Besides, most of our soccer games degenerated into free-for-alls anyway. Running back and forth and knocking the hell out of each other was good, clean fun. Well, it was fun anyway, even if it wasn't very clean.

Out on the west coast, I understand rugby was the big game. For the UDTs at the Creek, it was volleyball. One of the games the Team didn't play very well was basketball. But we entered a team in the base intramurals one year anyway. The Team was made up of men from both the UDTs and the SEALs, since we were both under the same command. Somehow, we ended up in the semifinals of the intramurals. We knew we didn't have a snowball's chance in hell of winning the game, so we just went to the club on game day. Our basketball team spent all afternoon getting drunk. We took cases of beer to the game with us.

From the beginning of the game until the refs finally threw us out of the gymnasium, we played SEAL style. Sometimes, there would only be three guys from our team on the court. The rest of us would be sitting down on the bench having a beer. To hell with having five men on the court.

The referee charged us with unsportsmanlike conduct and said we had forfeited the game. Not that it mattered to us, really. We had just gotten that far by sheer dumb luck. But the ref went over to the skipper of UDT 21 at the time—I believe it was Commander Robert Terry—and complained about our actions.

The main beef from the ref was our unsportsmanlike conduct. Terry wondered who had ever called us sportsmen.

"The problem with your men," the ref said, "is that they don't know how to lose."

"No, they don't" was Terry's answer. "They don't get much practice at it. Usually, what they do, they do very well, and they win." So much for basketball.

Fridays at 3:30, the work week was over. It seemed that the majority of the Team lived in the Princess Anne Plaza housing development, Malibu section. Only the young single SEALs lived in the barracks on base. And they would often gather together and just rent a place of their own. The young guys finally rented this place they called the Sugar Shack down on the beach. No furniture in the whole place, just wall-to-wall mattresses and a bar. A suitable abode for young and lively SEALs.

Because we all lived so close, we spent as much time together off duty as we did on duty. Even the single guys would come over to the neighborhood and start a party. First, the guys would go over to Art Hammond's house and sit down to have a drink. After they collected Art, the next stop would be my house, where they would do much the same. Moving on, we would usually go on to J. C. "Tip" Tipton's place and gather him up.

Tip's wife, Patty, was a partier too. One day, Tip was out in his front yard and he saw Sam Fournier, Art Hammond, myself, and others walking up to his place. All of us were half shit-faced and we were singing, playing guitars, and carousing. Going back into the house, Tip asked Patty, "Hey, Patty, do you want to go to a party?"

"Where?" asked Patty.

"Here, in about thirty seconds" was Tip's answer.

Tip's neighbor Annie also loved the Teams and enjoyed a good time. Annie had a pool in her backyard and she threw many a party for the SEALs. Most of the Team would show up for Annie's parties. There were only about twenty or thirty of us around back then and we could really have a good time. Those were good days.

THE DAY-TO-DAY RUNNING OF THE TEAM

After my first tour in Vietnam, I returned to Little Creek as a chief. Soon after I got back, Rudy took me aside one day to talk with me. Acting like a daddy—and he was the daddy to Team Two, though we called him Uncle Rudy—Rudy talked to me informally about what it meant to be a chief.

"Jim," Rudy said, "you earned the hat, bud. Now you're with us. You have a hell of a lot more leeway in how you act than you did when you were a senior first class. I don't care where you are or what you are doing. It doesn't matter if it's just you alone and you want to hang out and get drunk. But let me know where you're at so that I can answer for you. That's all you have to do, but you have to do it all the time. If you're at the club and you want to stay there, call me."

The one thing we all learned fast was that you could call Rudy, just as he said. But you didn't *tell* Rudy what you were doing; you *asked* him if it was all right. Calling up and saying, "Hey, Rudy, we're having a good time. Do you mind if we stay over?" was fine. But if Rudy said, "Look, something's happening, I need you back here," the decision was made. You didn't even go back and finish your beer. You returned to the Team ASAP.

When Rudy spoke, that was it. But just as often as not, Rudy would say, "No problem, see you in the morning." Officers came and went, but Rudy ran the Team. And he didn't rule with an iron fist, either; he just didn't have to. What Rudy used was a steady hand rather than a rough one, and that kept the respect of every man and officer who went through Team Two for almost thirty years. If Rudy walked by you and mentioned, "You do know where the barber shop is, don't you?" you had better take the hint and not make Rudy mention it again. A steady hand also meant that you could be sure of extra duty or anything else that would get the point across.

On the rare occasions that Rudy had to deal with an officer, usually one brand new to the Teams who was just too green to understand what was what, he didn't get face-to-face with him. For officers, Rudy worked through the exec, and he didn't have to do that often.

Rudy was one of a kind. That is not to say that each unit didn't have its own version of Rudy. Sam Bailey was Mr. UDT, Rudy's equivalent over in Underwater Demolition. But Sam, for all his skills and abilities, was not Rudy Boesch. He didn't have the finesse, closeness, or plain old experience that Rudy had.

Rudy rarely deployed away from the Creek. Running around on a deployment was not what Rudy was about. He stayed at the Creek and kept the Team humming. That is not to say that when the Team deployed as a whole, such as going down to St. Thomas, Rudy didn't come along with everyone else. And he didn't shirk his duty in a combat zone either. Rudy pulled his tours in Vietnam when his rotation came up.

Putting it as simply as I can, I don't think anyone will ever be able to fill the shoes of Rudy Boesch. Though other men will come along and do Rudy's job, and they will get the job done and have the same results, Rudy Boesch had a special understanding of his men, what they did, and why they did it. That is very rare. There was never a man more devoted to the Navy and the SEALs than Rudy, and his time in the service shows that.

Rudy understood what it meant to train all the time, or be on alert, and he would allow what he could to give his men time off. But you never lied to Rudy. If you didn't tell that man the truth, you might as well resign from the Navy.

The one excuse for time off that didn't work with Rudy was "I have to take the wife [or the kids] somewhere." From the first day of SEAL Team Two, Roy Boehm got the message out that there would not be a SEAL Team Two wives' club. On most Navy posts, there is an informal gathering of the wives of the officers and the enlisted men that has a ranking and set of traditions every bit as old and established as the Navy's. The women's ranks go according to their husbands', and the officers' and enlisted men's wives don't fraternize very much. This kind of organization can make or break a unit very quickly. And that situation was not going to be allowed at SEAL Team Two, not as long as Roy Boehm, or any of the men trained under him, had anything to say about it.

As long as I was in the Teams, up to 1972, there was no SEAL Team Two wives' club. There is such a thing today, but the Navy has changed a lot since I joined back in the 1950s. Today, even the UDTs are gone, having been absorbed into the SEAL Teams. On May 1, 1983, UDTs 11 and 20 were decommissioned, with their men making up the ranks of the newly commissioned SEAL Teams Five and Four. UDTs 12 and 22 were also decommissioned on that date, and their men made up the ranks of the new SEAL Delivery Vehicle (SDV) Teams One and Two.

Though the UDTs themselves eventually became SEAL Teams, the cooperation between the two was not always the best. In fact, during our first couple of years, there was downright animosity between the UDTs and the SEALs.

Most of the problems existed between the new SEALs and the older members of the UDTs, and things really were pretty bad during our first year as a SEAL Team. Some of the older guys said things like "Yeah, next year we're going to commission the WALRUSES," and other shit like that. But it was only a relatively few guys in the UDTs who were generating the friction.

And there were some grounds for the jealousy coming our way from the UDTs. Roy Boehm was seeing to it that the Navy bought us everything we needed, and more. Corcoran jump boots for our fatigues were just one of the uniform items we received, and everything we did get was top of the line.

The UDTs, right across the street from us, were still having trouble getting basic materials. The UDTs never had any money to speak of and the units would often work out of salvage, building what they needed when the Navy wouldn't go out and buy it for them.

The UDTs were like that for many years. And then along came

the SEALs, a bunch of fairly new kids on the block, receiving all the best toys. Although there were older guys in the SEALs, probably one third or half of the original plankowners had less than five years in the UDTs before the SEALs were commissioned.

The SEALs were a secret unit when we were first commissioned, just like the UDT during World War II. That caused more than a few problems with the high priorities we could get without having to explain ourselves to anyone. There were no news releases or much in the way of official public notification that we even existed. In fact, we were under orders not to discuss anything about what we did or who we were with the public at all, including our families.

On the other hand, Roy Boehm wanted us looking our best at all times and made sure we had the uniforms to do it in. We would walk around the base at Little Creek in polished jump boots, polished brass, a straight gig line (the line formed by your pants fly, buckle, and shirt buttons), and starched, pressed fatigues. Any of us could have been used as a Navy recruiting poster. Roy liked it that way and that was what he got—especially with Rudy Boesch backing up Roy's wishes.

This special treatment caused a lot of the friction between the UDTs and ourselves, because the UDTs had a very relaxed dress code. Most of the time, the UDT men were in bathing suits. If it was chilly, they would put on a green fatigue jacket over a T-shirt. Though we relaxed our dress code in the SEAL Teams over the years, some of the UDT guys really considered us a bunch of prima donnas, in part just because of the way we wore our uniforms.

It's possible that our problems with the older guys in the UDTs were because they couldn't see why we had been picked for the SEALs and not them. To cut down on the friction, and to build up our unit integrity, we came up with a new hangout for the SEALs during our off-duty time.

There was a joint just down the road from the base, kind of a combination motel/bar, called the Flamingo, but we called it the Redbird. The going question for a man leaving on liberty was "Going to the Redbird?" If the answer was yes, then another couple of guys would usually go along. When it came time for inspection,

Roy preferred to report "all present or accounted for," knowing we were actually at the Redbird having a beer, rather than have all his little SEALs stand in formation and butt heads during a personnel inspection by the Navy. It wasn't that we didn't respect the rules and regulations that governed our parent service; it was just that we didn't have time for them.

One Saturday, we were on an alert, standing by for God knows what. There were so many alerts we went through, and I had to get to Team headquarters. The only trouble was, my brother Bob was in town, getting ready to ship out for some time. But I had to go in to the Team, so I took Bob along with me.

On the way in, I picked up Tip and went into the Creek. Roy was there, along with some of the other guys, and we did whatever it was we had to do. Finally Roy said, "That's enough of this. Let's go to breakfast."

"Breakfast?" I asked. "Where are we going?"

"Redbird" was the answer that came back.

"Redbird?" my brother asked. "What the hell is a redbird?"

"You'll see when we get there," I answered. "Let's get going."

My brother was never much of a drinker, but I managed to uphold the family name despite that. When we arrived at the Redbird—which was east of the base, on Shore Drive—there were more than a few guys from the Team there, most of them ordering breakfast. The majority of the orders were for the traditional morning eats—bacon, eggs, whatever. As for Roy, Tip, Louie, and myself, up at the bar, we wanted a beer for the wait.

My brother was shocked. "What!" he said. "It's only nine-thirty in the morning. You just ordered breakfast. Ham and eggs with beer?"

Roy just looked at him and said, "Try it, son. There's two eggs in every can."

That was just the general feeling we had back then. We weren't only teammates; we were brothers. What Roy said, in that deep gravelly voice of his, was that we were "Man-o'-warsmen," Navy men inside and out. But more than anything else, I think we all considered ourselves brothers, with all of the petty bickering and head knocking that can go on among siblings.

In the SEALs, we never did tell very many people about what we were doing in and around Little Creek, not even our brothers in the UDTs. And they didn't tell us much either. Our lack of communication could lead to some bad situations, and I was involved in a really dangerous one.

In 1963, SEAL Team Two received a number of Powercat trimaran boats for testing and modification into SEAL Team Assault Boats (STABs). Before spending a lot of time and money modifying the craft to meet our specifications, we wanted to make sure they were up to the job. John Dearmon and I were given the job of testing the boats, and one of the things we needed to know was how stable they were in rough seas.

Ozzie Grant, a member of UDT 22 at the time, was conducting a night beach reconnaissance. The op was a standard castoff from a PL (Landing Craft, Personnel Launch) maybe a thousand to fifteen hundred yards offshore. The object of the exercise was to swim in and conduct a hydrographic reconnaissance/survey of Beach Seven under the cover of darkness. This kind of recon had been done by the UDTs since their first operations and consisted of carefully spaced swims measuring the contours of the bottom. Not a big deal, but the kind of operation that can make you feel very much alone in a great, big, dark ocean.

One thing that made the operation particularly difficult that evening was the rough condition of the seas. High waves are not the kind of water you want to swim through in the dark. No scuba gear of any kind was worn by the frogmen doing the op, just a regular mask and fins to get through the water and a wet suit for some protection from the cold.

Ozzie was one of the first people to cast off from the PL and head in to shore with his swim buddy, Nick Nault. Once at their proper location, the two guys would split off and measure the depth of the water with a lead line, just a lead sinker attached to a knotted cord, and write down the measurements on a plastic slate. Cartographers would later be able to put together an accurate chart of the water from the UDT information.

Once he was close enough to shore to hear the surf crashing on the beach, Ozzie kind of leaned back and rested in the water. He was trying to see if he could spot any of the other swimmers, when he started to hear a heavy pounding noise coming in over the water.

The sea and sky were the same color, black as hell, and Ozzie couldn't see a damned thing, especially not whatever it was that he was hearing. What Ozzie said later was that the pounding sounded like propellers cavitating (making air pockets underwater) as they bounced in and out of the water. But there weren't supposed to be any boats out in the water. And who would be driving a small boat around in seas like this anyway?

Not being able to see where the sound was coming from, Ozzie continued with his operation. All of a sudden, Ozzie saw a small boat coming in from his right side and bearing down on him. The boat was bouncing up and down in the water, smashing across the waves, with engines roaring as the propellers lost their grip on the water and spun in the air. Driving almost right at Ozzie, the boat was right on top of him in a moment, smashing him with the hull.

By pushing hard against the hull, Ozzie was able to force himself down and away from the boat. He desperately tried to get deep enough or far enough away so that the spinning propellers wouldn't chop him into shark food. As the boat passed so close that the prop wash pushed on one of his fins, Ozzie was able to get enough distance so that it didn't do much more than scare him out of a few years of his life.

Coming back to the surface, Ozzie saw the boat driving through the surf, heading back out to sea, when he lost sight of the craft. Looking around, Ozzie tried to spot one of the other swimmers on his op. On a hydrographic recon, the swimmers are spaced out evenly, twenty-five yards apart. Maintaining this interval and keeping things even is one of the reasons for practicing the operation.

Ozzie was a lot more concerned with where the other guys were in relation to that boat than how the recon was going. Ozzie hollered to another swimmer, "Watch out, there's another boat out here!"

But the only person to see the boat that night was Ozzie, not that any of his Teammates didn't believe him. Once back at the beach, Ozzie asked his swim buddy, Nick, whether he had seen the boat that had almost run Ozzie down. Nick hadn't seen the boat, but he'd sure heard it. Nobody knew who had been piloting the boat, but everybody was fairly pissed off about the incident.

After the recon was over, some of the guys in the PL got on the radio to find out who the hell had been piloting a boat with no lights or markings, off a Navy beach at night. I could have told them who it was, and they knew damned well it couldn't have been a civilian. Not in those waters at that time. Besides, Ozzie had seen the two huge black outboards driving the boat, and he knew the only people around with such a craft were the SEALs.

The next day, Ozzie came over to SEAL headquarters to find out who had been in the boat that almost sank him. "Steamed" is a good word to describe Ozzie's mood at the time. Since John Dearmon's boat was being worked on at the time, Ozzie figured that the pilot of the boat the night before had been me. He wanted a piece of my ass big time.

Things were soon set straight. Ozzie was told he wasn't supposed to be over at the SEALs' building and he was sent back to UDT 22, though he wasn't happy. Nobody was really mad at Ozzie for being pissed at the SEALs, but he wasn't supposed to charge over to our building, raising hell. Ozzie was right, however. The incident the night before had been a screwup, pure and simple. The only thing was, that particular screwup had damned near cost Ozzie a foot, if not his life.

What had happened was that John Dearmon and I had both been out the night before, running the Powercats. The seas being rough, it was a good opportunity to see what the boats could take. Basically, John and I were both trying to flip the boats over or pound the hulls into scrap. John's boat was out only for a while before he developed some trouble and had to go in to shore. I was busting around with my boat for quite a while, never knowing there were swimmers in the water.

The reason we were operating the boats at night was to keep from pissing off another sister service, the Coast Guard. Since the Powercats were to be used by the SEALs for clandestine operations, they had no markings whatsoever on them. Every time one of our boats was spotted, the Coast Guard called around, trying to find out whom they belonged to. When they finally tracked the boats down to SEAL Team Two, the Coasties wanted us to put U.S. NAVY or something on the craft to identify them. Well, identifying our boats was the last thing we wanted to do. So to avoid following the Coasties' instructions, but still not piss them off too much, we started doing some of our testing at night.

Another thing that pissed off the Coasties was the speed that we could travel in our Powercats. With twin hundred-horsepower Mercury outboards on the stern, there simply wasn't anything in the water that could catch our craft. And we enjoyed the hell out of them.

The particular night of the incident, the surf was up enough to give us a real good shakedown. The order of the run was to haul ass in toward the beach, screw around, and see if we could get through the breakers. The area where I ran into Ozzie had a water depth of maybe twenty feet. If I had run into him in the shallows, the story would have had a much worse ending.

When Ozzie was looking for me running across the water, I didn't have any of the running lights on—not exactly the safest way to travel across the water. But then we weren't going to be running SEAL boats near a public beach either. Naturally Ozzie could hardly see a black boat moving across a black sea. And I had no idea that he, or anyone else, was in the water at the time.

The lack of communication between the units was what almost caused a serious accident. In the Teams—both the UDTs and the SEALs—we came under the same overall command. But the right hand never told the left hand what it was doing, and vice versa. One result of the incident between Ozzie and me was a change in the overall method of operating between the Teams.

It was decided by the powers that be that if there were any more night operations—and the SEALs and UDTs operated at night a lot—one unit would tell the other at least where it was going to be operating. Much like the technique that we followed in Vietnam later, we requested an AO (area of operations) in order to pull a mission and not get shot by our own troops. We would let the base, or the people over in the UDTs, know what beach we would be working on. Our training and job were dangerous enough without our trying to kill each other, even by accident.

Years later, Ozzie Grant and I became good friends. Ozzie was on the board of directors for the UDT-SEAL Museum Association and I met him down in Florida. We've had many a good laugh over what happened that dark night so long ago. Ozzie has since taken me alligator hunting and out into the woods in Florida a number of times. I think he has forgiven me for almost running him over back then. But that time he left me in the field full of poisonous cottonmouth snakes makes me kind of wonder sometimes.

SEAL HUMOR

One of the things that always helped keep us going in the Teams was a good sense of humor. Or at least we considered it a good sense of humor. Pulling practical jokes was almost the rule at SEAL Team Two, and anyone could be a victim at any time. The more you made yourself a target, the greater the chance that you would take a hit.

It wasn't long after a new officer arrived at Team Two—I think it was about 1963 or 1964—that it became obvious to us that here was a new target. Black Jack was one of those men who, by the grace of receiving a piece of paper that said he was commissioned an officer and a gentleman, believed he was always right. Beside being correct, which a lowly enlisted swine couldn't be, Black Jack also always wanted to be at the center of attention, especially if the attention was from the public. The Teams were still very secret at the time, and chances for public recognition of the SEALs were few and far between.

Most of us in the Teams considered ourselves "quiet professionals" who didn't seek the public light or even approval. We did our duty as we saw best and our rewards came from the acceptance and support of our teammates. That may seem strange to a public that has been seeing the SEAL name tacked onto everything but breakfast food. Now books about the Teams, their history, and the stories of individuals who helped write that history are coming out constantly.

All that is true, but the one thing you will never see or read from an actual SEAL—and there are a hell of a lot of fake ones out there—is anything of a tactical or operational nature that is still being used today. And nothing is written that might be embarrassing to the reputation of the Teams either. Some stories might be around that serve as examples of mistakes teammates or even the Teams have made in combat or other situations. But that just means the SEALs are human too, much as we might try to ignore that.

In the early 1960s, a SEAL looking for publicity was a rare bird indeed. And when one came along who not only was image-conscious but also considered himself better than the men who had been in the Teams for years, that man was more than fair game— he was a priority target.

Sitting around the bar one day at the chiefs' club, a group of us was trying to decide how to take Black Jack down a peg or two. Everyone in the group, except for myself, had been in HALO (High Altitude, Low Opening, free-fall parachute) School with Black Jack and was really unimpressed with this particular officer. It was hard to understand how a college-educated man could ask, "If we're jumping from thirty-one thousand feet, can we see the ground from where we exit the plane?" It doesn't matter how high you are; you can always see the ground if no clouds are in the way. (Just ask one of the astronauts; it's hard to fly much higher than they do.)

It's hard to understand how some educated men don't have an ounce of common sense. But it sure can be fun to screw around with them. The idea that came to a bunch of us at the chiefs' club was to set up a phony newspaper interview. One of the guys knew several of the other chiefs on the base who could help us set up a phony SEAL interview. Laying out the bait wouldn't be a problem either. We would say that this was the first time any real public mention of the SEALs would be made in any newspaper. We were certain that our target couldn't resist.

When the phone call came into the Team to start the joke rolling, the "reporter" at the other end of the line asked for Black Jack, our operations officer. Identifying himself as being from the Norfolk *Ledger-Star,* the reporter told Black Jack that he would like to interview a couple of the SEALs for a Sunday supplement magazine story. The story would include photos of the kinds of equipment the SEALs were using and would be quite a good piece of press for the Teams.

Black Jack took the bait and ran with it. He said the reporter was talking to just the right person, and Black Jack would make certain that everything the man needed would be taken care of.

It was show time. To properly stage our little program, it had to look like an actual newspaper interview. Getting a chief from another part of the base wasn't a problem. The man we were using had never been around the Team area before and wouldn't be recognized. Another man was brought into the show and dressed to look like a photographer. Cameras and other gear were draped around our "photographer's" neck, the reporter was dressed up, and the appointment was made for the interview. All that remained was to brief our players properly.

Briefing done, our glorious leader met the newsmen when they arrived at the Team. Black Jack said he was going to handle all of their needs himself and there wasn't any reason to bother any of the other SEALs. The newsmen told Black Jack that they wanted pictures of the wet suits, the dry suits, and various types of breathing rigs. Black Jack damned near beat himself to death trying to give these men everything they wanted.

After some shots were taken of Black Jack in a dry suit, the reporter asked if he could put on a wet suit and wear the same breathing rig. This went on for some time, with Black Jack climbing in and out of different suits and gear, with all sorts of pictures being snapped. Too bad the camera didn't have any film in it; some of those pictures might be nice to have now.

Getting in and out of a dry suit was no simple matter. You had to climb into the bottom half, pull on the top half, and seal the two pieces together with a big gasket and a rubber ring. To make the rubber slip at least a little bit over the skin, you had to coat yourself with powder each time you put the suit on. And if you were sweating, it was that much harder. Of course, the day of the interview was a nice warm one.

It wasn't like Black Jack didn't add to his own misery. He had to be in every one of the pictures, and none of the other Team members could be involved. Into a wet suit with a Draeger rebreather, out of the wet suit and into a dry suit with the same Draeger. Do that whole sequence again, but this time use an Aqua-lung, then an Emerson. These guys were seriously messing with Black Jack, to the point that we thought he would catch on to the joke.

No need for us to worry. Black Jack was in his element, basking in the adoration of his public. He was going to be in the Sunday paper and that was worth all the trouble. If anything, that man was a bigger ham than I am, and that's saying something.

But all good things finally come to an end. The newsmen went back to their "paper" and we continued with our work at the Team. The prank started on a Thursday or Friday and Black Jack wasn't saying much around the Team about the newsmen or the story. Only a few of his friends were told to get a Sunday paper and see his big story.

Sunday came, but no story, no pictures, not even a little bitty one.

On Monday, Black Jack was steaming. He had put in three or four hours of really hard work into this story and nothing was in the paper. Calling up the *Ledger-Star,* our hero wanted to know where the story was. What happened to the pictures? And didn't the editors realize just how much time he had spent with their people? As it turned out, no, the editors didn't know how much time he had spent with their people. And what the hell was he talking about anyway? Did he have the right newspaper?

Black Jack was certain about the paper, and he told the editors so. There was not and would not be a story about the SEALs, Black Jack was told. The editors had no interest in a unit that couldn't be talked about much. But Black Jack kept asking them if they would be interested in doing a story anyway.

By this time, most of us had to leave. Things were getting too funny for us to keep operating with a straight face. In fact, things even got bad at the chiefs' club later. Do you know how hard it is to hold your beer steady when you can't stop laughing?

Just because I was involved in playing a number of jokes on the other guys didn't mean that I wasn't the target of a few gags myself. I had a little German NSU Prinz car at the time. Not even as large as a Volkswagen Bug, my Prinz had a two-cylinder dual-ignition engine with a five-gear transmission. The look of the car was such that you had a hard time telling from the outside whether it was moving forward or backward. Parking wasn't much of a problem since three guys could literally pick the car up and carry it away.

While I was at a party one day, my teammates picked up my Prinz and hid it in the bushes. Just scooped the little sucker up and stashed it away. When I came back from a tour in Vietnam one time, I found out my Prinz had gotten a new paint job while I was gone. Since I liked putting unit and school patches on my uniform, my car now had patches all over it: yellow polka dots all over the fire-engine-red body. Just another case of "let's fuck with Jim."

We always had something funny going on in the Team. Different things resulted when different people were messed with, and you could never tell when a good opportunity for a gag would come up. Once down in St. Thomas, one of the guys managed to get a date with one of the Dodge Girls from the TV commercials. To say that this girl was a looker was to say the very least.

A bunch of us were sitting in one of the bars in downtown Charlotte Amalie, the capital of St. Thomas. Besides myself, there was

J. C. Tipton, Louie Kucinski, Bill Brumuller, Jess Tolison—just the regular group who hung out together. Joining our little group was the SEAL and the Dodge Girl he was dating.

During the course of the evening, we heard the girl ask our friend if he would take her down to Katie's in the old Slave Market. That section of town was actually where the slave market had stood a hundred years ago. Now it was a large market area in general, where the locals purchased vegetables and other goods. In the market area was a notorious nightclub known as Katie's. It was strictly a gay and lesbian hangout.

Back then, things were a lot looser in St. Thomas than they were back in the States, where a place like Katie's would not have been a popular place to go. Down in the islands, you might get propositioned, but when your tastes were known, you would get mostly left alone. It was pretty weird for me the first time I was in St. Thomas and got propositioned by a guy. But what the hell, it wasn't the United States.

What we overheard was that this girl wanted to observe the behavior at Katie's, but she definitely wanted to be escorted. Our brave young SEAL agreed to escort the girl, and off they went to Katie's.

They weren't gone five minutes before things got set up on our teammate. Off the group went to Katie's, led by Bill Brumuller, who always seemed to be in the middle of these things.

We spotted the Dodge Girl and our teammate sitting at the piano bar in Katie's. Bill could put on the queer act in a fast heartbeat when he wanted to mess with somebody. Considering Bill is built like a barrel with arms and legs, he made a fairly dangerous-looking queer. The limp wrist and lisp he put on blended right in at Katie's. Approaching our teammate, Bill planted a big wet kiss right on our buddy's lips.

"You promised me you wouldn't cheat on me," Bill said in his best lisp, "and here you are out with this woman."

That Dodge Girl got up and ran out of the building. She was moving fast enough to outrun one of the Dodge trucks she was always pushing on TV. She may still be running for all I know. She never did appear in any more truck commercials that I know of.

That was just another example of the kind of fun we had over the years. The one rule was, never get pissed if you're had. You get pissed off and look out—that made you fair game for everybody, even the guys who didn't play practical jokes. If you took things as a joke, that's what was meant by them. In fact, if you weren't being screwed with, you didn't really feel like one of the guys. The jokes we played were never meant in a mean or vindictive way. They were never destructive and we never looked for real trouble. They were just a good way of blowing off steam in what was a pretty hazardous job.

There is one problem with putting these stories down on paper. All you can read is what we did, how we did it, and occasionally why we did something. What's missing is the feeling of camaraderie and closeness in the SEAL Team during those early years. Words just fall short in trying to explain how close we were to each other, much more so than even to family members. And maybe it was even because of this closeness that we messed with each other so much on a fairly regular basis.

Sometimes, it wasn't a particular person that was a target for a gag. On the proper occasion, we would mess with the entire Team. It all depended on the situation and how certain individuals might be feeling at a given time.

Dante (Stephensen) Shapiro was hot on physical fitness in the Team and was constantly trying to organize different events to keep us at our best. Dante set up intramural judo tournaments and other competitive sports to push us into being even more active than we already were. For me and several others, we were already too active. All of that PT was seriously cutting into our beer-drinking time. One time Dante set up a military pentathlon within the Team, setting one platoon against another.

The pentathlon was a series of events, each with a definite military skill involved. Some of the men in the Team had already been in an international pentathlon, where units from different countries

competed against each other, and they had brought back the idea
to Little Creek. What we were going to do was not only supposed
to be an individual competition, with each man trying to excel on
his own, but also a team competition. Our teams would be the platoons we were assigned to. Each man would run the course with a
buddy, and the points the two men earned would be added to the
overall score of the platoon.

Jess Tolison and I were very much alike. We had been to many
of the same schools together and had the same general outlook on
life in the Teams, especially PT and how to get out of it. For the
pentathlon, it was natural for Jess to be my buddy. What Jess and
I decided was to have our fun with the contest.

The pentathlon was set to start and end at the Team headquarters. First would be a timed run; then you would reach a certain
point and have to throw three hand grenades into a circle. Then you
would run to another point and paddle a one-man life raft across a
lake with just a single hand paddle.

Where Dante came up with those damned little rafts I never will
know. We soon found out that trying to paddle the raft in a straight
line with the single paddle was a real bitch. It turned out to be easier
to put the wooden paddle between your legs and just scull along
using your bare hands. Not very fast, but at least you went in one
direction, mostly.

After the raft paddle there was another run, this time down to
the beach for a distance swim. With the swim over, off you ran
again, this time to the rifle range. There you fired five rounds semiautomatic at the two-hundred-yard line with our new select-fire
AR-15s. The obstacle course was even part of the contest. My personal feelings aside, Dante really did a great job in trying to duplicate the international pentathlon and molding it to SEAL
operations. Only thing was, neither Jess nor I really wanted anything to do with it.

We decided, to hell with the whole thing. Since we couldn't get
out of the pentathlon, we were going to do it our way, by the numbers, exactly one step at a time.

This meant that we walked all the running portions. Getting to the grenade throw, each of us picked up one hand grenade. "Got your grenade?"

"Yeah, I've got mine."

"Okay. Ready, pull pin, one, two, three, throw."

All throughout the whole event, Jess and I did every action right alongside each other. I think we received the lowest score of the entire Team. What I do know is that our platoon was flat-out pissed off at us. It turned out that the platoon as a whole came to within a few points of winning. If Jess and I had just jogged the course, earning one more point, the platoon would have won. As it was, we lost, and nobody in Second Platoon appreciated our sense of humor that day. Dante got pretty pissed off at our attitude, but Rudy thought it was funny, and that was good enough for us.

TRAINING THE YOUNG LIONS

One action that we did on occasion in the Team was assist in training the new volunteers going through Underwater Demolition Team Replacement, the basic class that everyone had to take to get to the Teams. Anytime a class going through training got to Hell Week, the call went out for volunteer instructors. Since Hell Week effectively ran twenty-four hours a day for a week, the instructors ran in shifts to keep from getting tired. This was especially important later during the week, because the trainees would practically be zombies by then. You had to stay sharp to ensure nobody got hurt.

Volunteer instructors would come out of both the UDTs and the SEALs, but never included new teammates who were fresh in the Teams. Anyone who had been out of training for only a year or less might be too sympathetic to the new trainees and what we were putting them through.

My first time as an assistant instructor was a very interesting one. I knew someone who was going through training. One-Lump Williams had been in the SEALs since day one, assigned to us from the Army Special Forces. He didn't have to go through training when he joined the Navy; Roy Boehm had guided One-Lump through the recruiting process, making sure that he would go directly to the SEALs. But it was a measure of the quality of the man that One-Lump insisted on going through training just like everyone else. And we made it anything but easy on him.

The first time I was assisting, J. C. Tipton was working with me. Going down to the training area in our starched fatigues and spit-shined jump boots, we saw the trainees just getting ready to enter the mud flats. John Parrish always led the trainees through the mud flats in those days, so he was there, but no other instructors. The rest of the guys must have gone to lunch or something, so it was just John, Tip, and myself with this bunch of trainees. And the class had just gotten finished with the obstacle course so they were nicely winded by the time we showed up.

Off we went with John to the mud flats . . . to the flats and into them. Here we were, in starched uniforms, looking like we'd just stepped out of a recruiting poster, standing asshole-deep in the mud right alongside the trainees. That shocked the hell out of those trainees, exactly the effect we had been trying for. They must have though we were completely nuts. But John knew how to handle the situation.

"You trainees just lay down there in the mud," John said. "We're not going to let these instructors get their shiny boots muddy. You trainees make a chain across the mud with your bodies and these instructors will just walk across on you."

And that's what we did. Tip and I walked across the mud on the trainees themselves. As soon as we were across one man, he had to get up and hurry to the front of the line and lie down again. That way we had a continuous line of bodies to walk on. Of course, we got muddy all over anyway, but it still had a nice effect. Doing the unexpected was something we were good at, and it was fun to try to blow the trainees' minds.

There was one guy in that class with One-Lump whom I did not want to complete training. Jim Wallace had the same initials that I had and he looked like me as well. There was no way I was just going to let this man through training and into the Teams where he might cause people to confuse him with me. I already had received enough grief from having a Charles Watson in the UDTs and later the SEALs. I was constantly being mixed up with him.

This possibility was not going to continue. When I stepped on Jim Wallace, I stepped right on his head, driving it down into the mud. "Boy," I said, "you ain't going to make it." It became something of a personal obsession with me to try to drive Wallace out of the class. But I have to say this for him: With all the shit that I handed him, he never quit. Jim Wallace went on to graduate and join the Teams. That, of course, made him a teammate and I couldn't screw with him anymore. Or at least not as much as when he had been a trainee.

About the only thing we didn't do was actually blow up any trainees. Only the trained instructors would handle explosives during So Solly Day. On that day of Hell Week, the trainees are exposed to violent explosions almost throughout the entire day. Only the men who had been specially trained to set off charges close, but not too close, to the trainees handled any powder. But there was more than enough work for the rest of us in just generally harassing the trainees.

CHAPTER 6

Personal Problems and Their Effects

I N THE NAVY, there is an almost constant problem with marriages.
Only a strong and secure relationship will survive a "Navy marriage." Some wives have no problem with their husbands' going
away for long periods of time while their ships are on a cruise.
These women at least have the security of knowing where their men
are, or at least which ocean they are in. What's bad is where the
family can't stay together after the husband leaves the Navy. This
is where people find out that, although they may love their mates
greatly, they can't stand to live together on a long-term, day-to-
day basis.

The much more common problem in a Navy marriage results
from the partner in the service having to be away from home for
long periods. This is especially true with young couples. In a weak
relationship, the constant worry and wondering about her absent
sailor can lead to a young wife's imagination running away with
her. The idea can soon come to the mind of a Navy wife that her
husband is doing what sailors have done for centuries when in a
friendly port. The idea of "a girl in every port" can really tear a
marriage up, even when it isn't true.

The worst thing for a relationship is where the woman back at
the base is cheating on her sailor husband when he's away. This
not only destroys a man's morale, it can make it hard to keep his
mind on his job. Being distracted with a personal problem can be
just plain dangerous for anyone at sea, but for a man facing combat,
especially a SEAL, it can be downright deadly.

In the Teams, there's an additional stress put on a relationship that doesn't happen in other parts of the Navy. A SEAL or UDT man can be called away from home at literally a moment's notice. One minute, an operator can be planning a weekend away from the base with his family; then an alert goes down, he gets a phone call, and he's out the door. Because of security considerations, the wife doesn't have any idea about where her man has gone, what he might be facing, or how long he'll be gone from home.

We had kind of an unofficial network in place at the Teams. Men who were still at the base would look out for a deployed operator's family. This was fine for the day-to-day problems; washing machines that went on the fritz would get repaired, dripping faucets fixed, cars made to run. But there just wasn't much to be done about the worry that came with being a Team wife.

Some SEALs were real womanizers; a girl in every port just wasn't enough to describe their lifestyle. Other operators were absolutely loyal to the wives back home, and though they would go out and party with their teammates, extracurricular activities were where they would draw the line. The sexual urge would get pretty strong sometimes, especially after a hairy one when the platoon would be given some liberty time. Times like that were usually not given much thought afterward. Given the situation we were living and working in on a day-to-day basis, there just wasn't much time for guilt to slip in.

Time back at Little Creek after a deployment or tour could run very slowly for a family that was having trouble. More than one operator would volunteer for every assignment that became available, especially those in Vietnam. Some of these guys were hunters who wanted to take it to the enemy every chance they got. Other men just wanted to stay the hell away from home.

In the fall of 1968, I was the platoon chief for Sixth Platoon and we were getting ready to leave for deployment to Vietnam in December. As a platoon chief, I had a lot of say in who would be in, or out, of the platoon. When a platoon was getting ready to begin its refresher training prior to deployment, it was necessary to be sure all the platoon slots were filled. There usually wasn't any problem in getting enough volunteers. The hard part sometimes came in deciding who wasn't going to be part of the platoon.

We had one man in Team Two, Second Class Radioman Jack Rowell, who had a lot of difficulty getting into a platoon that was going to Nam. I had known Jack for a number of years. Though he wasn't a plankowner, Jack Rowell had been with Team Two since the early days and had shown himself to be a good operator. When Team Two had sent a detachment to the Dominican Republic in April 1965, Jack had been among the first guys to go.

During the Dominican crisis, Team Two got its first taste of combat. This wasn't anything much when compared to what came later in Vietnam, but to men who had mostly just trained for years, it was a baptism by fire. While in the Dominican Republic, Jack went with Georg Doran on a special undercover mission to search some caves for possible rebel supply caches. Though nothing was found, the mission was a hairy one, and I think both Georg and Jack came out of it with decorations.

This wasn't going to be Jack Rowell's first tour in Vietnam either. He had gone over with Seventh Platoon in the fall of 1967. Bob Gallagher had been the platoon chief of Seventh during that tour, and they don't come any better than the Eagle. Seventh had gone through the Tet Offensive and pulled a number of real hits against Charlie. One op was against a POW camp, and though no prisoners were found, Seventh Platoon did run into several battalions of VC. Bob had come out of the op with the Navy Cross, Mikey Boynton received the Silver Star, and the rest of the platoon held up its end of the fighting.

Jack Rowell had been part of all this. He'd even been wounded twice, but had come home to a real family problem. Though I didn't know anything about it at the time, life at the Rowell household had taken a real downturn while Jack was in Vietnam. The pressures of his family life had caused Jack to take on a different attitude, and one that didn't sit well with his teammates.

One thing that we did do in the Teams was respect each other's privacy. If a man wanted to talk, he would have little difficulty in finding a brother SEAL to sit down and share a few beers with. On the other hand, if a man didn't want to talk, he wouldn't be pressed to open up about what might be bothering him. I wasn't one of Jack's confidants and, though I had known him for a number of years and often jumped with him and the local parachute club, I had no knowledge about his family problems.

Jack approached me when Sixth Platoon was forming up. None of the others would take him with them when they went over. Jack had developed the reputation of being a bit of a crybaby in the Teams. Whenever something wasn't going right, Jack could always be heard complaining loudly about the situation. Though he had earlier shown himself to be a good operator, the change in his attitude had developed gradually since then and now was the only thing anyone noticed. This was what I knew when Jack came up to me at Sixth Platoon.

"Hey, Jim," Jack said, "can't I be in your platoon? Nobody will take me with them."

"Jack, there just isn't room over there for the kind of talk you do. You've got a rep for pissing, moaning, and groaning. That's why nobody else wants you."

Jack pleaded his case with me for some time that afternoon. Going home that night, I thought over what he had said to me. In the morning I came to a decision. Remembering the chance Roy Boehm had given me, I would do the same for Jack.

Calling Jack over to the side, I told him he was in. "Okay," I said, "I think everybody deserves a shot. You can come as part of the platoon."

I never regretted taking Jack along. During in the tour he won the Bronze Star, and I think the award should have been higher. When the chips were down, the man stood tall with a Stoner in his hands. In broad daylight, Jack stood on a rice paddy dike, just defying the bastards to come and get him while he covered our withdrawal.

During my tour with Sixth, I took over as the adviser to the Provincial Reconnaissance Unit (PRU) guys in Nha Be, where the platoon was based. While the platoon was operating, I also worked in the field with the PRUs, splitting my time between the two groups. Operating with the PRUs was exciting and we really took the war to Charlie's doorstep. Parakeet ops had been honed to a fine edge by Fast Eddie Leasure as well as a number of other SEALs earlier and I took advantage of that style of operating.

In a parakeet op, a single unarmed helicopter would fly along at several thousand feet, looking like any one of a hundred other birds that were in the air at any time in Vietnam. Inside that attack helicopter were several SEALs and an intelligence contact who could identify a target clearly, pointing it out to both the SEALs and the crew of the bird. When the target was spotted, the attack bird went in and landed as close to the exact spot as possible.

When the attack bird went in, the several gunship helicopters that had been flying low to the earth suddenly rose up and started circling the area. The target, usually a high-ranking VC, was snatched up as soon as he was identified, and the gunships made sure that the ground situation didn't get out of hand.

In the parakeets I worked, I was in the attack bird with one other SEAL, preferably a Stoner man, and three or four PRUs. When the attack bird swooped in to a target, we jumped out, sometimes right at the target hooch's door. As we went in, the four or so armed gunship birds that had been following behind zoomed up and flew cover, circling like great hawks.

The parakeet op was a really fast-moving, wham-bam-thank-you-ma'am kind of hit. Just the sort of thing I liked. On more than one occasion, my Stoner man, the only SEAL with me, was Jack Rowell. Jack had stood up well in the ops we had run so far and hadn't proved my judgment of him wrong.

On January 14, 1969, I went on a parakeet op with Jack acting as my Stoner man, supported by three PRUs. The target was a VC platoon leader, a worthwhile prisoner to snatch, who could possibly lead to more and bigger ops. The parakeet went well; the target hooch was pointed out by the agent who was in the bird with us, and we triggered the action.

The area was a familiar one, a number of native hooches surrounded by rice paddies with tree lines in the distance. Zooming in, we all jumped from the slick (an unarmed UH-IB helicopter). The

PRUs headed to the surrounding buildings, with Jack covering me as I busted in the door of the target's hooch. Only trouble was, I had kicked in the wrong hooch.

Flexibility is a virtue and thinking on your feet is drilled into you during SEAL training. We immediately moved out to the nearest hooch and I grabbed our targeted prisoner. The parakeet was running so fast, the man didn't have time to use his weapon. We had the VC platoon leader, some documents he had on him, his AK-47, some web gear combat harness, a .45-caliber pistol, and parachute grenades.

Unfortunately, we were farther away from the jump-off point than we had planned, and our actions had stirred up a real hornets' nest.

While we were running toward a point where the bird could come in to get us, the PRU man in front of me took a round in the leg. We were out in the open with no cover nearby. Diving down behind the injured man, I got on the radio. "Cover our ass with the guns. I have a man who's hit. Get the slick back in here."

The regular ARVN (Army of the Republic of Vietnam—that is, South Vietnam) troops had no respect for the PRUs and wouldn't give them support when they needed it. I knew I had to keep the respect of my PRU men to continue functioning the way I wanted to. When I carried the radio, I wore a headset to keep my hands free. While talking to the surrounding helicopters, I was quickly trying to patch up the man's wound. The PRU had taken a bullet in the upper part of the leg. I was on the ground, trying to get on a pressure bandage to stop the bleeding. Meanwhile, Jack stood tall. He literally straddled the two of us. Standing there fully exposed, Jack fired bursts into the area, keeping the VC away. Neither one of us knew what direction the fire had initially come from. But Jack fired his Stoner to let Charlie know just whom he was messing with. When a Stoner talks, everybody listens.

"Patch him up, Chief," Jack said. "I'll keep their fucking heads down."

In all the time it took the extraction bird to arrive (and it was a little while, with all the ground fire going on), Jack stood guard over me and my wounded man. He kept everyone away from us with controlled fire from his Stoner. It was a good fifteen to twenty minutes before we finally got out of there. Afterward, I wrote Jack up for the Bronze Star for the incident, and he got it.

Later, back at the Creek, guys would ask me, "Why did you write up that crybaby for the Bronze Star?"

I wouldn't let the conversation go much further. "Hey!" I answered. "That man stood tall and covered my ass when he was needed. Not like some other people we know that everybody thought were going to be heroes. When the pressure was on, they didn't show any backbone. He did."

But the personal troubles the man had earlier had almost kept me from taking him along with the platoon in the first place. Though I don't personally know of any SEAL who let his family life get in the way of performing his duty while in Nam, SEALs are human, after all. The pressures of married life, and the problems that come with it, can easily change a man without anyone noticing until the damage has been done.

CHAPTER 7

Atomic Demolition Munitions

T RAINING WAS, OF COURSE, something that went on all the time at the Teams, especially during the early years prior to Vietnam. Besides trying out different classes for possible adoption by the Teams, we also needed other much less exotic, more down-to-earth skills in the ranks of the SEALs. These needs were put forward by both the Navy and the Teams' command. The result was that a number of us were ordered to classes, sometimes on the base or nearby, but also at some distant locations.

In 1964, I took a number of classes that were less than exciting but offered experience needed by the Teams. I spent four days attending the Basic Mechanized Embarkation Data System Orientation Course. It gave me a fascinating overview of how to load and unload a ship. Not that loading a ship isn't a valuable skill in the Navy, it's just not something that was done in the Teams very often. That skill was a ticket punch that the Teams had to have in their locker according to the Navy, and I was just one of the SEALs who had to attend. Sometimes, we were told to attend such and such a class, without really knowing beforehand what it would be about. On one occasion, the subject matter was one of the most serious things I was ever involved in.

As SEALs, Jess Tolison and I had attended just about every service school together. So it was no surprise for us to be sent off to another. On one Friday afternoon in early February 1964, Jess and I were called in to Personnel and told that we would be reporting to the naval air station in Norfolk the following Monday morning to begin a new training course.

"Okay," I said. "What's the course going to be?"

"We can't tell you" was the astonishing answer.

Not being one to beat around the bush, I blurted out, "What the hell do you mean, you can't tell us?"

"Just be in dress blues and report to the classroom on Monday. Tell no one about the school. In fact, when you get done with the training, if anyone wants to send you again, you cannot tell them you've already been there."

Now things were getting more than a little bit screwy. "Say what?" was my witty comeback.

"The subject is highly classified; that is all you need to know at this time."

A cooler head than mine prevailed at that point and Jess guided me out of the door before I said anything to really get myself in trouble. True to orders, on Monday morning, we found ourselves in a regular classroom listening to a Marine gunnery sergeant lecture us. The classroom was a regular schoolroom, with desks and a blackboard. The class wasn't the most interesting one I had ever attended, at least not for the first few days.

On Monday and Tuesday we were lectured by this Marine on procedures. No charts, pictures, or training aids were visible. I've always been a hands-on type of guy and classroom work has never held much interest for me. By Wednesday, I had just about enough of all the lecturing and spoke up during a break.

"Jess," I said, "this is bullshit. All they're telling us is how to follow written procedures. We don't need a class to tell us how to read a list."

Jess had far more patience than I did. "Just cool it," he said. "They'll tell us more when they're ready."

Later that day, we started to get some real information about just what it was we were going to be working with. I think Jess and I both realized what the subject matter was at just about the same time. We were being taught how to enable and plant a bomb, a really big bomb. I raised my hand and was called on by the Marine instructor.

"Gunny," I said, "it appears obvious to me what it is we are being taught to use here, and I have two questions."

"What are those?" he responded.

"Number one," I asked, "if this thing screws up, just how far away do we have to be when it goes? Number two, just how long do we have to get there?"

"Don't worry about that" was the answer. "You'll never make it."

"Jess, I told you," I said, "we're in the wrong place."

"Just shut up" was Jess's answer. "They aren't starving us and they aren't beating us, so just sit down and pay attention."

This was good advice from a good friend. We were taught how to employ the SADM (Small Atomic Demolition Munition), also called a baby atomic bomb or backpack nuke. Eventually we were shown a training device and given hands-on experience with it.

Though I'm not sure of the designation and nomenclature of the weapon we were trained on, I have been told that it was most likely a modified W54 warhead as used on the U.S. Army's Davy Crockett weapons system. The weapon weighed around sixty to seventy pounds and had a yield of about 0.25 kiloton. The bomb had a cylindrical body with a flat head and rounded bottom. It was about a foot in diameter and two feet long, roughly the size and shape of a five-gallon bucket with a basketball stuck into one end. The flat end of the bomb had the controls for setting the fuze time delay and arming system.

The training itself wasn't really much. It was mostly about following directions read from a manual. And by following directions, I mean following them exactly. While one man read from the manual, the other performed the necessary tasks. Even how to get the darn thing out of the drum it came packed in was written down.

"Step one, take up Mark One Mod Two cutters. Step two, locate seal on locking ring at top end of barrel. Step three, place the seal wire into the jaws of the cutter. Step four, with a smooth, firm squeeze, cut through the seal wire."

On and on the directions went, and each step had to be followed without anticipating the step following it. An idiot could have done what we were doing up to that point. What you finally ended up with was a canvas sack containing the warhead—or a practice device, in our case.

This class came before the introduction of most fail-safe devices. In the flat end of the bomb were a number of controls, dials, and a combination knob, much like what you would find on a safe door. A combination had to be set into the knob to clear it, as I remember, and then another combination set in order to arm the bomb. Once the time delay was set, that was it. We weren't taught any shutdown procedures. And if you fucked up in setting the dials, the bomb could go off in your face.

A quarter of a kiloton may not seem like a great deal compared to strategic nuclear weapons that are measured in hundreds of kilotons or even megatons. A kiloton is equal to one thousand tons, or two million pounds, of TNT. Our little backpack nuke carried the estimated explosive power of one-half-million pounds of TNT, or a solid cube of explosive over 17.3 feet on a side. The Teams have a habit of overloading a target so that you don't have to go back for a second shot, but this was a bit extreme even for the SEALs.

Though we weren't told the yield of the device we were training on, we were told that "it could wipe a small city off the map." If we screwed up with this thing, Little Creek was only a memory.

On the more practical side, a padded harness for jumping with the bomb was included with the system, as well as a backpack for man-carrying the rig and another pack for swimming with it. All the transport systems were made of nylon webbing and plastic. The swimming rig allowed two people to grab handholds and swim along, towing the bomb between them. To my knowledge, nobody ever jumped with the bomb in the Teams. As a matter of fact, I don't think we ever even had physical contact with a real bomb. The few times we worked with the system, for an inspection or test, we used the training device, which was the same size, shape, and weight as the real thing.

After nine days, Jess and I graduated from the SEAL and UDT Nuclear Weapons (964) Course taught at the Nuclear Weapons Training Center Atlantic. We were each given a nice little diploma that we couldn't show to anyone, but it could go into our records. Not that anyone would have had any trouble figuring out what the diploma was for. Besides stating in plain English what we had graduated from, the document had the outline of a mushroom cloud in the background. So much for secrecy.

About a half-dozen SEALs became involved in the early SADM program. To make sure the Team could transport the SADM by small boat, we tested a rig while down at St. Thomas later in 1964. I did most of the running of the STAB for the tests at St. T, though they never gave me a bomb to play with. Instead of a bomb, the engineers put a whole bunch of indicators and sensors in the hull of the STAB. If a cradle for the SADM had to be made, these same engineers were going to be the guys who built it.

Eventually, we did determine that the STAB could not be used to transport a SADM: too much G-force. What startled the engineers was the readings they were getting from their sensors. As it turned out, the power of the STABs, along with the way we ran them, made for some much higher G-force and impact readings than expected. After making their report, the engineers told us that if a human being was securely strapped down to the deck inside the STAB, he would quickly be killed from the amount of force he was exposed to. Nobody had told us; we had just been running the boats the way we always did, cushioning any impacts with our legs.

When I first really thought about what we were playing with, I found it a very scary thing. I mean it was neat, and to be trusted with such a powerful weapon was no small honor. But here was THE BOMB, a very powerful thing indeed. This little devil's big brothers had literally changed the face of the world and affected the way governments would interact with each other forever. I had seen all the training films and heard the reports and had a real good idea of just what this little thing could do. Cuba was running pretty hot at the time, and Havana Harbor was a conceivable target for such a weapon.

None of us were very combat-experienced in those years. And we all thought about what such devastation might look like. No weapon has a conscience, but the man who employs it does. If a SADM was detonated, just how many innocent people would turn into dust in the blast? If it was in Cuba, how many of those people killed would have had no real influence in the Communist government? Turning people into their component atoms just because of where they happened to live wasn't exactly what I wanted to do. Qualifying with this weapon was one of the SEAL firsts I could have done without.

Boy, I thought, *if you ever have to work with this, don't fuck up.* An atomic bomb is not very forgiving and mistakes will blow you and a lot of other people away.

I often wondered how Jess and the other guys felt about what it was we had been trained on. Not everybody in the Teams was qualified to employ a SADM, and I didn't particularly want the honor. But asking the guys their own thoughts just wasn't done. I hoped and prayed that I would never be asked to employ the damned thing.

Despite the serious nature of the weapon, there were still some lighter moments. Though the Team never used the real thing, we did have to pass our first Nuclear Weapons Acceptance Inspection (NWAI). For the inspection, a group of qualified SEALs prepared the bomb for employment. Though the device we used was only a training model, it was treated just like the real thing. Security had to be tight and all the *i*'s dotted and *t*'s crossed on procedures. Grading for the inspection was strict; a bad mark could be received for something as simple as passing a pair of pliers to your partner over the bomb rather than around it. Later, the Team would have annual Nuclear Technical Proficiency Inspections (NTPIs), which tested our procedures and ability to maintain, arm, disarm, and prepare for employment the B54 practice weapon.

In the summer of 1967, I was the Ordnance chief for Team Two, trained and ready for our first NWAI. There was an ammunition depot in the Norfolk area that stored the training device for our Team, and it sent over the dummy weapon for the inspection. The Ordnance locker for Team Two was still in the first building we ever had and the device was delivered to us there. A big deal was made about transporting the device; armed guards escorted the truck, which had red flashing lights on it. Everything had to be signed for, and serial numbers on the sealed container were checked and rechecked. There was nothing particularly rah-rah to me about the training model; our security was tight and nothing was going to happen.

The drum was unloaded and we took the container into the Ordnance locker to prepare for the inspection. Securing the building and locking everything up, we went off to do some more immediately pressing business. That afternoon, my workers and I went back into the building to open the container and prepare things. Surprise was the least of our reactions when the drum was opened: It was empty! Our supersecure fake baby A-bomb was missing.

Immediately securing the area and telling my men to stand by, I went to a public pay phone to call a friend of mine over at the ammunition depot. Giving the man my number at the pay phone, I told him to get to another public phone and to call me back. Public phones are not subject to security types listening in, and this conversation was one I wanted kept private.

When my friend called me back, I told him the situation. To say he was concerned is understating his reaction considerably. He asked me how many other people knew about the situation. I told him that only my men and I knew what was going on. He said he would check on the situation from his end and get right back to me. Hanging up the phone, I lit a cigarette and sat back to wait.

My wait was a short one. The phone soon rang and my friend was on the other end. It seemed that the training device had been left in the middle of some packing material at the ammunition depot. Guys were just going about their duties with this superclassified doodad just sitting on the garage floor. Needless to say, my friend had quickly secured the device and called me back. After we made arrangements to meet, the ammunition man would bring the device over to me without anyone else being the wiser.

The second delivery was quite a bit different from the official one made earlier. A taxi came up to the Ordnance shed and my friend got out with his seabag. Inside the seabag was our missing little toy. This would have given the officers fits if they had known. But that's one of the reasons that chiefs actually ran the Navy back then. Sometimes it's just better to get the job done and not make the higher-ups sweat the details.

We did pass the inspection, with an "excellent" rating. To tell you the truth, we probably could have prepared the bomb with a hammer and blacksmith's tools and still passed. It seems my friend from the depot held some influence with the inspectors. I've been party to some pretty weird things during my career, but having a lost A-bomb delivered in a taxi ranks right up there with the stranger ones.

CHAPTER 8

Briefings

O VER TIME, as we continued our operations in Vietnam, we used briefings more and more to get information across in the most efficient way. In most briefings, we would receive detailed information on an upcoming mission. In proper military parlance, the briefing told us what the mission was, who would be involved, what the transportation to the target site would be, what our support was, and how we would leave the target area after the mission was completed. Additional details would include our order of march, who would carry what and how much, code names, radio frequencies, emergency procedures, and rendezvous locations.

At first, in training, we played the game, followed the official outlines, and gave our briefings according to the numbers. This was another thing I had picked up in Army Ranger School back in early 1965. While our training went on, we had instructors who would grade us on the completeness and orderliness of our briefings.

As we operated together as a unit during predeployment training however, the briefings became considerably shorter. Rick Marcinko was not one for a lot of unnecessary talk prior to a mission, whether it was in training or out in the jungle. Rick made sure that we knew everything that we needed to know and ignored most of the military formalities. As we continued to operate together, we became tighter with each other and operated like a smooth, well-oiled machine.

This ease developed within a platoon when it was preparing to leave for Vietnam. Everyone would learn what the platoon's strengths and weaknesses were during predeployment training. Once you were in Vietnam, skills were honed so that you automatically knew what the other men would do in a situation. Combining this with the general experience of operating almost on a day-to-day basis made a detailed briefing just unnecessary.

While we were in training, a briefing would last for about twenty minutes to a half hour and follow a standard military format. The standard briefing in Vietnam, after the group was humming, lasted maybe five to ten minutes for Team Two platoons. Certainly bigger operations would take longer briefings. But for the most part, we employed the KISS principle—Keep It Simple, Stupid.

In later tours, officers who were fairly new to the Teams would be tagged as platoon leaders or assistant leaders for deploying platoons. These young men would have to learn to depend on the experience of their older senior petty officers and chiefs.

The best way for one of these young officers to learn the ropes was to be paired as the assistant leader to an older and more experienced officer. A good example of this occurred during my third tour in Vietnam. They don't come much better than the platoon leader of Sixth Platoon in 1970: Lieutenant Louis H. Boink. The assistant platoon leader was Warrant Officer Henry S. "Bud" Thrift, Jr.

Bud was a young guy on that trip, but he fit in well with the squad and platoon. Even though he was relatively inexperienced at the time, Bud quickly caught on to more streamlined and mission-oriented ways of doing things and conducting briefings. Bud's advantage was that he went on a number of ops with Lou in charge and was able to see how Lou did things.

In conducting his briefings for a mission, Lou kept things simple and concise. Here's where we're going; this is what we are going to do. Pointing things out on a map or aerial photos, Lou would indicate the important points for the mission, such as where we would insert, the location of the target, and where we would extract. Most of the time, the same man carried the radio, or acted as point, or held rear security. It was these sorts of things that we were supposed to have learned in training, and not taking advantage of that experience would have been wasteful.

Individual actions at the target would be detailed a little more. "At the target," Lou would say for a possible snatch op, "this guy will go here, and that guy will go there. Myself and [whoever] are going to bust the door in."

Standard operating procedures (SOPs) were developed and usually followed for an entire tour. The lessons learned by the platoons that had been there before us had been learned well. We were professionals who didn't have to sweat the details; we attended to them automatically.

If aerial photos were available, they were passed around the group as Lou gave the briefing. The age of the photos was important, as the situation could change if too much time had passed. So we were told if the shots had been taken yesterday or even earlier on the day of the briefing.

We normally tried to operate only on the freshest intel available. Any intel that was available from our source was normally passed on to us during the briefing. If the source had produced any sketches or maps, they would also be passed around for all of us to study. This helped each of us to get into his head as solid an idea of the layout of the target area as possible. Every man in the patrol had to pick up and continue the operation if someone was hit or otherwise put out of action. And it just made plain good sense to have the area you were going to operate in clear in your head. This was Charlie's playground, and we were going to crash his party. It helped to know the way home.

Getting to the target site was always the trickiest portion of an operation. Most of the mistakes made on ops that I was involved in centered on some error in locating the target. Though it sounds like a simple rule, you had better be sure of the hooch you were going to hit. They all looked the same in the dark and the VC didn't put out mailboxes with their numbers on them.

The very best way to go in to a target was to have a guide. Whenever possible, we would have the intel source himself guide us in to the target. Without a doubt, this man would know his neighborhood just like we knew the area around Little Creek. Not only could a native guide walk to the target practically blindfolded, he would also know where the boobytraps and other pitfalls were.

Of course, there was a risk involved in using a Vietnamese guide. We always were very cautious with a guide, especially one who we had not used before. Later, after he had proved himself on an op, we had more confidence in a given source. But we never relaxed and trusted one of our sources completely. There was always the thought in the back of your mind that this might be the time that he sold you out.

But these were factors that were considered by the officer in charge before the briefing was put forward to the men. The quality and completeness of the intel had been checked and possibly cross-checked and confirmed. Support in the way of helicopter gunships or gunfire support had to be put on, and arrangements for insertion and extraction completed. These were only part of what had to be done before the briefing was called together.

One advantage we had while we operated in Vietnam was working with each other every day. The twelve or fourteen men in a platoon became very close in a way that is hard to duplicate today. Nothing causes the deadwood to be shed faster than a combat situation. The requirements for lengthy and finely detailed briefings just didn't exist for the most part in Vietnam, and things were simplified accordingly.

In the Teams today, I understand the briefings are long and complicated affairs. Without doubt, the new breed of SEALs have a lot more details to attend to than we old-timers did. But there is also another factor to consider. With the rather small number of hot missions today's Teams have to perform, especially compared to our almost daily ops in Nam, how much of the briefing is due to the leader's own inexperience? There are young officers in the Teams today every bit as competent and hard charging as the best of those we had leading us in Vietnam. But the sheer volume of experience just isn't available now.

Today, after a briefing, a platoon is put on hold and told to wait for the go signal. While on hold, the platoon is put into isolation. Isolation is a separate room within a Team's headquarters containing bunks, cooking facilities, classroom materials, and sanitary facilities. Men eat, sleep, and work together, isolated from any con-

tact with the outside world or even much contact with their teammates. While in isolation, the men go over their plan together,
practicing and otherwise memorizing what they were briefed on. At
the headquarters building, isolation can be a pain. When a platoon
is deployed on a ship or other location, it can be downright
maddening.

It is not unknown for a platoon to be put into isolation for a
month or more and then have the op canceled. It stands in the
young lions' favor that they operate so well with all the restrictions
placed on them today. The Teams of my day wouldn't have stayed
together with those rules for very long. A whole month with no
beer!

CHAPTER 9

The RAG Boats

T HE MISSION of stopping seaborne infiltration of supplies to the VC in South Vietnam was given to Task Force 115 under the name Operation Market Time. TF 115 continued this mission from 1965 through to 1973. Part of the reason for bringing the SEALs to Vietnam was to take the mission of TF 115 farther inland.

TF 115 used bigger ships than the others that we had regular contact with in Vietnam. The Navy had assigned destroyers to TF 115 and we made use of their accurate 5-inch guns whenever we could. Additional forces were assigned to TF 115, including ships from the U.S. Coast Guard. These ships included 82-foot cutters assigned to Coast Guard Squadron One and based at An Thoi, Danang, and Cat Lo. The cutters were used by the SEALs, mostly from Team One, for general transportation.

The only Coasties I had direct involvement with were the men manning the high-endurance cutters based at Subic Bay in the Philippines. The high-endurance cutters were from two classes of ships, the 327-foot Campbell and the 378-foot Hamilton. Both of these classes mounted one 5-inch, 38-caliber gun as their heavy punch. In Navy parlance, the length of a cannon's barrel is given in calibers, which are multiplied by the diameter of the shell fired by the gun to get the barrel's length in inches. For example, a 5-inch, 38-caliber gun has a barrel 190 inches (5 times 38), or 15 feet 10 inches, long.

However you measure it, those Coasties could man their guns. During my third tour in Vietnam, I had occasion to use the "center-of-sector" technique to confirm our location while on an op. Center-of-sector involves calling in a round of white phosphorus from your artillery support unit, aimed to land in the center of the sector in which you are operating. The Willy Peter round is used because it not only produces the noise of its impact and explosion, but creates a column of white smoke as the phosphorus burns.

Needless to say, you need to know that you are not standing in the center of your sector when you use this technique, and you have to have faith in your gunfire support. There was no trouble with the accuracy of the naval gunfire support the one time I used center-of-sector. The firing ship was the Coast Guard cutter USS *Dallas,* one of the 378-foot Hamilton-class ships, and the Coasties were right on the money.

The *Dallas* also supplied fire support for other SEAL operations, but I'm certain of using her only on that one op. Destroyers were also used for fire support, such as the USS *Southerland* (DD 743) a 390-foot, modernized Gearing-class ship that Lieutenant Boink used on a POW rescue op.

Other fire support was available from the Navy, but I never got a chance to use it personally. It must have been quite a sight to have the 8-inch, 55-caliber guns of the Salem-class cruiser USS *Newport News* (CA 148) at your command. She operated in Vietnamese waters in 1967 and 1968.

But the biggest bangs in the waters of the South China Sea came from the nine incredible 16-inch, 50-caliber guns on the Iowa-class battleship USS *New Jersey* (BB 62). That huge mother could throw her 2,700-pound 16-inch shells some twenty-three miles inland. Twenty-seven hundred pounds is heavier than some of our fully equipped boats weighed with a whole SEAL squad on board. Though she was in Vietnamese waters only from September 1968 to February 1969, the *New Jersey* could stir the heart of many a SEAL, all of whom are sailors under their Tridents.

Several other types of boats were assigned to Task Force 115, the most infamous of which had to be the Nasty-class boats. The Nasty boats were fast patrol boats (PTFs) the Navy had purchased from Boatservice Ltd. of Norway. The eighty-foot PTFs were modern torpedo boats and could really haul ass, moving out at about forty-five knots. Guns on board the Nastys varied and could include

40mm and 20mm cannon, an 81mm direct-fire mortar, and at least one .50-caliber machine gun.

The big thing about the Nastys was their mission, which was to attack supply centers in North Vietnam. Personnel aboard the Nastys who would land and attack targets in North Vietnam were LDNNs (Lien Doc Nquoi Nhia, "soldiers who fight under the sea") who had been trained by SEALs. I never particularly liked the LDNNs, who were supposedly the South's answer to our U.S. Navy SEALs. I was possibly influenced by Roy Boehm, who really didn't trust the LDNNs, even though he had helped set up their training and school back before the SEALs deployed to Vietnam.

One rumor that regularly surfaces is that the Nasty boats transported U.S. Navy SEALs into North Vietnam for missions behind the lines. My answer to those rumors is that I just don't know. SEAL Team One personnel did go out on Nastys during some missions, but supposedly as advisers. They never left the boats.

My own experience with the Nasty boats was very limited and came about from what was really just a sightseeing trip near Danang. It was during my first tour in Vietnam with Rick Marcinko and Second Platoon. I had taken a Caribou flight up to Danang in order to pick up some special equipment we needed for a planned mission. While I was in Danang I stayed over with the guys from the local Boat Support Unit and they gave me a grand tour of the area.

Besides showing me the local hangouts, the BSU people took me out into the countryside a bit. We went up on Monkey Mountain and Marble Mountain. This area was really SEAL Team One's stomping ground. In fact, I had picked up our gear in a sealed box at the Team One location in Danang. Team One was running the LDNN school nearby. Also nearby was the base for the Nasty boats.

Though the base was partially run by SEALs from Team One, supposedly no American was ever allowed to go out on one of the Nastys' runs to North Vietnam and leave the boat. Though it was never talked about in the Teams, things didn't always work that way. But those missions would have been pretty hairy. If a SEAL did go into the North and was lost, that would have been just about it for him. "Joe who?" and "Team what?" would have been heard coming out of the U.S. State Department. To the best of my knowledge, the Nastys were stripped-down PTs that were funded and operated by the Agency (as we called the CIA), not the most trustworthy people for the SEALs to operate with in the first place.

But as it was, the closest I came to the Nastys was just to look at the fence that surrounded the base where they were. The Nasty base was at the foot of one of the mountains near Danang, but little activity could be seen inside the base from the mountain. And you sure couldn't see into the base from outside the fence. The fence—more of a wall, really—completely surrounded the small base and blocked off any view of what was going on inside. You could listen and tell a boat was leaving. Those Nastys had two big eighteen-cylinder Napier-Deltic diesels cranking out 6,200 shaft horsepower to two screws, but nothing was visible. Security was tight around the Nasty base and I never did get in to see any of the boats or go on board.

Funny thing was, we had trained the Nasty boat crews at Little Creek back around 1963. Our part of the Nasty crews' training involved teaching them combative measures, hand-to-hand, and small arms and other weapons use. There were only about fourteen or fifteen sailors in the training as I remember, led by a couple of lieutenants. After they completed their training with us, the Nasty crews moved on to Coronado, California, for additional training and deployment.

The big thing that the public knew about involving the Nasty boats (though their actual part in the incident didn't come out until years later) was that in 1964 the Nastys were conducting operations off North Vietnam, destroying supply centers, POL (petroleum, oil, lubricants) dumps, and generally raising hell with the North Vietnamese Army (NVA). The actions conducted by the Nastys were part of the Operation Plan 34A program, which outlined a number of sabotage and destruction missions to be conducted against North Vietnam by South Vietnamese LDNNs.

The NVA took only a little while to start reacting to the actions of the Nasty boats. On August 2, 1964, at about 1600 hours, the

U.S. destroyer *Maddox* (DD 731) was attacked by a number of North Vietnamese P-4 patrol boats. The *Maddox* had been patrolling the waters off North Vietnam and was considered to be in international waters at the time of the incident. The P-4s were responding to attacks against shore installations by Nasty boats just a few days before, and they probably thought the *Maddox* was leading the much smaller Nastys.

The incident itself didn't last very long. The *Maddox* took some fire from the P-4s, but the small patrol craft were not much of a match for the U.S. destroyer. On August 4, there was another action by North Vietnamese patrol boats attacking U.S. ships. The results were much the same, with the U.S. craft emerging the undisputed winners of the engagement.

The idea of the relatively tiny North Vietnamese Navy taking on the United States didn't sit very well with the U.S. Senate or House of Representatives. By August 7, the Tonkin Gulf Resolution was passed by Congress. The resolution authorized the president of the United States to use U.S. armed forces to assist in the defense of non-Communist governments in Southeast Asia. This was used as the legal basis for President Johnson to start sending U.S. troops into Vietnam and was effectively the beginning of active U.S. combat involvement in the war. The name of the resolution was taken from the body of water where the Nastys had been operating when the *Maddox* was attacked. It was a tiny little battle that had massive consequences.

Along with the Nasty boats, TF 115 had another class of patrol boat that earned a good reputation in Vietnam, though not as notorious a rep as that held by the Nastys. To increase its ability to operate and patrol close to shore, the Navy ordered the Mark I Swift boats in 1965–1966. The Swift boats were a modified design taken from the all-metal boats that supplied the offshore oil wells in the Gulf of Mexico. Called PCFs (Patrol Craft, Fast), the Swifts earned a name for themselves operating in the near-shore waters and rivers of the Mekong Delta.

Personally, I never operated off a Swift boat. But a number of SEAL operations by both Team One and Team Two started with insertions from Swift boats. The waters I worked in were always a little too shallow for the Swifts, but when they had the water they needed to work in, the Swifts did a good job.

The twin GM diesels on board the Swifts put 960 shaft horsepower into the boats' twin screws and would push the metal hull through the water at up to twenty-eight knots. A Swift's six-man crew operated the boat and her twin .50-caliber machine guns in a gun tub on top of her pilot house, as well as the Mark 2 Mod 1 81mm mortar on her rear deck. The Mark 2 Mod 1 mortar was different from the Mark 2 we had aboard the Mike boat, in that it also held a .50-caliber machine gun mounted piggyback on top of the mortar. This arrangement of the over/under .50 caliber and 81mm mortar, as well as the gun tub, gave the Swifts three .50s and the mortar. This firepower was augmented by whatever small arms were available to the crew and anyone else who might be aboard, such as a SEAL squad.

The South Vietnamese Navy had been running small boats in the rivers and canals of the Delta since it inherited the craft from the French in the 1950s. The South Vietnamese units were called RAGs, for River Assault Groups, and were made up of a wide variety of small craft. Many of the RAGs' small craft were modified American landing craft, usually LCMs (Landing Craft, Medium) and LCVPs (Landing Craft, Vehicle and Personnel). The boats were armored and had a number of weapon-mounting points added for .30- and .50-caliber machine guns. Some of the larger RAG boats also mounted 20mm and 40mm cannon. Run by the South Vietnamese Navy but often carrying U.S. Navy advisers, the RAGs were intended to be able to lift a Vietnamese infantry battalion and move it through the riverine environment to a point where it could engage the VC. By 1966, the RAGs were performing their primary transportation mission about 10 percent of the time. The rest of the time they were conducting support operations and escorting commercial watercraft.

The SEALs would use the RAGs on occasion for transportation or even close-in fire support. Missions where the SEALs were working with local ARVN groups and Regional Forces (RFs) were often carried on RAG boats. During one operation conducted by Sixth Platoon in July 1970, Lou Boink and Fast Eddie Leasure were working with a group of South Vietnamese from the 974th RF company. Lou and Fast Eddie, the only SEALs on the op, were acting as advisers to the company commander and coordinating artillery and gunship support. This was part of the Vietnamization effort, which was increasing South Vietnamese involvement in their own defenses.

The operation was an area search with the target the Z-10 NVA battalion, which was suspected to be in the area. After about a one-kilometer patrol, the men boarded three RAG LCM-6s for extraction. The boats were from RAG 25 based in Ca Mau. While moving down the Kang Chac Bang canal, the RAG boats were ambushed. The lead LCM-6 took a hit on the port side forward from a heavy weapon that wounded twelve RF troops. The firefight got heavy fast, as the RAG boats took both sides of the canal under fire from their 20mm cannon, .50-caliber machine guns, and the small arms of the RF troops on board.

In the aftermath of the fight, ten VC were known dead and an unknown number of additional enemy troops were killed or wounded. Moving in to shore after leaving the ambush site, the ARVN wounded were treated and a medevac called in to remove eight of the most seriously hurt. To give the medevac birds room to land in a secure area, the little flotilla moved to a Thoi Binh District town just a short distance away.

It was during the helo extraction at the town that Lou and Eddie had their turn at almost becoming additional casualties. The helo they boarded for extraction caught one of its skids on the barbed wire circling the perimeter of the secure town, aborted its takeoff, and crashed into the nearby canal. Lou and Eddie got up, boarded the second helicopter, and returned to base. It's interesting to look at Lou Boink's remarks on the Barndance card for the operation. Barndance cards were the operation reports we kept for use by the Teams themselves, to keep track of mistakes made, lessons learned, and who did what. On Barndance 6-38, dated July 19, 1970, under

"Remarks," Lou wrote, "2 helo gunships took hits and out of order—some days chickens, some days feathers."

The RAGs were considered a good idea by the Navy planners back in the United States and efforts were made to field a U.S. version of the boats early in the war. Task Force 117 was a combined Navy and Army effort to eliminate the VC influence in the Delta area of South Vietnam. In September 1966, Task Force 117 of the Mobile Riverine Force (MRF) was commissioned; it first reached Vietnam in early January 1967. The Navy units immediately began incountry training in the Rung Sat area with the Army component of the force, the 9th Infantry Division.

The MRF inherited much of the mission of the earlier RAGs and was itself broken down into smaller groups. Task Force 117 was divided into two squadrons, River Assault Squadron 9 and River Assault Squadron 11. The squadrons broke down into two river assault divisions each. River Assault Divisions 91 and 92 were part of Squadron 9, and Divisions 111 and 112 were under Squadron 11.

TF 117 fielded many of the very unusual boats seen in the rivers and canals of South Vietnam. The monitors were highly modified LCM-6s. Considered the battleships of the riverine fleet, monitors were very heavily armored and packed serious firepower. The guns on board a sixty-foot monitor in 1968 included an Army 105mm howitzer, two 20mm cannon in rotating armored turrets, three .30-caliber machine guns, and two 40mm high-velocity grenade launchers in the turrets next to the 20mms. Some monitors mounted M10-8 flamethrowers in place of the 105mm howitzer and one of the 20mm guns. The flamethrowing monitors were called Zippos and could really clear out a riverbank.

Additional TF 117 craft included Armored Troop Carriers (ATCs), Command and Control Boats (CCBs), and Assault Support Patrol Boats (ASPBs). These craft all shared several characteristics: They were ugly, were armored like a bunker, and carried every weapon the Navy could fit on board. Some of the ATCs had a specially reinforced overhead on the troop well, intended to accept helicopter landings and takeoffs. The platform-equipped ATCs were unofficially called ATC(H)s and were the smallest "aircraft carriers" ever in the Navy.

The riverine gunboats were used by the Teams, primarily for fire support, whenever they were operating in the same area we were. The TF 117 craft the SEALs got the most use out of were the support ships, especially the self-propelled barracks ships (APBs) used by TF 117 as floating river bases. During my third tour in Vietnam, I spent several weeks operating off APB 35, the *Benewah*. The APB would sit in the middle of a river like a big mama duck with all her little ducklings surrounding her—only in this case, the "ducklings" were monitors, ATCs, and other such nasty little craft.

CHAPTER 10

PBRs and the Brown Water Navy

T HERE WAS PROBABLY no waterborne branch of the Navy that the SEALs spent more time with, or owed more to, than the PBRs of Vietnam. The PBRs (Patrol Boats, River) were the heart and soul of what is now called the Brown Water Navy and was then officially called Task Force 116.

The River Patrol Force was established on December 18, 1965, to control the inland waterways of South Vietnam. The River Patrol Force was a major part of Task Force 116, which had been created for Operation Game Warden. With Task Force 115 and Operation Market Time blocking the infiltration of supplies to the VC by sea, TF 116 was to extend the actions against the VC to inland waters. TF 116 effectively made the Navy the policeman of the inland waterways, swamps, and rice paddies of the Delta region.

The Navy needed a new kind of boat to operate in the shallow, cramped waters of the Delta. By the spring of 1966, the first of the Mark I PBRs were delivered for service in Vietnam. As boats, the PBRs were never very much to look at, but their performance was really something to see. The thirty-one-foot hull of the PBR was fiberglass and carried a GM 220-horsepower diesel truck engine on board. The truck engine drove a Jacuzzi water-jet pump, which shot out a stream of water to drive the boat forward at up to twenty-eight knots.

With the water-jet drive system, the PBRs didn't need a propeller that could foul on all the debris in the water of the Mekong Delta. But that debris tended to clog up the intake vents for those same water jets. The junk in the water would also break down and chew up the blades of the impeller inside the water pump. This cut into the drive's ability to push the boat through the water.

I never saw a PBR, either the early Mark I or the later, improved Mark II, ever really use its top speed very much. The boats couldn't go that fast because they were usually overloaded with weapons and ammunition. This was actually a mistake on the part of the PBR sailors. The boat was designed for X amount of weapons and ammunition, and the sailors always seemed to overload the boats. The only time I remember seeing a PBR running at close to twenty-eight knots was after a heavy firefight when the men on board had expended about 80 percent of their ammunition.

The PBRs were almost direct descendants of the World War II PT boats. And like some of the PT crews back then, the PBR crews never felt they had too much firepower. The weapons that were part of the boat's standard load were nothing to be sneezed at. In the bow deck of the PBR was a Mark 36 mount, a sunken gun tub holding twin .50-caliber machine guns, and five hundred rounds of ammunition.

Amidships on the PBR were two pedestal mounts sticking up like pieces of pipe. The amidships mounts could accept either an M60 machine gun or Mark 18 Honeywell 40mm hand-cranked grenade launcher. The M60 would have several hundred rounds of ammunition linked up to feed it, and the Honeywell had an ammunition box that held a forty-eight-round belt of 40mm grenades.

Originally, the Mark I PBRs were to have a .30-caliber machine gun mounted on the after pintle, but this was changed to a .50-caliber machine gun before the boats went to Vietnam. The after gun mount was a Mark 26 pedestal mount, kind of a tall tripod holding the .50 up high enough for a standing man to operate it. Almost any weapon the PBRs had available could fit in the after mount—the M60, the Mark 18, the later Mark 20 40mm machine gun, the .50, and even a Mark 4 60mm mortar.

Most of the PBRs I operated with had a standard .50-caliber machine gun on the after mount. Starting early in 1967, a Mark 46 mount was issued to the PBRs that would allow a 40mm Mark 18 or the later Mark 20 to be mounted above the .50-caliber gun. This system allowed the PBRs to have an over/under 40mm/.50 caliber covering the rear.

In addition to the standard weapons, each of the four PBR crewmen was issued an M16, and several had sidearms as well. Extra 40mm M79s, M60s, M16s, AK-47s, and shotguns, as well as an assortment of grenades, all found places on board the PBRs operating in Vietnam.

The first group of PBR sailors received their boats and began operations in Vietnam in March 1966. TF 116 was divided into two smaller units: TF 116.1, the Delta River Patrol Group; and TF 116.2, the Rung Sat Patrol Group. Of the 120 Mark I PBRs in Vietnam, 80 boats were assigned to TF 116.1 and operated in the Mekong Delta; the other 40 boats went to the Rung Sat and TF 116.2.

Very soon after beginning operations in Vietnam, the SEALs from Team One, Detachment Golf, were working with the PBRs in the Rung Sat. The mission of TF 116 was to enforce curfews for shipping on the water, interdict VC infiltration, prevent VC tax collectors from extorting money and supplies from the people, and generally counter VC movements on inland waters. This was just the kind of job that the SEALs were best able to help conduct at the time, going on land while Navy forces backed them up on the water.

Team Two SEAL platoons started arriving in Vietnam early in 1967, and we were assigned to operate with TF 116.1 in the Mekong Delta. SEAL Team One platoons had been conducting their operations mostly up in the Rung Sat during 1966 and 1967, and had been pretty successful in taking the war into Charlie's backyard. It was to continue the SEALs' success with TF 116 and expand it into the Mekong Delta that Team Two was brought into the war. The number of SEALs in existence in 1967 was low, around two hundred operators total. This meant that to increase the scope of operations in Vietnam, both Teams would have to be used. After Team Two became actively involved in the war in 1967, we remained so until the U.S. Pullout in the 1970s.

When I arrived in Vietnam with Second Platoon in January 1967, most of the detachment went up to the Rung Sat to get broken in by the Team One platoon there. Bravo Squad and yours truly were left back at the PBR base at Tre Noc. The first experience we had with the area was when Rick Marcinko and Bob Gallagher talked their way on board a PBR going out on patrol.

Rick had picked the PBR carefully because of the chief who ran it. Chief Ed Canby had been a Junk Force commander and was a PBR boat captain in 1967. Canby had been in Vietnam for about three years before Rick met him and was already something of a legend. It shows the closeness of the PBRs and SEALs better than anything I can say that the first real combat training we received in Vietnam was at the hands of a PBR boat captain. There was no question that Chief Canby knew the river like the back of his hand and he was absolutely the man to buddy up with. We could operate, but we had to learn the river first.

For all of the good feelings that developed between the SEALs and the PBR sailors, things didn't start out very well. When we arrived in Vietnam, we were told that we were there to operate in support of the PBRs and riverine operations—not in conjunction with, not alongside of, but only in support of the PBRs. That wasn't what we had trained for those long months back at Little Creek. Lieutenant Commander Hank Mustin, the operations commander of the base, kept harping on the rules of engagement we would have to operate under and how they hadn't been completed yet. Here we had been preparing back at Team Two since September the year before, and they weren't ready to give us the rules we were going to fight under?

Needless to say, that situation didn't continue. With Chief Canby's guidance, Marcinko's Marauders went out in our own STABs and raised merry hell with the VC. But that didn't sit well with the people in charge and Bravo Squad of Second Platoon soon found itself sent out to My Tho to operate there.

At My Tho there was another PBR base, again part of TF 116.1. The only thing really different was that the My Tho PBR commander wanted us to begin operating right away, the sooner the better.

It wasn't as if the PBR sailors didn't ever get out on dry land to fight. The PBR crews did occasionally get out and play games with Charlie when the opportunity presented itself. When river and canal patrols took them alongside villages that were right on the shore, some crews would arm themselves and go out hunting.

However, that was against the rules for the PBR sailors. They were not supposed to leave their boats and engage the enemy. One boat crew out of My Tho made a regular thing of nosing in to shore and having a couple of men go out to sneak and peek. The crew didn't make any great secret of its actions. After the sailors had a few beers in them, they'd relax and start talking. "Boy we went into this village last night and really stirred things up," one of them would say while sitting around the bar.

We didn't think much about these guys going against their "rules of engagement." After all, we thought the rules were just a bunch of political horseshit anyway. But we had the training to operate on land; the PBR sailors didn't. The more those sailors got to know us, the more they realized that they weren't trained for that kind of operating, and just how dumb it was to try it without training. With no idea about fields of fire, no plan, not even any basic intel for a real op, all the sailors were doing was getting ready to walk into a meat grinder. It wasn't long before the PBR sailors just stayed on their boats and left the walking, or crawling in the mud, to us.

But when it came time to do their job from the PBRs, those sailors were real operators. There wasn't anything those boats could do that the PBR sailors weren't willing to try. Many were the times that they came in and pulled the SEALs' chestnuts out of a VC fire. The PBRs would operate in pairs, and while one PBR was laying down covering fire, the other would nose in to shore to extract a SEAL unit that was in trouble.

Mostly, we used the PBRs for infiltrations and extractions. The PBRs operated up and down the rivers of South Vietnam all the time. Though Charlie had a world of respect for those little boats, they didn't elicit any particular curiosity. Unlike a Mike boat, which stood out like a whore in church, a PBR was just part of the everyday traffic on the river. When you're playing games in somebody else's backyard, you had better blend in. This kind of invisibility, combined with firepower, made the PBRs ideal insertion and support boats.

Depending on the kind of insertion planned, either the PBR would nose in to the bank to let us off, or we would slip over the side as the boat passed our insertion point. If we used the nose-in approach, we would be able to go in drier and heavier, and the gear and ammo wouldn't drag us down into the water (in spite of a life jacket). But on a nose-in insertion, we had to sit there on the shore longer, just quietly listening in case Charlie heard the boat stop.

The PBR insertion technique we liked more was the pass-by. The PBR went by the point of insertion at a medium cruising speed and we'd slip over the sides or stern. Because the water-jet propulsion didn't have any screws, there wasn't any danger of being struck by a prop. The boat continued on its way, and we slipped in to shore. A regular UDT life jacket was worn during an underway insertion, two jackets for a man armed with a machine gun. Once we were onshore, the jacket was deflated and carried in a large pocket. The underway insertion technique was very much a modified version of the old UDT style of rolling off a rubber raft tied to the side of the boat, modified to fit our situation in Vietnam.

Riding a PBR could get a bit cramped. The thirty-one-foot boats were already crammed with gear, weapons, ammo, and crew, so adding a squad of six or more SEALs really filled them up. When moving on a PBR, we tried to stay out of the way of the crew, especially the gunner in the forward gun tub. Those twin .50s in the bow of the PBR were a major part of the boat's firepower and we didn't want anything to get in their way.

In the case of a hot extraction or ambush, all of the SEALs' weapons fired over the gunwales, adding their weight to the firepower of the boat. But usually, a couple of SEALs would ride inside with the coxswain and the rest would just find a place around the back of the boat. If the shit hit the fan, we would mostly try to stay out of the way. It was the PBRs' job to get us to and from the mission site, and we would be happy just letting them do that.

Though a good boat, the Mark I PBR demonstrated its short-comings early in 1966. By December of that year, a new PBR, the Mark II, was arriving in Vietnam and it became the boat we worked off the most. The Mark II PBR had a Jacuzzi Mark IV water jet, an improved version over the earlier model, as well as more powerful engines to drive the jet.

The hull of the Mark II was still fiberglass but had an aluminum gunwale for added strength. The firepower was pretty much un-changed except for the replacement of the bow gun tub with a Mark 56 gun mount. The Mark 56 still held twin .50s but was lower in silhouette and also carried five hundred rounds of ammunition for its guns.

The Mark II PBRs were faster and easier to maintain than the Mark I model. If a crew didn't mind getting wet, a PBR could re-verse course in her own length while traveling at speed, and stop dead in the water within ninety feet, also from top speed.

The new hull design of the Mark II PBR had been adapted some-what from that of the Nasty boats, but someone hadn't paid atten-tion where he should have. The deck around the bow gun tub was sunken an inch or so on both the Mark I and Mark II PBRs, making a raised lip around the edge of the deck. This edge lip was even more pronounced on the Mark II, showing that the designer proba-bly had never been shot at. Why? Because PBRs patrolled in canals where branches hit both sides of the boat. In these tight quarters, a firefight could get messy real fast. If a VC on the bank was lucky enough to land a grenade on the bow of the boat, a grenade couldn't roll off into the water, because the designer had been kind enough to put that lip along the edge.

But the PBRs and the sailors who manned them proved to be a perfect complement to the SEALs. As the Task Force 116 Game Warden forces expanded, so did the SEAL commitment to Vietnam. By mid-1968, the Game Warden forces, which were assigned a large number of PBRs, were divided into different area (river) patrol groups with each group containing a mix of forces. Each patrol group consisted of a PBR unit, a helo unit (the Seawolves), a SEAL unit, a SEAL support unit, and an LST (Landing Ship Tank) or mine countermeasures unit.

Though the SEALs had initially been sent over to Vietnam in support of the PBRs, by mid-1967 we had turned that around completely. Now the PBRs operated in support of the SEALs. One of the missions given to Roy Boehm after he left Team Two was to help set up a major portion of the PBRs' training at Mare Island in California. Roy recognized the value of the PBRs right away and knew what they would be able to do with the SEALs.

Starting almost from the beginning, Roy directed the PBR training with the knowledge that the Teams would end up stealing them one day. Having already spent time in Vietnam, Roy saw which way the war was going, at least for the Teams. We were not going to operate well just going after snipers who messed with the PBRs, though we would do that at any time during the war. What we did best was take the war to the enemy—kicking ass and taking prisoners. And the PBRs would do best in cooperating with the SEALs as transportation to and from an action site and supporting us where possible.

It wasn't six months after Team Two arrived in Vietnam that we did exactly what Roy had said we would do. We stole the PBRs and used them for our support.

Nobody was better at his job than the PBR sailors. It annoys me how some people say, "I was a SEAL and I was the best we had in Vietnam," though I have been guilty of that once or twice myself. The truth is, the Teams lost about forty-nine men total in Vietnam. That's the total casualties of the UDTs, Team One, and Team Two. The number would have been double—no, quadruple—what it was if it hadn't been for the support we received from the PBRs and the Seawolves.

Ninety-nine times out of a hundred, if a SEAL unit had bitten off more than it could chew and had to hotfoot it out of an area, the PBRs or the Seawolves, most often both, would come in to get it.

It didn't matter what the situation was. If you could get near the water, a PBR would show up, probably with a Seawolf covering its ass from the air. Bullets would be flying, but those fiberglass bathtubs would come in close. In a firefight, you would instinctively duck down behind the plastic hull of a PBR. Nothing but a quarter inch of fiberglass, but you would be glad you had it. It was a kind of ostrich mentality—if you couldn't see them, they couldn't see you. We used to laugh about it afterward.

The fiberglass hull of the PBRs actually did have an advantage. An RPG (rocket-propelled grenade) or recoilless rifle shell could hit the hull and go right on through without detonating. The plastic hull just didn't have enough resistance to set off what was effectively an antitank round. Of course, if the shell hit something substantial, like the engine or gun mounts, it would go off and rip the boat to hell. But more than one PBR came back to base with two holes in the hull, one where the shell had come in, and the other where it had gone out.

CHAPTER 11

Equipment for Operations

T HE FIRST WEAPONS we had in the SEALs were fifty-five AR-15
rifles that Roy Boehm had gone out and purchased for us on
the open market. Roy bought enough AR-15s to outfit both SEAL
Team One and Team Two within a few weeks of our being commissioned. The word was that we would be going into Cuba almost
right away and Roy wanted us to have the best light automatic
weapon that was available on the market at the time. Without question, that weapon was the selective-fire AR-15.

Right from the start we never had any trouble with the AR-15.
The gun was light and handy, and could spew out twenty rounds
of 5.56mm ammunition in a little under one and a half seconds.
The little 5.56mm bullet was considered too light by the military
thinking of the day, but it was as destructive as hell within the
short—up to two-hundred-meter—range at which we were expecting to engage the enemy. Up close, within thirty meters, the AR-
15 would literally tear a target apart with its high-velocity
ammunition.

The Army had all kinds of other bitches about the AR-15 and
its oversized .22-caliber ammunition. One pet complaint was that
the small barrel of the AR-15 would get clogged with water too
easily just by being out in the rain and would blow up the first time
an operator tried to fire it.

Fact is, the SEALs work in the wettest environment there is,
and Roy knew this when he checked out the AR-15 at a dealer in
Baltimore. Roy took a couple of men whose opinions he valued
with him to Cooper-MacDonald in Baltimore, where they put the
AR-15 through its paces. They threw the weapon into the surf, with

the sand swirling all around, and found that it worked just fine. Using his open-purchase account, Roy bought over one hundred of the rifles, as well as spare parts and magazines, to split between SEAL Team One and Team Two. He also made sure that we had a supply of ammunition. All of this years before the Army wanted anything to do with the AR-15.

It was Roy's end run around the established weapons community in the military that ended up helping to get him transferred from the Teams. The higher-ups don't like being made to look like fools, even if they do make it very easy sometimes.

Along with the AR-15s, we also received a couple of shorter AR-15 carbines and CAR-15 submachine guns. The AR-15 carbine had its barrel cut off just beyond the front sight and the flash hider reattached. Though it was four inches shorter than the standard AR-15, we didn't think much of the weapon, and I don't believe many more than one or two were ever in the Teams.

One AR-15 variation we did like was the CAR-15 submachine gun. The Model 07 CAR-15 had a solid stock that could be slid open or closed about two inches and locked into place. The barrel was only about ten inches long and had a special shortened pair of triangular handguards. In spite of having a large muzzle blast, the CAR-15 was a very handy weapon with a good deal of firepower. We used the original Model 07 CARs in the Teams until they were literally falling apart.

The Army finally got in on the act and was issuing the M16, a modified version of the AR-15, by the time Team Two became involved in the Vietnam War. Along with the M16, the Army had its own versions of the CAR-15 designed, the XM177 E1 and E2. Though they had a few more bells and whistles than the SEALs thought necessary, such as a forward bolt assist to help close the breech on a dirty round, the Teams accepted as many XM177s as we could get. Those weapons were also used till long after the Vietnam War had ended, when they were finally replaced with a new version, the M4 carbine.

The only other small arms we had at the beginning of the SEALs were some M3 .45-caliber submachine guns, commonly called greaseguns, that the Navy had issued us. Though I used them in training, I never carried an M3 or the later M3A1 submachine gun in combat. Early on during our weapons training at Fort Bragg, I had developed a taste for submachine guns. But the greasegun was just too heavy to carry, for the firepower it gave. The thirty-round magazines for the greasegun were very heavy as well, the .45-caliber M1911 ball ammunition weighing almost twice as much as a round of M193 ball 5.56mm M16 ammunition.

What Roy Boehm had done was see to it the SEALs had the best weapons available right from the beginning, and the Navy punished him for it. Later on, when the Army and everybody else in the U.S. military were using the M16 as their basic weapon, no one remembered that it was a Navy lieutenant who had gone out on a limb and gotten those first weapons for us. But all of us in the Teams knew we owed our best chunk of firepower to Roy Boehm, with a little help from Eugene Stoner, the designer of the AR-15.

For machine guns, we didn't have much in the Teams until about 1966. One of the first military schools we were sent to after the Teams were commissioned was the Army Jungle Warfare School near the Panama Canal. It was at that school that some of us first used a light machine gun on land rather than mounted on board a ship or boat.

At Jungle School, classes were taught on all aspects of jungle operations and survival. We learned how to conduct ambushes and how to counter them. Small-boat operations, communications, the effects of heat on the body, guerrilla operations, and jungle navigation were all taught. We also got to use some of the Army's toys, since we were not allowed to bring our own weapons down with us from Little Creek.

Sometimes, the lessons didn't quite go as the Army planned. On one training patrol to an ambush site, Louie Kucinski was carrying an M14 rifle while another member of the patrol had a Browning M1919A6 .30-caliber light machine gun. The A6 is anything but a very light weapon. Weighing in at about thirty-three pounds empty with its metal stock and bipod, it's a "light" conversion of an earlier tripod-mounted weapon.

"I tell you what," Louie said. "I'll carry the A6 if I get to shoot it when we get there." Not having any difficulty with this offer, the man with the A6 traded weapons with Louie.

When we finally reached the ambush site, Louie set down the A6. "All right, you carried it, you shoot it," said the kid who originally had the A6. Getting down into position, Louie fed a belt of ammunition into his weapon. When the ambush started, Louie just held down the trigger of the gun until he had gone through the entire 250-round belt. Normally, you fire a machine gun in short bursts to avoid overheating the barrel. Chalk up one barrel for Louie.

The instructors on the operation with us weren't very pleased with Louie's trigger control on an A6. But that was part of the game, to piss off the Army. We would listen to the instructors carefully. They knew how to get by in the jungle much better than we did then. But we were SEALs. We had to stretch out now and then. Besides, long-standing tradition held that the Army was a Navy target at all times.

We got a little more experience with machine guns courtesy of the U.S. Army. While down at Fort Bragg in the fall of 1962, all of SEAL Team Two took the Special Forces course in U.S. and foreign small arms. For over a week, we all spent time field-stripping, firing, and familiarizing ourselves with all kinds of small arms. It was during this training that Team Two racked up its first deer, taken out on the .50-caliber machine gun range. It was also during this time that I developed my taste for submachine guns, finding the small, light chunks of firepower handy and easy to carry and use.

But in the Teams, we didn't have an issue machine gun until about 1966. At that time, it was obvious that we were going to be deploying to Vietnam soon. To add to the firepower of a squad and platoon, we began receiving M60 light machine guns.

The M60 had a much more modern design that the Browning M1919A6, which was the only other light machine gun we had really used up until then. Made from metal stampings and precision castings, the M60 weighed about ten pounds less than the Browning and was designed to be carried and operated by one man. Instead of being fed from a large metal ammunition can, ammunition for the M60 came in hundred-round belts packaged in a small box that could be mounted on the left side of the weapon. Not quite as strong as the Browning, because that reduction in weight had to come from somewhere, the M60 was a much handier weapon that could be fired from the hip, shoulder, or its built-in bipod.

The Teams used the M60 through the Vietnam War and still have it in the inventory today. It wasn't long before we were modifying the M60 to make it lighter and easier to carry. Modifications were done according to an individual SEAL's taste and ability. As long as the weapon still operated dependably, and the man could keep up with his job, SEALs in the Teams were given a lot of freedom in their equipment.

Within a short time of our beginning operations in Vietnam, the selection of weapons for a patrol became routine. You didn't have to tell a guy what we needed to carry in the way of weapons, ammunition, or grenades. A guy carried what he knew he could handle while moving quietly through the brush.

A good example of this was Dave Hyde, a big ol' country boy who was with me on my second and third tours in Vietnam. Standing about six feet one inch tall, Hyde at that time weighed in the neighborhood of two hundred pounds. Always a big fan of the M60 machine gun, he lavished time and skill on his weapon. To modify his M60, he took an older-style mechanical M60 buffer and replaced some of the internal buffer pads with nickels. With the modification, Hyde's M60 fired over eight hundred rounds per minute, up considerably from the normal six hundred rounds per minute.

To help lighten his M60 and make it more maneuverable, Hyde cut back the barrel of his weapon to just in front of the gas system. Rethreading the barrel, Hyde reattached the flash suppressor. By shortening the barrel, he removed the bipod, front sight, and about four inches of barrel. This took several pounds off the gun. With the front sight gone, the rear sight could also be removed, dropping another couple of ounces. These modifications to save weight were pretty common in both SEAL Teams during the Vietnam War.

Every little bit of weight saved on the gun meant something particular to Hyde. It meant he could carry more ammunition.

To feed his machine gun for a good length of time, Hyde made a U-shaped aluminum canister that would hold a five-hundred-round belt of ammunition and feed it directly to the weapon. To carry his rig, he fixed a harness to the aluminum belt box that would hold the whole mess around his waist like a thick belt, while still feeding the ammunition belt onto the left side of his M60.

With all of this ammunition and a heavy weapon, Hyde still didn't feel he had enough stuff with him. As well as his modified M60 and his ammunition harness, he carried a sidearm, hand grenades, knives, and miscellaneous gear. The man ended up looking like a popular cartoon of a SEAL that was circulating among the Teams. In the cartoon, the SEAL is outfitted with everything that might be used on a mission and looks as if he couldn't take a step. Even with all of his stuff, however, Hyde never did have any trouble taking steps.

The one time I said something to Hyde about the amount of gear he carried, he came back with an answer I couldn't argue with. "Chief," he said, "when I can't keep up with you, then you can tell me what I can't carry."

And I learned from that. Hyde had no apparent difficulty keeping up with the patrol. Whether it was moving fast and hard or slow and quiet, he would always be right where he was supposed to be. If that equipment was what he wanted to carry, no problem. The answer for the leader was, don't piss your troops off; let them carry what they're comfortable with.

As a platoon chief, I preferred leaving the choice of what weapon a man wanted to carry up to the individual whenever possible. If a man wanted to use a Stoner, and I knew the man was competent with the weapon and would take care of it, I didn't tell him, "No. I want you to carry an M16."

Saying something like that would disrupt a man's mental attitude and maybe even lower his self-confidence. As long as the general needs of the platoon or squad were met, and I had available what I would need according to what the target was or who was in the area, I let the man carry what he wanted. My attitude was common throughout the Teams on both the east and west coasts. This is one thing that I understand is still done in the Teams today. The men carry what they want, which helps increase their confidence, a very important point in a combat situation.

And a combat situation was not the only place in Vietnam where we might need a weapon. It was common practice for SEALs to be armed at all times while in Vietnam. Even when we were just taking it easy in places that were supposed to be secure, like downtown My Tho during my first tour, we usually went armed. As our reputation grew, SEALs became more and more of a target no matter where we were in Vietnam.

When we spent time in town off duty, we would just strap on a sidearm. In My Tho, Bob Gallagher and I slipped on issue holsters with Smith & Wesson Model 39s in them. It was one of the few times that I carried that particular handgun, and that was because it was Team issue and available. For most SEALs, sidearms were carried more often while in town than out in the field. Even in Saigon, with military police all over the place, we would usually have sidearms stuck into our belts, underneath our uniform blouses, in spite of the fact that it was against regulations.

No matter where you were in Vietnam, there could be a VC agent just across from where you stood. More than one U.S. soldier was killed in Saigon, despite its being a secure city. For the SEALs, having a pistol on you, whether it was a .45, a Smith & Wesson Model 39, or a Combat Masterpiece .38 revolver, just became part of the uniform.

Most of the SEALs who operated in Vietnam had a wide choice of sidearms they could carry as backup or off-duty weapons in Vietnam. Battlefield souvenirs also were popular with some SEALs, especially the Chicom Type 51 (7.62mm Tokarev), which was common, and the Type 59 (9mm Makarov), which was really pretty rare. The Teams had a good assortment of issue sidearms available. The Smith & Wesson .38 Special Combat Masterpiece revolver had been in the SEALs and the UDTs for a number of years. Also avail-

able was the 9mm automatic pistol and the standard-issue
M1911A1 .45 automatic.

I carried either a .45 or an Agency-issue 9mm Browning High
Power. My preference was for the Browning High Power but only
the Agency issued them. My opinion is the Browning High Power
is one of the finest handguns ever made, back then and even now.

When Sixth Platoon arrived in Nha Be in 1968, we learned that
the local Provincial Reconnaissance Unit was in need of an adviser.
In spite of being the platoon chief for Sixth, I wanted to operate
with the PRUs, so I accepted the job as their U.S. adviser. The
Agency ran the PRUs as part of the Phoenix Program, supplying
them with materials, weapons, and support. As a PRU adviser, I
was able to draw what I wanted from the Agency stores, and what
I wanted was a Browning High Power.

As a PRU adviser, I was issued a Browning and happily carried
it during my time in Nha Be. The only bitch was that I lost it during
my second tour when I was wounded in a water mine explosion. I
shouldn't complain much; after all, I was the only person to have
contact with the mine who survived the incident. But when I was
medevaced out to the MASH unit at Ben Wha, somebody took my
Browning and either kept it or turned it in to the Agency people. I
didn't get another one until the 1990s.

Each SEAL tended to have his own taste in weapons, and I
wasn't any different. In spite of the short CAR-15, and the later
improved XM177 E1 and E2, I didn't particularly like the M16
family of weapons. I much preferred a 9mm submachine gun for
some of the operations I went on. The Teams had some 9mm submachine guns available, most of them World War II designs like
the British Sten gun, the German MP-40, and French MAT-49, but
we didn't take any of these weapons with us to Vietnam. After fa-
miliarization training at the Creek, most of the submachine guns
we had went back into the armory to wait for the next class. There
were a few Swedish Ks in the Teams, and those were the weapons
I preferred to carry while on point.

The Swedish K, also called the Carl Gustav M45, was a simple
weapon with a thirty-six-round magazine and a side-folding stock

that could make it a very compact package. You could easily hold a submachine gun like the Swedish K with one hand and fire it while it hung from a sling around your neck. This was one of the things I liked about submachine guns: They would put out a lot of fire and still leave one hand free to grab your radio or anything else you needed.

Only the Agency had Swedish Ks in any decent numbers, and it issued them to its PRU advisers and SOG (Studies and Observation Group) people. Even the Ks the Agency had got short in number after the Swedes refused to sell any more of the guns to the United States since we were a "belligerent" country. In 1966, the Navy tried to buy a number of Swedish Ks for the Teams but ran into the same problem the Agency had. To fill in the gap, Smith & Wesson back in the States began designing its own submachine gun, the Model 76, after a request from the Navy was made to the president of the company. The Model 76 was like a smaller, lighter Swedish K but was American made, which eliminated any foreign supply problems. Smith & Wesson made about six thousand Model 76s between 1969 and 1974. The Teams purchased a number of Model 76s during the Vietnam War and the weapons remained in the active SEAL inventory until the early 1980s.

The Smith & Wesson Model 76 was available to us in the field in only limited numbers. A handful of prototype weapons were tested by the Teams in 1967. Design changes suggested from the Vietnam field trials were incorporated into the gun, and the modified S&W Model 76 went into production in 1969. Each weapon was issued with a special barrel and noise suppressor in addition to a regular barrel. Since suppressed weapons were always in fairly short supply, the S&Ws we had were reserved for use as suppressed submachine guns.

Though the suppressor made the S&W fairly quiet, it also added several pounds to the weapon and really made the thing muzzle-heavy. The special barrel used with the suppressor was ported near the chamber to bleed off propellant gases. Standard 9mm ammunition would leave this barrel below the speed of sound, eliminating the sonic crack.

Most of the suppressed weapons we had during the Vietnam War, except for the Hush Puppy (the suppressed S&W Model 39), were heavy because of their suppressors and not very comfortable to carry. Except for one operation during my first tour, I didn't really have a need for a suppressed weapon, though there were times when having one available would have just been a nice thing.

What I liked carrying most of all, especially during my second and third tours, was a radio. It may sound strange, me preferring to run as light as possible and all. But the radio was absolutely the biggest "gun" you could carry. At the other end of that communications line was your fire support, air support, and means of escape from a bad situation. Even when I was acting as the patrol leader during my later tours and sometimes still working as the point man, I operated with a radio on my back.

Depending on the operation, I was armed with either a shotgun, a Stoner, A CAR-15, or just a sidearm. During a busy operation, such as my POW rescue attempt, I was too preoccupied with giving orders and coordinating over the radio to be bothered with a long gun. In those situations, I tended to have at least one or two bodyguards nearby, preferably SEALs with one or more Stoners. All I carried was a pistol, usually an issue .45, for protection if the shit hit the fan.

On snatch ops, I usually carried my pistol-grip Ithaca shotgun with a duckbill attachment. For close-in engagements, there isn't anything better, in my opinion. If we were operating in more open areas, such as rice paddies, I carried a CAR-15 for its longer range. Either way, I was always capture oriented and the first one to bust in the target hooch.

That was kind of a dumb thing to do, looking back on it. The patrol leader, and the radioman, shouldn't have put himself in the most dangerous position by being the first man through the door. If he was taken out, the patrol lost its leadership and communications at the same time.

But I have always been a hard-headed chief and preferred to be the one who busted in the door and grabbed up the target. With that completed, it was time to call in our extraction and get on home. Besides, when I busted in the hooch, it was my decision as to who in the hooch got taken out and who was captured. What I didn't want was for somebody to go in and blow everybody away, killing the guy we wanted to talk to. I cannot emphasize too much that the SEALs in Vietnam were capture oriented. It was through our prisoners that we worked our way up the chain of command of the VC.

There were operations where I didn't feel a CAR-15 or even my shotgun was enough firepower. When I worked with the LDNNs in Cambodia, I carried a Stoner most of the time. My custom shotgun put out some real fire, and my LDNNs knew that. But a Stoner could cut down trees and small buildings, and that was something the LDNNs really respected. Roy Boehm had never trusted the LDNNs out of his sight, and he'd helped set up their training school. If they were enough to make Roy distrust them, they made me absolutely paranoid. Just because you're nuts doesn't mean somebody isn't out to get you.

One of the things we were always trying to do in the Teams was operate smarter and not harder. Running as light as possible but still carrying enough equipment to get the job done was one of the best ways to operate smarter. To help us accomplish this, the people back in the States at China Lake, California; White Oak, Maryland; and other places were constantly coming up with different equipment for us. Regular-issue signal flares were heavy, and the ones that were light needed a special launcher. Developed especially for us was a family of signal cartridges that fit our standard SEAL weapons.

The signal ammunition came in two calibers, 9mm and .38 Special. Those two calibers fit the majority of the popular SEAL handguns. The .38 Special signal cartridges were the Marks 130, 138, 139, and 140. For the most part, these were not much more than fancy bright tracers in different colors. The Mark 130 burned red, the Mark 138 yellow, and the Mark 139 green.

The Mark 140 signal cartridge was special in that it didn't start burning brightly until it had traveled fifty to eighty feet from the weapon's muzzle. The other signal rounds started burning brightly right from the muzzle. The Mark 140 also burned in two colors; for the first three seconds of flight the projectile had a green trace, and then it had a red trace for the remaining three seconds.

Another group of signal rounds was loaded in the 9mm Parabellum, the standard 9mm cartridge. The 9mm rounds were the Mark 121, 122, and 123 signal cartridges. Colored traces were red for the Mark 121, green for the Mark 122, and yellow for the Mark 123. The 9mm signal cartridges had very bright traces, but the cartridges didn't have enough recoil to operate the slide in most 9mm handguns. When you fired a 9mm signal cartridge, you had to pull the slide back manually to extract the empty case and load another round.

The intention of the rounds was to give us a signal flare that was able to punch through a jungle canopy. It was a sound concept and some SEALs did use the signal cartridges while in Vietnam. Though the trace of the signal rounds was bright, it wasn't really a replacement for even a pen-gun flare and certainly not a standard pop-flare. I never used any of the signal rounds while I was operating in Vietnam.

Other special kinds of ammunition were designed for the SEALs, some of which never made it out of the United States. An experimental bird-shot pistol round was suggested for our use, but I don't think anyone ever picked up on it. Though a bird-shot handgun round might have had its uses in a survival situation, I can't think of much use for such a thing in a combat zone.

When a point man was leading a patrol, you wanted that man to move as lightly as he could and still carry as big a punch as he could handle. Firepower was what he needed, in terms of a high volume of initial fire with a lot of effect on the target. Shotguns, CAR-15s, submachine guns, and 40mm grenade launchers all had their place to fulfill a point man's needs. The shotgun was what I soon settled on as my primary weapon while on point. Other SEALs liked the XM148 grenade launcher, which I tried but found too heavy and limited for my taste.

The CAR-15 was short and handy, and had a good deal of firepower in a small package. These features made it a popular weapon with other point men in the Teams. To increase the initial volume of fire from both the point man's and the squad's weapons, a larger magazine than even the thirty-rounder was needed. By 1969, we received a small number of fifty-round magazines that fed dependably in our M16s and CAR-15s. Issued out in Vietnam, many of the fifty-round magazines found themselves in the weapons carried by the point men on patrols.

Overall, we went through several different mods of fifty-round magazine from 1969 to 1972. The design of the fifty-round magazine did need some improvement, but with the cutbacks in military funding after the Vietnam War, the project was shelved. The Teams today have not given up on trying to find new ways of increasing their firepower.

Most of the large 75- to 120-round drum magazines made for the M16 today are intended primarily for the civilian market. Almost none of these overlarge magazines are rugged enough for use by the Teams. One magazine is an exception, the 100-round C-MAG double drum magazine made for the M16 by the Beta Company.

The C-MAG has two small drums that sit on either side of the magazine well of an M16 and do not stick out from the bottom any farther than even a normal 20-round magazine. Feeding from either drum into a central extension, the C-MAG will feed 100 rounds dependably and is stronger than some parts of the rifle. The C-MAG is not available on the civilian market at all but has been used for a number of years by the SEALs and other Special Warfare units.

One thing we never ran light on while on patrol was ammunition. Through all of my tours, the amount of ammunition I carried remained about the same, depending somewhat on the weapon I was carrying and the type of op being conducted. The minimum amount of ammo I would carry when armed with a CAR-15 or M16 was 200 rounds loaded into ten 20-round magazines. If you were lucky enough to have one, and I mean one, of the 30-round magazines for an M16, that was the magazine you carried loaded into your weapon.

The damn 30-round magazine was one of the hardest things to

come by. We couldn't get them issued to the platoons, but the Air Force guards at the air bases all had 30-round magazines. According to Colt, the 30-round magazine was still being developed and only the Air Force had accepted the early model. Nobody asked us; we would have taken all we could get. What we ended up doing was trading, cumshawing (Navy scrounging), and just plain stealing whatever few 30-round magazines we could get.

In the 20-round M16 magazines, we loaded a full 20 rounds. None of this 18-round bullshit to save the spring; we never had trouble with fully loaded magazines. The early 30-round M16 magazines did occasionally give some problems when topped up full, so we loaded them with only 29 rounds. What we didn't have any trouble with was making the early 30-rounders fit into our AR-15s, M16s, or CARs. The early large-capacity magazines had a curved design that the Army said wouldn't properly fit in all the weapons that were being issued in the military. Because of a problem that we never had, the Army didn't approve a 30-round M16 magazine design until 1968. And even then, we had to wait months before the new magazines were available for issue in the Teams.

When the new 30-round M16 magazines arrived, there weren't any ammunition pouches available to fit them. Some SEALs had been using AK-47s and carrying their long magazines in the three-pocket chest pouch the VC used. The pockets of the AK-47 magazine carrier were too deep to carry the 30-round M16 magazines, and filling the bottom of the pocket with something to make the magazines stick up was just a pain in the ass.

What did work was the canteen cover that fit on a pistol belt. Intended to hold a one-quart canteen nested in a canteen cup, the cover held three or four 30-round M16 magazines securely. If you left the top of the canteen cover open, you could get five 30-round magazines into it, but they didn't travel as securely. It wasn't long before we started getting the new issue 30-round magazine pouches at the Team, but the new pouches held only three magazines. Even after the new pouches were available, some guys still used the canteen covers as carriers because they held several more magazines.

To carry our dozen or so 20-round magazines while on an op, in

Team Two we used the issue M1956 universal ammunition pouch modified slightly to fit our needs. The universal ammunition pouch could carry two M14 magazines, three 40mm grenades, or four 20-round M16 magazines. The M16 magazines tended to fit low in the pouches, so we fitted tape pulls that you could yank to help pull the magazines out of the pouch. The magazines were carried bottom-up for fast reloading and also to help water drain out.

The sides of the M1956 and later pouches had special straps that held a hand grenade and secured the fuze against being dropped or accidentally activated. On the average operation, I carried four M26A1 fragmentation grenades attached to my pouches. On snatch operations or when we knew we were going to run into bunkers, I would add a couple of Mark 3A2 concussion (offensive) grenades to the frags I was already carrying. Sometimes, especially during my first tour, I would also have at least one M15 or M34 white phosphorus grenade on my rig.

At least one knife was also an integral part of a SEAL's basic load in Vietnam. Most of the guys carried the issue Mark 2 Ka-Bar and were well satisfied with it. Other SEALs would use whatever knife they had brought from home or picked up in Vietnam. I carried a Sykes-Fairbairn commando knife that my uncle Buck had given me before I left for my first tour in Vietnam. Uncle Buck had been in the Army Rangers in Italy during World War II where a British commando had given the knife to him. In turn, I carried that same knife through three tours of Vietnam.

Most of the Ka-Bars the guys carried were taped to the upper left front strap of the load-bearing harness. The Mark 2 Ka-Bar had a hard plastic sheath, so tape didn't squash the sheath and make the knife hard to draw. The sheath was mounted handle-down for a fast draw in case you needed that knife in a hurry. There wasn't any problem with losing the knife while on patrol. Besides using the snap-strap that came with the sheath, most guys put a couple of rubber bands around the handle of the knife and the bottom of the sheath.

One thing that you always carried with you while on patrol was a Mark 13 day/night flare. This signal was small, light, and handy as all hell. The Mark 13 made orange smoke for a day signal when you pulled the ring on one end. If you pulled the ring on the other end, the one that had a ring of raised dots around it, you ignited a red flare for night. The body of the Mark 13 was designed to stay cool while the signal burned so you could hold it in your hand without any trouble. Besides being a signaling device, the Mark 13 flare burned hot enough to start a good fire even in wet materials.

A Mark 13 was always taped to the sheath of a knife while on a swim in the SEALs or the UDTs. That habit remained in Vietnam, and many of the SEALs there carried Mark 13s taped to their knives. I always carried at least two Mark 13s when on patrol.

One trick we had when using a Mark 13 for signaling in the jungle was not to use the day (smoke) end much. Even on the brightest day, the red flare of the night end of a Mark 13 could be seen by overhead aircraft. Only the SEALs and the UDTs carried Mark 13s, so we could be quickly identified by an extraction bird or a gunship coming in on a run. By using the night end of the Mark 13, we also avoided having a lot of orange smoke lingering around our position, giving it away to any Viet Cong or NVA who might be nearby.

In addition to the Mark 13s, we usually had at least a few pop-flares in a squad while on patrol. The flares were aluminum tubes, about a foot long and an inch and a half in diameter. By taking the shipping cap off one end of the tube, placing it over the opposite end, and striking it sharply with your hand, you ejected a rocket that would go up several hundred feet before releasing a burning flare.

The drawback of the pop-flares was that they were heavy and bulky objects for just launching a flare. But the rocket put out by the pop-flares would punch through most jungle cover and eject a bright parachute flare for illumination or signaling. Normally we carried a couple of white parachute flares for illumination and a red parachute flare for signaling. The aluminum bodies of the pop-flares were bright silver and we would have to cover them with tape or paint them over to hide the shine. The flare would be taped to one of the straps of your carrying harness while on patrol.

Several items that everyone carried were standard pieces of first-aid gear. A canister of serum albumin would be taped to the upper back of each man's load-bearing harness. The serum albumin was a blood expander that each SEAL was trained to use to relieve shock in any man who was hit badly. The small, gray metal canister with a turn-key opener held a bottle of serum albumin and everything you needed to treat a man with it.

In addition to the serum albumin, each man had a square first-aid pouch attached to the upper part of his harness, right behind the neck. The pouch contained a couple of medium battle dressings, and a few morphine Syrettes if you were the corpsman. We examined a waterproof first-aid pouch in 1968. I even took a trip out to a factory that had some prototypes for us in September of that year. But a waterproof pouch was more trouble than it was worth, and all of our battle dressings came sealed in a plastic pouch anyway.

The first-aid gear was among the few items that each SEAL was trained to carry in the same place as everyone else in the patrol. When it was necessary to treat a wounded man, there wasn't any time to look around for gear.

To be sure we all knew how to use the first-aid materials we carried with us, part of predeployment training included a course in combat medicine taught by the platoon corpsman. In February 1970, Sixth Platoon was preparing to deploy on what would be my third tour in Vietnam. The platoon went down to the Marine base at Camp Lejeune, North Carolina, for a four-day course titled Field First-Aid Procedures for Nonmedical Personnel. The course was intended to teach us how to start an IV, administer serum albumin, and perform other sophisticated lifesaving techniques.

The powers that be were now going to see to it that, after two tours in Vietnam, including getting wounded myself, I would officially learn how to use the equipment I had been carrying around for years. We had been taught how to use the gear we had with us right from the beginning, but now we would have a piece of paper that said we knew what we were doing.

The most fun part of the training was learning how to give each other injections. Whether you were a big, tough SEAL or not, those damned needles hurt, especially when wielded by some of our more ham-handed operators. When they teach diabetics to give themselves insulin shots, they start out with sticking the needle into an orange or something like that. Not us; we teamed up and stuck each other.

My training partner was Slaytor Blackiston, a third-class quartermaster at the time. Slaytor wasn't particularly interested in sticking it to his platoon chief, especially right before we deployed to Vietnam. So when it came time to inject me with his syringe full of sugar water, Slaytor pretended to stick it in me and just emptied the needle along my arm. Then he just looked up at me and smiled.

When it came to be my turn to give Slaytor a shot, I paid him back in true SEAL fashion. I drove that needle right through his arm. "Never give a sucker an even break, Slaytor," I said.

Slaytor's answer was a bit loud and I don't think he was showing quite the proper amount of respect for a Navy chief petty officer. But as long as he said "Chief," everything was all right.

When it came to operating in the field, just like most everything else, the actual web gear that a man wore was usually left up to the individual's taste. Most often, the standard Army pistol belt was worn along with an H-harness, four or more ammunition pouches, and whatever other gear the man had. Canteens were not worn as a matter of course. I don't believe I ever wore a canteen on my rig in Vietnam and I don't remember any of my fellow SEALs carrying one. Water is very heavy and we didn't want the extra weight. Everybody carried a small vial of iodine tablets as part of his kit and there was water available in the areas we operated in. If we needed water while on an op, we would just use whatever container we had handy and use the iodine tablets to purify the water.

Next to water, one of the heaviest things you can carry on a patrol is food. The more compact and lighter dehydrated rations weren't available for my first tour in Vietnam. Even if the lighter rations had been available, we wouldn't have carried them while on a patrol. Rations were just too heavy to bother packing around.

When I was working with the LDNNs especially, if we needed a meal while going in on a target, we would move up to a hooch and have a mama-san cook us up a batch of rice. This action was not as insane as it sounds. We would always put out a perimeter and secure the area. But I wouldn't let the men do anything to terrorize the inhabitants of the hooch. It was bad enough that we knocked on these people's door in the middle of the night; I sure as hell wasn't going to let my LDNNs give them a bad time.

When we did the same thing with a patrol of SEALs, we just let our interpreter do the talking. My squad wasn't going to do anything more than stay alert and watchful. It wouldn't do to make enemies of these people anyway. After an op, we might have to come back along the same way we went in and pass the same place again. That wasn't how things were planned, but shit happens.

When we had a mama-san fix us some rice, we always left something in exchange. Money in the form of piasters was something either I or the patrol leader always had with him. But it wasn't always as easy as paying somebody for something. In the boonies of Vietnam, the locals subsisted on a barter economy. Money wasn't exactly worthless, but it sure didn't have the same value as it did in the cities and towns.

Bud Thrift always carried piasters with him to pay locals for materials or information. But we never did get into the barter system very well. There was no way we would leave someone a piece of our equipment, no matter what he told or gave us. And giving something like a flashlight or lighter really didn't work out very well, if you thought about it. Here were these people, so far out in the sticks that they didn't use money as a normal means of exchange. You give someone in that situation a flashlight, and what is he going to do for batteries later on? Or lighter fluid, for that matter? The American soldier's standby, candy bars, didn't work either, because they just melted in the heat, and you couldn't carry them along with you for the same reason.

Though it wasn't the best answer, we would just pay for things with money. You would always do what you could to just say, "Thank you. I'm sorry I disturbed you, but I was hungry." For the most part, the average Vietnamese was between the jaws of a vise, with us on one side and the VC on the other. It was all some of these people could do just to survive on a day-to-day basis. The basic idea was to use your common sense when you had to deal with the locals. The rule was, don't piss the people off; you might need them again in the future.

The SEALs had no trouble following that rule. And when you were working with the LDNNs, and some PRUs, you made sure that they knew where you stood, and you kept the worst ones on a very short leash.

One odd thing we carried on a regular basis, starting with our first tour, was handcuffs. Taking a page out of the police hand-books, we had brought several pairs with the platoon. Snapping a pair of handcuffs on a VC prisoner would make him much easier for one man to secure, and they were fast and convenient.

During my second tour, we were still using steel handcuffs to secure prisoners. On one op out of Long An, I was leading the patrol, which had Chuck Fellers, David Hyde, Clayton Sweesy, and the rest of my squad from Sixth Platoon, along with our interpreter, George. The op was a body snatch, and we got our prisoner and his weapon without any major incident. Grabbing our man up, I secured him with a pair of my Smith & Wesson steel handcuffs.

Though handcuffs were useful in securing a prisoner, they did have some drawbacks. For one thing, the steel cuffs were heavy and expensive. The Teams then were not as well supplied as they are today, and equipment seemed to always be in short supply. We always had the money we needed for the large items, but the little stuff, like lumber or handcuffs, we had to argue for. If one of the higher-up nonoperators in the supply chain couldn't understand why we wanted something, the bean counter would turn our requests down.

Handcuffs were just like everything else, and we had only a couple of pairs in the platoon during my second tour. Smith & Wesson did have a lightweight alloy set of handcuffs on the market, but they were even more expensive than the steel set, so we just put up with the weight of the steel cuffs.

One problem we never could solve about the cuffs was the way the metal shined. Highly polished steel might look good in the civilian world, but that was the last thing we wanted with us in combat. Nothing we did really seemed to help very much; paint just rubbed off and tape gummed up everything.

So here we were, extracting from a snatch with our prisoner secured at the rear of the column with our nice shiny handcuffs. With me leading the way, our patrol was heading out to the extraction point when shit started to happen. As I had learned long before, an extraction is the most dangerous part of an operation. You've made it known that you're in the area, and anybody who wants your ass will be riled up and moving in on your last known position.

The patrol started taking fire from the rear and it was time for us to get the hell out of Dodge once again. The interpreter, George, was at the rear of the column, securing the prisoner and moving him along with the rest of us. I don't know what happened, but as we were moving out, suddenly I had George up front with me.

Whatever our VC had done, he was no longer our prisoner but now listed as an enemy KIA (killed in action). George knew I was limited on handcuffs and had come up to me to tell me what had happened and ask for the key. Now was not the time for me to ask for details about what the hell had gone on at the back of the column; all I did was reach around my neck for the chain that I kept the handcuff key on. Only thing was, no chain and no key.

"Forget about the damned handcuffs," I told George. "We're moving out right now." With that, I signaled the patrol that we were moving on. The area was still hot and I figured the prisoner had tried to make a break during our confusion. It wasn't like we were taking direct fire, but we could hear the VC moving about and occasionally firing their weapons, sometimes in our direction.

We had gotten a couple of hundred meters on down the way when George came back up to me at the head of the patrol. Without a word, he handed me my handcuffs back, still locked and more than a little bloody. George was a PRU interpreter and less squeamish about some aspects of getting the job done than even a SEAL could be. I just took the cuffs and kept them for the next job, never asking any questions and not getting any answers volunteered.

George just didn't want to see his chief lose his handcuffs, and it wasn't like our ex-prisoner was going to need them any longer.

Later on during the war, we started using the long plastic strips that are intended to secure bundles of electrical cables in the place of steel cuffs. The idea of their use had come out of one of the R&D groups back in the States, possibly China Lake. The tie strips can be tightened into a loop easily but cannot be loosened; they have to be cut to remove them. Even the strongest man cannot get enough leverage to break a pair of the bigger tie strips without busting up his wrists all to hell. Convenient, cheap, and already in the supply system, the plastic tie strips also made it unnecessary to keep track of a handcuff key. Today, these same strips are still used in the Teams as well as in police departments to secure large groups of prisoners.

One thing that nobody carried with them while on patrol was dog tags. Those two identification shields worn on a chain around the neck carried your name, rank, service number, blood type, and religious affiliation if any. Though you could cover them with tape or plastic, dog tags could rattle if they struck together. We also didn't want any form of identification on us when we went out on operations. It has long been a tradition in the Teams that no one is ever left behind, living or dead. If I was captured in Vietnam, all I felt a dog tag would do was give more information to my captor.

We wore standard fatigues with a name tape and U.S. NAVY over the pockets when on base or in town, but we didn't have any type of regulation uniform while we were on an operation. Like the choice of a weapon, the uniform a man wanted to wear was mostly up to him. With all the time spent training long before we ever got to combat, the last thing you had to worry about was what a man might wear on an op. Some guys had little superstitions about what kind of headgear or other item of clothing they should wear. Frank Moncrief had a kind of cowboy bush hat with the sides folded up that he always preferred to wear when he went out into the field.

Things like footwear were left completely up to a man's individual taste. I preferred the canvas coral shoes issued in both the SEALs and the UDTs. The coral shoes had a light, flexible rubber sole with a low-cut, laced canvas upper. They were very much like a gray gym shoe. When you were wearing corals, your feet had a certain amount of protection, but you could still feel the irregularities of the ground through the sole.

Some guys wore jungle boots, coral shoes, or sneakers, and some even went in their bare feet. Going barefoot had its advantages when you were traveling through mud and other surfaces that would just pull a shoe right off your foot. But for the most part, men tended to wear something that protected the foot from thorns, rocks, splinters, twigs, and things like that. The jungle boot had an armored sole with a steel plate in it to protect you if you stepped on a punji stake. At the same time, the boot was so stiff that you wouldn't feel it if you were just starting to pull on a trip wire with the top of your foot.

My own uniform tended to be blue jeans (Levi's) and a black pajama top of a tiger-stripe camouflage shirt. My headgear was initially a soft cap with a bill, or a black beret. After an adventure with some ants falling down my neck, I learned the value of an all-around brim and started wearing a floppy bush hat when on patrol.

It was funny, but regular civilian Levi's wore better than any other pants we had available in Vietnam. And we were never able to convince the government about that. If we wanted Levi's, and we did, we had to buy them ourselves. It wasn't like the Teams owned stock in Levi Strauss and Company; it was just the cloth Levi's were made from wore better in the brush.

If you wore the 1967-issue uniform into a mangrove swamp, that would be the last time you wore that particular set. The thorns and other vegetation in a mangrove swamp would just tear the hell out of a set of jungle fatigues. Later during the Vietnam War, ripstop uniforms became available, and these lasted longer in the brush. But there never was anything issued that would wear better than regular Levi's. Before we went over on our first tour, guys from Team One suggested that we take a bunch of Levi's with us, and they were right; the darn things wore like iron.

In general, we carried four sets of fatigues with us when we first deployed to Vietnam. There wasn't any way we were going to stand any inspections or parades, so there wasn't a need for a dress uniform.

That did cause a small problem, however, if a man was wounded and sent home. If the wounded man was a litter patient, there was no problem—the guy would just wear what the hospital gave him. But if the man was walking wounded, he would have to wear a dress (Class A) uniform in order to ride on most military flights. Most of the time we traveled in civilian clothes or just plain fatigues, so if a man needed a uniform to travel in, we had to scrounge one up for him.

Some funny things got their start in Vietnam and are still around to make trouble for the SEALs today. One of these "traditions" is the wearing of a triangular bandanna wrapped around the hair in place of a hat. Personally, I didn't wear a "rag" tied around my head—I just preferred a hat—but there is no arguing the advantages of having a patrol rag snugged in place.

First of all, the triangular bandanna lay flat against the forehead with the ends tide off at the base of the skull, just above the neck. Wearing the rag in this manner helped add to an individual's camouflage and keep his profile low. In addition, the rag kept any perspiration from running down his forehead into his eyes, possibly blinding him at a very bad moment.

The rag was also useful in other ways. It could be turned into a very quick tourniquet, and when you need one of those to stop the bleeding, you want it right now! The rag could also gag or secure a prisoner, wipe off a weapon, or even be used as a triangular bandage. Since the SEALs were so flexible in what uniforms were allowed on a patrol, the rag became something of a symbol of special operations forces. And this was what caused trouble for the Teams recently.

During the Somalia landings, the SEALs were sent in ahead of the Marines to scout and secure the landing beaches. This is a normal part of a SEAL mission profile and is no big deal unless the area is heavily defended. The beaches at Somalia weren't heavily defended; they were occupied by something much worse—newsmen.

When the SEALs landed, they had newsmen and cameras all over them right from the git-go. It is a big point in those young lions' favor that they didn't shoot some of those jerks who shoved their cameras and lights right into the SEALs' faces. If there had been some resistance on the beaches from the Somalian warlords, those same cameramen would have turned to the SEALs to protect them. But the SEALs would have been completely blind in the dark from having all those bright lights pointed at them.

What was funny about part of the operation was the orders that had gone out from Army General Carl Stiner, then the man in charge of SOCOM, the Special Operations Command in Tampa, Florida. General Stiner did not want to see one bandanna worn by any of the SEALs who would be in public view. Bandannas made the SEALs look like pirates and the general would have none of that. (What the hell was this anyway, a military operation or a dog-and-pony show for the media vultures?)

Of course, the first thing shown by the news media on television was a bunch of young U.S. troops, huddled in the glare of camera lights and trying to do their job. Besides the confused look on the operators' faces, the bandannas wrapped around their heads stood out in plain view. The general just about went ballistic; somebody in the Teams had flagrantly disregarded orders and heads would roll.

The investigation that followed didn't last long. The men who had been filmed were U.S. Marines, part of the long-range reconnaissance units that were augmenting the SEALs in securing the beachhead. No SEALs had been caught wearing bandannas, and the Marines had never been given the order not to wear them.

Nice to know that some things never change, and that the Army can still be more concerned with appearances than with getting the job done.

CHAPTER 12

Shotguns

D URING OUR FIRST PREDEPLOYMENT TRAINING at Camp Pickett, Virginia, we spent a whole week just firing weapons to get a feel for which ones we would like best in Vietnam. We didn't have much in the way of the exotic weapons that would later become almost a trademark of the SEALs. What we did have was AR-15s and M16s, the little shorty CAR-15s, M79 40mm grenade launchers, M60 machine guns, and 12-gage Ithaca Model 37 shotguns.

Supposedly, the Navy—and the SEALs—ended up with the Ithaca shotgun as the result of some kind of political maneuvering in Washington, D.C. A politician wanted the Ithaca Gun Company to receive a military contract and the Navy was tagged to receive the riot-gun version of the Ithaca Model 37. If the story is true, it's one of the few times I know of that some pork-barrel politics did the fighting man some good.

The Ithaca Model 37 is a tough, pump-action, 12-gage shotgun holding four rounds of ammunition in its tubular magazine underneath the barrel. With a round chambered and the magazine topped off, the Ithaca carries five rounds ready to go. The design of the Ithaca leaves only a single port in the bottom of the smooth-sided receiver. That single port is where fresh ammunition is loaded and fired casings are ejected—an odd system and a unique one in the shotgun field. But the Ithaca has a machined steel receiver and the single port helps keep dirt and other gunk out of the action of the weapon.

The specific model of Ithaca we carried the most was the Featherweight Riot Gun. The riot Ithaca had a 20.1-inch barrel, no sights except for a bead at the muzzle, and a gray, parkerized finish. Overall, the gun was 40 inches long and weighed 6.3 pounds empty.

The pump action of the Ithaca was operated by a wooden grip that slid along the magazine tube just underneath the barrel. One of the real advantages of a shotgun was the fact that you didn't have to worry about whether the gun would jam up from the mud, like other automatic weapons. With an Ithaca, even if it was covered in mud, chances were the gun would fire, if you had the strength to jack the slide back and forth. And if you had the opportunity to wash off a shotgun in a stream or canal, all you had to do was swish it around in the water to get it clean enough to operate in an emergency.

Some Ithacas didn't have a disconnector as part of the weapon's trigger mechanism. A disconnector forced you to release the trigger and pull it again for each shot as you operated the weapon. Without a disconnector, all you had to do was hold the trigger back and operate the slide. Each time a round was loaded and chambered, the gun would fire. By holding the trigger back and working the slide quickly, you could fire a shotgun as quickly as some automatic weapons.

Bob Gallagher and I had heard about the nondisconnector Ithacas and did talk about them a bit. We both figured that the holding-the-trigger-back-and-firing trick would just waste ammunition and possibly leave you with an empty gun in a bad situation. What we did instead was train with the shotgun until racking the slide and releasing the trigger became second nature. Constant dry-firing drills, working the slide and moving your trigger finger back and forth, created a muscle habit that made it difficult to fire a shotgun any other way. You had to work at it to screw up.

One drawback we noticed early on with the Ithaca was its limited magazine capacity. Full up, it took only five rounds, and the way the barrel was attached at the front of the magazine made enlarging the magazine a difficult proposition.

What we did to make up for the limited magazine capacity of the Ithacas was practice reloading on the run. Even with the weapon up to your shoulder, you could keep slipping rounds into the bottom port with your left hand after a little practice. I quickly picked up the habit of keeping a few rounds between the fingers of my left, nonfiring hand. Anytime there was a lull in firing, I would slip a few more rounds into the magazine. By topping up your shotgun's magazine automatically, you almost felt the gun would never run dry.

After my little adventure with the ants falling down my neck, which made me accidentally discharge a 40mm grenade at my feet, I was looking for a different weapon to carry while on point. The CAR-15/XM-148 was just too big and powerful for what I really wanted. At that time the 40mm buckshot rounds that were available were being held back from issue to the troops in the field, including the SEALs.

If the 40mm buckshot round had been available, I might have rethought my attitude toward the XM-148. The buckshot round would have made it a devastating close-in weapon without the danger of using an explosive shell. But, since a shotgun-type round wasn't available for the XM-148, I did the next best thing and started carrying a shotgun while on point.

The shotgun I used during my first tour was the regular Team-issue Ithaca Model 37. By the middle of March, we received a brand-new type of shotgun from our support people back in the States. The Remington Arms Company had developed the Remington 7188 series, a gas-operated shotgun capable of full-automatic fire.

The Remington 7188 Mark 1 was a modified version of the company's Model 1100 sporting shotgun. In place of the regular safety behind the trigger was a selector switch. With the switch pointing rearward, the shotgun was on safety. With the switch pointing down, the weapon fired one shot for each pull of the trigger. But pointing the switch forward put the gun on full automatic, and it fired at a cyclic rate of about 420 rounds per minute.

In addition to the selective fire capability, the Remington 7188 Mark 1 had some other nice touches in its design. The weapon had an extended magazine tube going the entire length of the barrel. With the long magazine, the 7188 held seven rounds in the magazine with an eighth round in the chamber. Rifle sights were fitted to the barrel for exact aiming and the barrel had a protective hand guard over it. There was even a lug under the barrel for mounting a bayonet, not that the SEALs were known for bayonet charges.

Bob Gallagher immediately grabbed up the 7188 as soon as it arrived. As far as the Eagle was concerned, the weapon was the best thing since sliced bread. On an ambush on night, Bob let loose with his shotgun on full automatic and that bitch really hummed. The blast from a machine shotgun is unreal, with what the weapon does to a target area. But full-automatic fire did empty the gun within a few seconds, and you still had to load the rounds one at a time up through the bottom of the receiver.

What Bob really thought was that the 7188 would be the ideal weapon for me to carry on point. The power of the 7188 was without question, but I just didn't like the weapon for point. It was heavier and larger than the Ithaca and my pump gun was much more reliable.

Even Gallagher gave up on the 7188 after carrying it on a number of patrols. As the weapon picked up dirt and mud in the field, it would jam up even on semiautomatic fire. The design was just too sensitive to dirt. Bob finally quit carrying the 7188 and switched over to an Ithaca like mine. During other tours, other SEALs would carry the 7188 while on patrol. Both Mike Boynton and Fly Fallon used the 7188 on at least a few ops. But the drawbacks of the design just couldn't be dealt with in Vietnam, and only a dozen or so 7188s were even made, to my understanding.

What I came to like the shotgun for was its devastating power in a close-in fight. When an op took us through an open area, such as rice paddies, I would carry a CAR-15 or even the occasional M16. If we were going to be in the bush, on a snatch or hooch searches, I would carry a shotgun. Even when I later became a platoon chief, I would still walk point and carry a shotgun when the situation called for it.

Things happened so fast when we busted a hooch or initiated an ambush that there wasn't time for a VC to be impressed by the three-quarter-inch hole in the muzzle end of a shotgun. But the sound of a shotgun firing sure impressed the VC. We soon learned that the VC and NVA had a healthy fear of a shotgun. What we also heard was scuttlebutt about what the VC would do to a man who was captured with a shotgun.

The rumors came from up north in I Corps and other areas. Up there, the U.S. Marines were operating heavily and many of them carried shotguns. We heard that if you were taken prisoner and were armed with a shotgun, the VC used your own weapon on you.

That was a story I heard more than once: Don't get caught with a shotgun because they will use it on you. Rumors like that were not something you could let affect you on your job. And the NVA and VC already had a big reward out for the capture or confirmed kill of a "green face," as the SEALs were known. But the effectiveness of a shotgun was proven more than once in Vietnam and I still prefer the weapon today.

During my first tour in early 1967, the Team had a much smaller selection of shotgun ammunition types than was available to us later in the war. For the most part, we had 00 buckshot in several different loads. Since the days of the Old West, 00 buckshot has been the standard combat load for 12-gage shotguns. Called "blue whistlers" back then, 00 buckshot is composed of 0.33-inch diameter lead pellets, normally loaded nine to a cartridge.

Some of the 12-gage 00 buckshot rounds we had were the all-brass-cased M19 rounds that were first designed back during World War I. The only nice thing about them was that the all-metal case was intended to keep the round waterproof, an important consideration back when all other shotgun shells were made of paper that would swell up when wet.

We did receive some new rounds that were just as waterproof as the earlier M19 ammunition—even more so, because the new rounds had a better seal on the case mouth. The new rounds were plastic-cased 00 buckshot ammunition that was no different from the commercial ammunition you could buy in any hardware store back in the States.

A new military buckshot round, the XM162, became available in 1967 and was issued to us while we were incountry. The XM162

12-gage shell was one of the new designs coming out of Winchester and was made especially for the military. The 00 buck that was in the XM162 was made of a hard alloy and the pellets were packed in a plastic sleeve to keep them from rubbing the barrel of the shotgun as they were fired. This still-round buckshot would fly straighter and farther than the earlier loads.

The ammunition I liked best for my shotgun was the XM257 buckshot round. In the XM257 were twenty-seven pellets of special hardened number 4 buckshot carried in a plastic sleeve and protected against deforming when the round was fired. Using the latest sporting ammunition technology, Winchester made the XM257 round for the military, to be effective at a longer range than the older ammunition designs. The first rounds we received were even loaded in the red plastic cases Winchester used for its Mark 5 sporting ammunition. Later, production XM257 ammo was in a black plastic case with a brass or gray steel head.

The XM257 also eliminated any problems with the Geneva Conventions, in which shotguns are not outlawed for use in combat, but soft lead ammunition is. Lead bullets deform when they hit, the same as a soft-nosed round, and they are specifically banned from use in combat. The hardened pellets of the XM257 round do not deform and are also more effective at longer ranges than the old soft buckshot.

In my opinion, the round was dynamite. Any opponent I hit with that swarm of twenty-seven 0.24-inch-diameter pellets tended to go down and stay down.

Some weapons experts today swear that the only shotgun ammunition worth anything in a fight is 00 buckshot, with its 0.33-inch-diameter lead pellets. Others go even further and say that the 000 buckshot round, with its 0.36-inch-diameter pellets, is the only effective fighting round for a shotgun.

Far be it from me, a simple Navy chief, to argue with many of these armchair experts. But I didn't find I needed the extra penetration you get from the larger sizes of buckshot. Instead, I liked the dense pattern of shot from the XM257 round. The nine pellets in a standard 00 buckshot round, and the eight pellets in a 000 buckshot round, just don't have as good a chance of hitting the target as twenty-seven pellets of number 4 buckshot.

I may not have spent as much time as some so-called experts reading and playing with all the numbers on ammunition that are out there. But I have been a Navy SEAL, and one with three tours of combat experience behind him. The smaller-stature Asians we were fighting were taken care of very effectively with the number 4 buckshot round I used, almost to the exclusion of any other rounds we had available.

As time passed, we did have different rounds available for us and our 12-gage shotguns. The fléchette round was supposed to be the great shotgun round, tearing up the enemy and extending the range of a shotgun close to that of a rifle. As far as range went, I couldn't say, as I never used my shotgun except for close-in fire-fights. When I did try the fléchette rounds, I found they didn't have any real knock-down power.

A regular buckshot round could really tear a hole in a guy, busting him up pretty bad with just one good hit. The fléchette round fired all of these little finned nails, maybe an inch long and a tenth of an inch or less in diameter. All the little needles did was poke a bunch of holes in the target. Sure, a VC was going to bleed to death in maybe fifteen or twenty minutes, but the fléchettes weren't going to knock him down. The fléchette rounds just weren't worth the trouble, in my opinion.

Solid-slug ammunition was also available to us for our shotguns. The slug round is a single cylindrical hardened-lead "bullet" that has tremendous knock-down power on the target. A solid 12-gage slug will just smash through things, tear locks off doors, or blow someone right off his feet. But a 12-gage slug is still nothing more than a big bullet, and a real heavy one at that. Slugs tend to weigh in the neighborhood of an ounce or more apiece. Add that to the weight of a shell, and it doesn't take more than eleven or twelve 12-gage slug loads to weigh a full pound.

After my first tour was over, I returned to the States and started working as the research and development chief for Team Two. A number of new projects were in the works to increase the firepower available to the SEALs. Two types of special shotgun rounds were designed and used by the Teams in Vietnam: CS rounds and several different colors of flare shells.

The CS round launched a thumb-sized canister of CS composition tear gas that would burst after hitting a solid object. Acting like a miniature tear gas grenade, the 12-gage CS round was just the thing for firing into bunkers and shelters that we didn't want to enter ourselves.

The CS rounds were much more convenient to carry than a full-sized tear gas grenade. They were powerful enough to drive out any hidden Vietnamese in an enclosed area without our having to use lethal force. That not only helped add to our bag of captured VC, it also kept down the injuries to any innocent villagers.

The red, green, and white flare rounds launched a single burning star up to an altitude of a hundred yards or so. The flares had enough power to penetrate the jungle canopy so we could identify ourselves to any incoming aircraft. Though they weren't very bright, the 12-gage signal flares could be seen for a good distance at night. Much lighter than even a standard XM257 round, the 12-gage flares were much easier to carry then the issue pop-up flares, though we would often carry both, just in case. In a pinch, the flares could even be used to set fire to a hooch or other building's thatch roof from a distance of thirty yards or so.

One particularly neat round of ammunition never made it over to Nam, where it might have had a lot of appeal to guys like me. AAI in Baltimore came up with a silent shotgun shell in late 1967 or early 1968. The round apparently made little noise, no smoke, and no flash when it was fired. And the round worked in any shotgun, especially a manual repeater such as the Ithaca that I already preferred.

The silent shotgun shell launched a number of buckshot pellets with a plastic piston. The body of the cartridge was steel and was sealed against any gas leakage. When you fired the round, gas pushed the piston forward but never left the sealed cartridge casing. No gas leakage, no noise.

Only about two hundred of the special rounds were ever made

and all of those were used up in testing at White Oak and places like that. Apparently there was some trouble with getting the round to work effectively and still be silent. It didn't matter how quiet a weapon was if it couldn't get the job done with a single shot. A wounded sentry could start yelling or even fire off his own weapon. All in all, the special round was a good idea that never made it over to Vietnam. Which was too bad; a silent round that could fire in a shotgun and still blow away a target would have been real popular in the Teams.

In early December 1967, I traveled up to Fort Dix, New Jersey, to the experimental range there run by Frankford Arsenal. The folks at Frankford Arsenal had been working on an Air Force requirement for a shot-spreader attachment for their guard shotguns. Frankford had also been spending some time addressing the requests for equipment and modifications put forward by SEALs in Vietnam. On this trip, I would be picking up two new modified shotguns.

The modifications Frankford had come up with for the Ithaca impressed me quite a bit, especially after I had spent some time with the weapon out on the range at Fort Dix. One of the better changes to the weapon was an extension to the magazine, increasing the number of rounds that could be loaded, ready for use.

A kind of kit had been made up that could be used to modify existing shotguns. A long extension tube that could be screwed onto the end of the existing magazine of the Ithaca was part of the kit. Because the front magazine cap is part of the barrel retention system in the Ithaca Model 37, mounting the magazine extension required some permanent changes to the barrel of the weapon.

Changes that were needed included removing the old barrel lug and attaching a clamp between the barrel and the new magazine extension. These changes could be easily done in a field repair shop, and the necessary kits later were forwarded to Vietnam. With the extension in place, the magazine of the Ithaca could now hold seven rounds, with an eighth round in the chamber.

In addition to the magazine extension, a longer magazine spring, and a barrel clamp, the kit also included a new kind of muzzle choke device that I particularly liked. The choke device was a four-inch-long extension that had to be brazed onto the muzzle of the shotgun's barrel. The long cylindrical choke had a deep V-notch cut into it back from the muzzle. The V-notch split the choke into upper and lower halves, like the open end of a duck's bill. Since the choke looked so much like an open duck's bill, that was the name that stuck to it: the duckbill.

What the duckbill did was change the pattern of the shot spreading from the muzzle of the shotgun from a circle to an oval. Instead of a forty-four-inch circular pattern at thirty yards with number 4 buckshot, the duckbill-equipped weapon would have a pattern ninety-six inches wide and only twenty-four inches tall at the same distance with the same load.

The first time I was told what the duckbill would do, I didn't believe it. But firing the weapon on the range made a believer out of me. The wide pattern would greatly help in hitting a running man with the blast from my 12-gage. Instead of having to calculate a lead distance, you could just point and shoot a shotgun with a duckbill on it. And the duckbill worked best with number 4 buckshot, already my favorite combat load.

I picked up the two modified shotguns at Fort Dix and took them, along with a couple of unmounted duckbill chokes, back with me to demonstrate at Little Creek. After we accepted them, a number of the kits were made available to both Team One and Team Two. A total of about fifty Ithaca Model 37s were modified in the Teams.

The weapon I wanted for use while on point was as short and handy a shotgun as I could get. What I didn't want to do was lose the extra magazine capacity of the extended magazine, and I really liked the duckbill attachment. Since the magazine extension now went all the way to the end of the twenty-inch barrel, there was no way to shorten the weapon by cutting the muzzle back. Instead I took the stock and cut it down to just a pistol grip.

Exactly what I did was cut off the wooden stock just behind the pistol-grip portion. Sanding the grip round, I replaced the long stock bolt with a shorter one that would extend into the receiver and hold my pistol grip securely on the weapon. Taping the hell out of the grip gave it a little padding and covered up my carpentry work.

By attaching my pistol grip to a duckbill Ithaca, I took off about nine inches of overall length and dropped about half a pound of weight. Running a heavy string from the muzzle back to my pistol grip gave me a simple sling that could go behind my neck and carry the shotgun at waist level, ready for use. The sling also freed my left hand from having to hold up the weapon. Now I could reload, signal, or draw another piece of equipment with my left hand without having to lower my weapon.

My duckbill-modified, pistol-grip Ithaca became my "Sweetheart" during my second and third tours in Vietnam. The lack of a stock never bothered me because I would normally carry a shotgun only when I expected to be in close quarters. Close up, I could point my shotgun from the waist and blow away any target I had in front of me out to twenty or thirty yards without any trouble. When I carried a shotgun, twenty yards was a long way. If the op was such that I carried a shotgun, the average engagement distance was more like five yards or less. At that close range, the duckbill acted more like a big buzz-saw and could cut a man almost in half with a single shot.

I demonstrated my modified Ithaca to my brother SEALs to kind of sell the weapon to the Team. Those men who had liked the shotgun to begin with loved the idea of the duckbill. The shotgun men in the Team actually liked the new extended-magazine Ithaca better than the Stoner light machine gun. You could put as much lead into an area with the long magazine as you could with a belt from the Stoner. Twenty-seven pellets of number 4 buck multiplied by eight rounds gave you 216 "bullets" sweeping an area within a few seconds of each other. The longest belt carrier we had for the Stoner at the time held only 150 rounds of 5.56mm ammunition.

As far as my pistol-grip modification went, most of the guys thought I was crazy. At that time, there wasn't any such thing as a 12-gage pistol-grip shotgun. Even sawed-off shotguns still had a minimal kind of stock. Different guys in the platoon, including Bob

Gallagher, tended to have the same opinion: "You're going to blow that gun right out of your hands," he said, "and bust your wrist all to hell in the process."

The first time a group of us went to the range and I demonstrated the weapon, the guys were all impressed that I didn't break my wrist. What I wasn't going to do was hold the weapon up like a pistol and fire it. Instead, I cradled it with my left hand and held it tight against my body with my right. The technique was very much like the instinctive shooting style we had learned from the British SAS back in the early 1960s.

For the most part, the duckbill-modified Ithacas were a success throughout the Teams. Both Team One and Team Two fielded them in Vietnam from 1968 till the end of the war. In the 1970s, the weapons the Teams had were getting pretty worn and were eventually replaced, primarily with Remington 870s. And when the Ithacas left the Teams, the duckbills went with them, a modification that I am sorry to see is not in the Teams anymore.

But for all of the success of the duckbill modification, the design did have some drawbacks. Only the XM257 round with its number 4 buckshot really worked well in the duckbill. Even 00 buckshot, which the Team had loaded in the XM162 12-gage round, didn't spread properly through a duckbill. And the special 12-gage CS tear gas and flare rounds absolutely couldn't go through a duckbill choke. I don't know if firing a CS or flare round through a duckbill would actually hurt the weapon or injure the operator, but the projectile would be torn up going though the choke.

On missions where we knew we would be searching hooches and bunkers, I used the 12-gage CS rounds. On those missions, I carried the standard, unmodified five-shot Ithaca. With the open cylinder bore on the standard Ithaca Model 37 Riot Gun, the CS rounds could be used without any problem. All you had to do was load the CS round as the last shell into the magazine. That way, pumping the action would load the CS round into the chamber for firing. If any bad guys came out shooting, the rest of the magazine would be full of XM257 buckshot rounds for combat.

Another problem with the duckbill choke was that the open end tended to catch on brush and plants as you moved along on patrol. After extensive firing, the choke would also start to spread apart, greatly changing the shot patterns. China Lake redesigned the duckbill late in 1968, eliminating the problems of the open muzzle. The new duckbill choke had a ring around the muzzle, closing off the front portion of the side slots and eliminating the spreading apart of the bill.

During my third tour in 1970, I ran into a little bit of trouble because of my taste for shotguns. I was just coming off an advisory tour with the LDNNs during which we had pulled a number of missions in Cambodia. When the tour was over, I was called in to NAVSPECWARGRUP-V (Navy Special Warfare Group—Vietnam) in Saigon for a debriefing. It was at the airport in Tan Son Nhut that I ran into an Air Force colonel who wondered just who I was.

Looking back on things, I was probably a pretty weird sight even for Vietnam. Here I was climbing out of a helicopter wearing Levi's and a black pajama top. On my head I had a black LDNN beret with lieutenant's bars on it, and around my neck was my shotgun, Sweetheart.

A jeep pulled up to give me a ride in to headquarters. With a big grin on my face I saw that Rudy Boesch, the bullfrog of Team Two, was incountry on a tour and driving my pickup jeep. It was quite a feeling seeing Mr. SEAL sitting there in the jeep waiting for me. As I walked over to the jeep, looking forward to seeing Rudy, this colonel came up to me and asked just what the weapon I had around my neck was.

"That's my Sweetheart," I said. "My twelve-gage."

Well, this colonel had never seen a weapon like mine before. And chances were he would never see one like it again. Sweetheart was custom-made and I had the only one like her in Vietnam. Then this officer went on to ask me if I knew that shotguns were against the Geneva Conventions.

Who was this jet jockey, some desk-bound officer who saw more action in the officers' club than anywhere else? "Colonel," I said, "if they ever send me to Geneva, I'll leave her at home. But between now and then, she and I just don't part company."

He really didn't like my answer, but what could he do about it? Leaving the flustered officer behind me, I continued on to the jeep, where Rudy was having a real hard time holding a straight face.

The Air Force colonel probably had never seen close combat in his life. Not to put down what the Air Force does; those flyboys have saved more than one SEAL who got in trouble in Indian country. But if a man doesn't understand another man's job, he should just keep his opinions to himself. The only defense I will put up for that colonel is that he probably thought I was one of the cowboy plumbers (CIA men) who were making such a "name" for themselves in Vietnam.

CHAPTER 13

Hand Grenades and
Grenade Launchers

O NE OF THE IMPORTANT CONSIDERATIONS we had for our weapons in Vietnam was how much they could add to the firepower of a SEAL squad in combat. Firepower in the classic Navy definition is the weight of shot, or number of shells, that can be put out of a single ship in one salvo. For the SEALs, it was just how much ammunition we could put downrange in the shortest amount of time. Being able to overwhelm a target area by saturating it with a hail of bullets either eliminates an enemy threat right away, or it makes the enemy keep their heads down long enough for some outnumbered SEALs to beat feet the hell away from there.

Firepower in terms of volume of fire was supplied to the Teams in Vietnam in the form of extended-magazine shotguns, Stoner and M60 light machine guns, and extra-large magazines for our M16s and CAR-15s. It was the assurance of putting out a heavy volume of fire for a good length of time that made us carry such large quantities of ammunition with us while out on an op. But the effectiveness of what we fired at the enemy was at least as important as the amount of fire we could put out.

The biggest storm of bullets in the world won't do a thing for you if they aren't powerful enough to damage the target. The high-velocity ammunition fired by our M16s, Stoners, and M60s could tear a target area up big time. And I learned just how effective a shotgun could be in sweeping an area in a sudden, eyeball-to-eyeball encounter. But not all of our targets were right out in the open where we had a direct line of sight. The VC were just as interested in firing from behind cover as we were. To cover your ass in combat, you also needed weapons that could go around cover, such as inside a bunker or behind a rice paddy dike.

For real close-in fighting behind cover, there was nothing quite as handy as a frag grenade. Instead of having a cast-iron body like the old Mark II pineapple grenade, the M26 grenade we used in Vietnam had a thin sheet-metal casing around a steel coil and the explosive charge. The steel coil was a roll of square wire, notched every quarter inch or so along its length, that broke up into hundreds of fragments when the grenade detonated. The blast of an M26 fragmentation grenade covered a thirty-meter-wide area with small, high-velocity steel fragments, whereas the Mark II spread maybe a couple of dozen fragments over a twenty-meter-wide area.

The M26 and improved M26A1 were used by the Teams as our standard fragmentation grenades throughout the Vietnam War. Everybody in the squad carried at least a couple of frag grenades on just about every op. An integral part of the SEALs' firepower, the use of fragmentation grenades was part of our standard operating procedure for ambushes.

As part of an ambush, the two men on either flank would each throw a fragmentation grenade after firing a single magazine from their weapons. Everybody else who was part of the ambush would fire two magazines. This was done to help ensure that the kill zone of the ambush was saturated and that no targets had been missed because they were behind a body or some other cover.

On one operation during my first tour, I was one of the men on the squad's flank when we pulled a hasty ambush on Ilo Ilo island. Everybody's eyes got real big when one of the grenades thrown during the ambush—I think it was mine—hit a tree limb and bounced back at the squad. The damned thing sailed right over our heads as we buried them in the mud of a canal bank, praying our own grenade would not kill us all.

Landing in the water of the canal behind us, the grenade detonated harmlessly, spraying us with little more than stinking mud and dirty water. We were lucky that time. More than one soldier has been killed by his own grenade when something went wrong.

The violent little bombs are designed to maim and kill, and they don't care whom they do it to.

For the most part, though, we didn't have any trouble using fragmentation grenades. You couldn't beat an M26 for making sure a bunker was clear after you threw tear gas into it. You could slip up along the wall of a bunker and just toss the grenade around the corner. Nothing more than your arm would be exposed to possible enemy fire, and even that was only vulnerable for a second at most. The blast of an M26 combined with its fragmentation would either kill or stun anyone in the enclosed area of the bunker.

Grenades were also great for tossing over a paddy dike when you knew there was a VC on the other side. On one op, I watched Bob Gallagher sneaking along a paddy, trying his best to nail a guy on the other side without getting hurt himself. After I shouted at him, Bob looked at his situation and tossed a grenade over the dike. Scratch one VC.

Fragmentation grenades were also neat to use for a quick booby-trap. When you were deep in Indian country, you couldn't be bothered bringing out the bodies of any VC you nailed. After searching the bodies for intelligence material, however, every now and then we would take a page out of Charlie's rules of warfare. The VC would occasionally boobytrap the bodies of U.S. servicemen killed in combat. Later, when the bodies were recovered, the VC would manage to get one or two more GIs. Following in Charlie's footsteps, there were times when we left a little calling card, a grenade under a VC body.

If you pulled the pin on a fragmentation grenade and placed it underneath a VC body, the weight of the dead body would hold down the spoon of the grenade. When the VC picked up their dead, moving the body released the spoon and the grenade detonated just a few seconds later. By following this procedure only in free-fire zones where there were no villages, we made sure that only the VC would be the ones to move a boobytrapped body.

Fragmentation grenades worked so well as improvised booby-traps that we had some M26 grenades specially made just for that use. The special M26 grenade looked exactly like a standard grenade except that there was no delay element in the fuze. When the pin was pulled and the spoon released, the grenade went off. Carefully packaged and marked so that they were not confused with our regular munitions, the zero-delay grenades were being used in Vietnam by mid-1968.

A grenade without a delay in the fuze is absolutely deadly if you let it get mixed up with any normal grenades. Following all the rules, we didn't fool around with such deadly devices and used them only for the situations they were intended for. Besides being useful as a boobytrap, a zero-delay grenade could be left behind, "accidentally" dropped in an area where only the VC could find it. But in spite of everything we did, nothing is completely foolproof. Never underestimate a fool.

On one operation being conducted by Third Platoon in September 1968, a SEAL squad was recovering sensor devices that had been planted in the Rung Sat. When the sensors were planted, a zero-delay grenade had been placed underneath each one to prevent the VC from tampering with or recovering the classified devices.

In spite of the boobytraps, picking up the sensors was not a big problem with the technique Third Platoon was using. With one end secured to the pickup boat, a 150-foot-long line was tied to the sensor device. The PBR would get under way with the SEALs on board and just pull the sensor from the mud. The grenade would go off at some point in the procedure, but everyone involved would be far enough away that none of the fragmentation could normally reach them.

After pulling out two sensors without incident, however, the squad ran into some trouble on the third device. Instead of falling away like the earlier grenades, the third grenade stuck to the mud on the sensor and wouldn't come off. When the sensor was pulled on board the PBR, the grenade came along with it. The RIVDIV (River Division) lieutenant who was on the PBR pulled the grenade free of the sensor, keeping the spoon secured in his hand. All that had to be done now was secure the spoon somehow, perhaps with a pin taken from a smoke grenade, and everything would have been all right. This was where the fool part of "foolproof" came into play.

That lieutenant knew the grenade had a zero-delay fuze on it. Instead of doing the smart thing, he figured he could throw the grenade far enough away so that when it went off, it wouldn't hurt anyone. I wonder what part of "zero delay" that officer didn't understand.

As soon as the grenade left the lieutenant's hand, the spoon came up and the grenade went off. Four men, including one SEAL, were seriously wounded by the explosion. Another four men, including a Vietnamese LDNN, were slightly wounded. The SEAL who was badly injured, Carl "Skip" Isham, had to be medevaced out and eventually lost an eye from his injuries. And the lieutenant who had caused the incident was injured badly, losing a portion of his arm. When that officer was visited in the hospital by some SEALs later, his comment to them was "If I had only thrown it harder."

It didn't matter how hard a zero-delay grenade was thrown; it would go off as soon as it left your hand. But some guys just never learn. The only trouble is that they aren't necessarily the only ones who pay for their mistakes. Skip Isham eventually had to leave the Teams and the Navy because of his injuries.

But not all of the grenades we used were so deadly, though they all could be dangerous. One particular one we carried a lot was the Mark 3A2 offensive grenade, commonly called the concussion grenade. Designed to have almost no serious fragmentation, the Mark 3A2 grenade was little more than a half-pound cylinder of TNT held in a cardboard tube with a regular pull-ring fuze on one end. The concussion of the TNT charge detonating could stun a VC without killing him or injuring him severely.

The concussion grenade was particularly useful on a sampan ambush. If we tossed a Mark 3A2 into the water, any VC who had dived from the sampan to take cover in the water would be driven to the surface by the shock of the explosion. Using a concussion grenade against a suspected tunnel would have the same effect, driving the VC out to where we could capture them.

Though not as sophisticated as the antiterrorist stun grenades the Teams use now, the Mark 3A2 concussion grenade helped us capture a number of VC in Vietnam who would have otherwise been killed or lost. Usually several concussion grenades were carried in a squad, and those proved to be enough for the average operation.

On one operation during my third tour, I ran out of concussion grenades while we were investigating a suspected tunnel complex as part of an Army operation. Officially, the narrative on the Barndance card for the operation read: INSERTED TWO SEALS, TWO PRUS, ONE POW, LINKED UP WITH "A" CO. POW LED TO FOUR TUNNELS. USING "A" CO. FOR SECURITY, SEALS/PRUS SEARCHED AND DESTROYED FOUR TUNNELS, CAPTURING ONE NVA.

We actually captured the NVA prisoner without the Army's help. He was an NVA officer who had been left behind because of a wound in his leg and an infected arm that prevented him from keeping up with his unit. The Army hooked up with us mostly just for political reasons. The colonel in charge of the Army unit just seemed to want to be able to say his men had been on an operation where an NVA was captured. Not that the capture itself was any big deal.

We had a POW who led us straight to the spider hole where the wounded NVA was hiding. A spider hole was not much more than a foxhole with a woven bamboo or grass mat covering it for camouflage. When we approached the hole, we just lifted the mat and the wounded NVA man surrendered.

The rest of the operation consisted of going through the area and investigating a "VC tunnel complex," as it was called in an Army report. This was in the middle of the Mekong Delta. The average height above sea level was maybe a foot, and that was only when the area wasn't actually below sea level. The idea of there being a tunnel complex struck me as almost funny. The only way to build a tunnel around here was if the VC used submarines, and I didn't think the Russians or Red Chinese had supplied them with any of those.

What the prisoner did was point out the tops of spider holes around the area where he was captured. With the Army company supplying security, we checked out the spider holes the simple and secure way. We threw grenades into them.

Using concussion grenades was the most effective way of clearing a spider hole. And though I still don't think there was a real tunnel complex there, some of the spider holes seemed awfully deep. Some of the grenades went down a long way before they blew, and the explosion was a muffled thump, not the same kind of blast that a grenade going off underwater would make. Smoke would eventually rise back out of these spider holes, indicating that the hole wasn't flooded. And that was something I just couldn't understand, given all of the rice paddies that were around us. But neither I nor any of my PRU men were willing to go into a spider hole to find out what was there. And none of the Army men were about to go into them either.

The one thing that really stands out in my memory about the op was running out of concussion grenades while checking out the holes. There was an Army second lieutenant standing on a rice paddy dike maybe forty yards from where I was standing next to a spider hole. When I called over to the lieutenant to ask if he had any concussion grenades, the silly bastard threw one over to me. Instead of walking over and handing me the grenade, he tossed a live explosive grenade over to where I was. At least the simple son of a bitch left the pin in it! This was not the kind of person I wanted to operate with. And I believe it was the last time I operated in the field with an Army unit.

Later, I watched the Army unit interrogate the NVA officer we had captured earlier in the op. Not only was I disgusted with the rough way they handled the wounded, weakened prisoner, but I never received any intel back on what information they received from the NVA. I just couldn't convince the officer in charge that we could act on intel much better and quicker than the Army could. The colonel wouldn't have any of that, so I never received a written report on the results of the op.

Besides the standard-issue hand grenades we had available, the men at China Lake and elsewhere came up with several special-purpose grenades for our use. One of them was supposed to help us with destroying VC food caches. Most often, a food cache would be bags of rice, sometimes hundreds or even thousands of pounds of it.

In a village, a normal amount of rice wouldn't draw any attention from us. But if the area was a known VC location, and the rice was much more than the villagers could use themselves, we knew it was an enemy food cache. Simple economics would make a village sell any major rice surplus it had to meet the rest of the village's needs. Having a very large excess quantity on hand meant that the village was full of VC sympathizers and they were just waiting for the VC to come through and eat.

We couldn't poison the stuff; we may operate on a hard-core basis, but that's a little rough even for the SEALs. Besides, the higher-ups wouldn't have let us do it. And when you found a large cache of rice—once we found over five hundred kilos of it in one cache—you just couldn't haul it all out. Putting explosives around it would blow a mess of it all over the place. Pouring gasoline on it would set fire to part of the rice, but it wouldn't burn enough to destroy the entire cache. The only thing you could do that would guarantee the destruction of a rice cache was to take it over to a river and dump it in. But when things were getting hot, you sure as hell didn't want to get caught hauling heavy rice bags around.

The boys back in the States tried issuing AN-M14 TH3 thermate grenades to us, in part for destroying rice caches, as well as just setting fire to enemy hooches. An M14 thermate grenade burns at something like 4,000 degrees Fahrenheit for over half a minute, spreading molten iron around while burning. But the damned grenades also weigh something like two pounds, and they were just too heavy to be worth the trouble. Setting fire to a hooch could be easily done with a Mark 13 flare, especially with the addition of a little gasoline when we had a boat nearby. But even burning thermate wouldn't destroy rice completely.

A special grenade that was made up for us to use in destroying caches was a napalm grenade we received as a kind of kit. By just adding regular gasoline to the grenade casing, it would make napalm gel, just like what was dropped from planes. The grenade worked like a regular pull-ring hand grenade, only when it went off, it spread burning napalm over a fairly wide area. This was great for burning bunkers and hooches, but even napalm couldn't handle a rice cache. The napalm grenade from China Lake was dropped as being just not generally useful enough. And we never did come up with a good way of destroying a rice cache.

There was another special grenade made for us that I thought was really neat. The chemists at Du Pont back in the States came up with this stuff they called TIARA, for Target Illumination and Recovery Aid. TIARA was a liquid chemical that would glow blue-green when exposed to air.

The stuff was issued to us in two ways, in a spray can and in a canister-type hand grenade. With the spray can, all you had to do was hose down an area and it started glowing. If a VC stepped into the TIARA, it stuck to his feet and he left glowing footprints behind him as he ran. This made it very easy to follow a subject.

The other way we used the TIARA compound was in the hand grenade China Lake loaded for us. A gray canister with black markings saying NWC MARKING GRENADE, the TIARA grenade would explode and spray this chemical all over the inside of a hooch or bunker. Since the stuff wasn't poisonous, we didn't hurt any innocent civilians hiding inside when we tossed in a TIARA grenade. But the glowing chemical made anyone who was touched by the stuff stand out in the dark jungle.

When we hit a hooch at night, any VC inside could run right out through the back wall sometimes, and you just couldn't see them, wearing their black pajamas, at night. By tossing in a TIARA grenade first, it didn't matter where they ran, we had no trouble spotting these blue-green ghosts running in the dark. And trying to rub the stuff off just made it glow brighter. Personally, I used a TIARA grenade on only a few ops. But on the occasions that I did use one, I found it to be a good device and one that had a number of uses. But for some reason, after the Vietnam War ended, they just stopped making the stuff.

Besides hand grenades, a very popular weapon with the SEALs

was the 40mm grenade launcher. The M79 was the first 40mm launcher to fire the little high-explosive grenades that proved so popular in Vietnam. The weapon was first developed in the early 1950s, to fill in the space between how far an average soldier could throw a hand grenade and the minimum range of a 60mm mortar. The SEALs never carried anything as big as a 60mm mortar while on patrols, but we really loved the power of the little grenades thrown by the M79.

We took M79 40mm grenade launchers with us to Vietnam as part of our equipment during my first tour. The M79 is like a large single-shot break-open shotgun that fires a high-explosive grenade out to four hundred meters. A good man with an M79 can practically drop a round into a hat at over a hundred meters—the weapon is that accurate. The single-shot capacity of the M79 was too much of a liability for me to consider carrying one while on point. I did use one when I operated as a coxswain on the STABs we had also brought with us.

We had modified the STABs so that the coxswain sat in the front center of the console, protected by a small fiberglass hood he could pull up behind him. The hood was more to keep hot brass from falling down the coxswain's neck than for any fragmentation or bullet protection. But in the middle of a firefight, that quarter inch of fiberglass felt great, and I was glad to have it.

In order to let the coxswain feel he was part of a firefight and not just steering the boat, we kept an M79 and a case of ammo up in the bow of the STAB. You couldn't fire the M79 very accurately with one hand, but when we were putting out fire into an ambush, every little bit helped. The M79 was a pain to use while sitting down. By clamping the launcher between your knees, you could break the weapon open, extract a fired casing, and load in a fresh round; then you pulled the gun up to shoot. And the coxswain did all of this while he was steering the STAB.

The M79 was all right in general, and the 40mm family of grenades had a great design. Besides the high-explosive rounds, there were also buckshot rounds, flares, and CS tear gas shells available.

The real disadvantages of the M79 were its size and the single shot you had available before you had to reload.

Early in our first tour, a new weapon was sent over to us from the States that used the same ammunition as the M79. The XM148 was a 40mm grenade launcher that you mounted underneath the barrel of an M16 or CAR-15. The new launcher still had the single-shot capability of the M79, but since you carried it mounted on another weapon, you could just switch over to the other weapon after firing your grenade.

For lightness, most of the XM148s we received in the Teams ended up being mounted on CAR-15s, especially the later XM177E2. The combined firepower of the 40mm and 5.56mm CAR-15 appealed to a number of SEALs, myself included. Soon after the XM148 arrived in the platoon, I started carrying one while operating on point. Later I gave up on the XM148 and started carrying a shotgun. For the squad, however, the XM148 could really add something to the overall firepower of the unit. There were not a lot of the XM148s available, so the M79 continued to be carried, usually as a secondary weapon in combination with a CAR-15 or M16.

The overall design of the XM148 was a little flimsy, though we didn't have much trouble with it in the Teams. The Army gave up its XM148s in 1968, waiting for over a year until a better weapon was available. By 1969, the new M203 40mm grenade launcher was available for issue, the first weapons going to the Army. The Teams started receiving the new grenade launchers in 1970 and we used them right alongside the earlier XM148.

The M203 had a stronger design than the XM148, with a sliding barrel assembly and trigger group that fit in front of the magazine well on an M16. Designed to fit underneath the barrel of any M16-family weapon, the M203 was most often mounted on an XM177E2. By the mid-1970s, the XM177E2 and the earlier CARs were being replaced with the longer-barreled M16 carbine, now called the M4 carbine. The M203 mounted under the barrel of an M4 carbine has become one of the most popular pieces of firepower in the SEALs' inventory. Whole platoons of SEALs have gone out on operations with almost every member of the sixteen-man platoon armed with an M203.

The idea of fourteen or more 40mm grenades raining down on an ambush site really brings to mind the idea of firepower. The only way to get that kind of target saturation with single-shot launchers is to have a large number of men armed with them. During the Vietnam War, we experimented with a number of variations designed to increase the firepower of the 40mm grenade launcher.

By early 1964, the Honeywell company came up with what it called a multiple grenade launcher, later adopted by the Navy as the Mark 18 Rapid Fire Gun, but most everybody referred to the weapon as the Honeywell.

About the size of two shoe boxes stacked on top of each other, the Honeywell was a manually operated, hand-cranked weapon that was fed from a twenty-four- or forty-eight-round fabric belt. The hand-cranked aspect of the Honeywell hadn't been seen in the military since the Gatling gun, but it kept the weapon simple and fairly reliable. Able to be used from any mounting that could accept the recoil of a .30-caliber machine gun, the Honeywell looked like an ideal boat gun to the Teams.

Before Second Platoon left for our first tour in Vietnam, we took a couple of Honeywells out to the range to try them out. Operating the Honeywell from a tripod was easy, only you had to crouch over the weapon, because you couldn't very well lie down behind it and work the crank. The low tripod mounts made it difficult to aim the Honeywell using its sights, but experience with the weapon made instinctive aiming easy.

After a fairly complicated loading procedure, firing the Honeywell was just a matter of reaching down the right-hand side and turning the crank. For each half turn of the crank, the Honeywell fired one shot. The firing rate for the weapon was determined by how fast you turned the crank. Rates of fire could range from single shots up to a cyclic rate of about 250 rounds per minute. During most combat operations, the Honeywell was fired at a rate of about 100 rounds per minute. One drawback of the Honeywell, which we didn't mind in the Teams, was that the weapon could fire only the 40mm HE and practice rounds. All of the flare rounds were too long and the buckshot and fléchette rounds too short to feed through the action.

One thing that the Honeywell had was firepower, both in volume of fire and effectiveness on the target. By cranking up the weapon to its maximum elevation and gradually bringing it down as you fired it, you could put out an entire forty-eight-round belt before the first round hit the ground. Fired properly, a Honeywell could cover an area the size of a football field with 40mm grenades, and all of the grenades would impact at about the same time. The biggest pain in the ass with the weapon was loading and reloading the fiberglass belts. Once a belt had been fired, you had to remove the fired casings and then insert fresh rounds, making sure each round was pushed in correctly. Worn belts would cause jams and the Honeywell itself was not really rugged enough for the Vietnamese environment.

Though the Honeywell saw use throughout the Vietnam War, by the late 1960s it was being replaced with a new grenade launcher, the Mark 20 Mod O Grenade Machine Gun. This was a full-automatic weapon firing 40mm grenades from a metallic link belt. The metal belt used by the Mark 20 made the weapon a lot more reliable and easier to use than the Honeywell. Roughly two feet long and six inches square, the Mark 20 had two spade grips at the back of the weapon and a simple sight arrangement. A little practice with the Mark 20, much like the Honeywell before it, and then you really didn't use the sights much. Firing from either a twenty-four- or a forty-eight-round belt, the Mark 20 had slightly lower rate of fire than the Honeywell, but it really added to the firepower of the SEAL support boats.

First available in August 1967, the Mark 20 was very popular with the later Mark 2 STABs, also known as the LSSC or Light SEAL Support Craft. There are pictures of STABs operating near the Cambodian border in 1970 where the boats are carrying as many as four Mark 20s along with a number of M60D machine guns.

Both the Mark 20 and Honeywell grenade launchers added a lot to the volume of fire we could get from our support boats, but they didn't do much to add to the firepower of a SEAL squad. New weapons were always something we wanted to examine at the Teams, and something I personally took a big interest in.

In April 1968, while operating as the research and development chief for Team Two, I took my first trip out to China Lake in California. The engineers there were trying to come up with answers to some of the requests that were coming in from the platoons in Vietnam. Team Two sent me out to China Lake to give the men there some feedback from the east coast.

China Lake had been known to Team Two for a short time as an experimental ordnance lab developing various goodies for the Teams. The official name of the organization we were interested in was the Special Operations Branch (Code 3567) of the Naval Weapons Center, and the people there were just as interested in us as we were in them. It wasn't just that they wanted to talk to us on the east coast; we wanted to find out what was available or would be in the future.

China Lake was in never-never land, absolutely the middle of nowhere in southern California, only one small mountain range away from Death Valley. The isolation was probably the reason the Navy had chosen the place to set up its airborne weapons development program. One nice thing about the California desert: There isn't much trouble finding a place to fire small arms.

My meeting there on my first trip was really just a get-to-know-each-other sort of thing. The China Lake people showed me what the facilities were and what they could do for us. My mission was to learn all I could and then go back to the Creek and report it all to the higher-ups at the Team.

The most fun I had there was during the more informal meetings with the engineers. The technical end of war was something I was just starting to learn. Up until then my general image of warfare was to carry a weapon and kill whoever was trying to kill me. But the engineers I met at places like China Lake, Frankford Arsenal, and some of the other private companies that developed things for us were opening my eyes to the nuts and bolts behind our hardware.

The engineers and developers were sharp, and so refined in their work that they were in danger of becoming separated from the real world. It was while having a few beers at the local club that I would talk to the makers about what went on in the field. Not many of the engineers drank, and of course I was just an average SEAL social drinker. Altogether, it was a nice, warm, comradely atmosphere to talk about better ways to kill people.

One of the things I was asked about was the different weapons we used, how much we liked them, and how they could be made better. The 40mm grenade was still a new item in combat and the engineers wanted to know what we would like to launch it. The M79 was popular in the Teams, and we already had the XM148 from Colt. But the firepower of the 40mm was limited to just a single shot in both the M79 and XM148.

"Hey," I answered, "the M79 is just fine. But just this one shot doesn't get it. That's why we prefer the XM148 underneath the '16. Now, if you had a grenadier who could fire more than one shot without having to reload his weapon, that would be great. The M79 is a nice weapon, but it would be better if it held more shells. Isn't there some way you could make it a repeater?"

As I remember it, I was sliding my hands back and forth like I was operating the slide of a shotgun. The engineers listened to what I had to say, made their notes, and the evening went on. The variety of boobytraps, fuzes, and other ways of committing mayhem I was shown looked very good, and I delivered a very complimentary report to headquarters when I returned to Team Two a few days later.

During the first week of June 1968, I returned to China Lake to examine some of the new materials they had developed for us. Since the SEALs were operating under a high priority and the engineers and technicians were working almost exclusively for us, the Special Operations Branch at China Lake was able to turn out materials at an incredible rate.

The traditionally slow Navy way of doing things was what I

was used to, and what we tended to rebel against in the Teams. What a surprise it was to arrive at China Lake and see what was waiting for me. Along with a number of different boobytraps and fuzes, some of which are still classified even today, were two different models of repeating 40mm grenade launchers.

One of the grenade launchers was a triple-barrel affair that fit underneath the barrel of an M16 or CAR-15, just like the XM148. Only the tri-barrel launcher could put out three 40mm grenades as quickly as you could pull its trigger. An extended trigger ran from behind the receiver of the tri-barrel to just underneath the trigger of the rifle it was mounted on. Without changing your grip very much, pulling the launcher's trigger would operate a rotating hammer and fire each of the three separate barrels in turn.

Overall, the effect of the tri-barrel launcher was neat, but it did suffer from a number of drawbacks, some of which I could see right away. The three open barrels of the launcher had to be short to fit underneath the M16 hand guard. The very short barrels cut down on the muzzle velocity of the 40mm grenades so much that the tri-barrel had only two-thirds the range of either the M79 or the XM148. The open mouths of the barrels could quickly clog with jungle crap, mud, muck, leaves, and all the assorted gunk we found ourselves crawling through on almost every op in Vietnam. The single open barrel of the XM148 was trouble enough to keep clear; the three open muzzles of the tri-barrel were like walking around with a small bucket underneath your weapon. A very few of the tri-barrel launchers were tested in Vietnam but were not very popular. Though the tri-barrel 40mm did add to the firepower of a squad, the drawbacks of the design kept it from being very fieldworthy for the SEALs or anybody else.

The other grenade launcher China Lake had available was a different story altogether. What the guys at China Lake handed me was a 40mm pump-action grenade launcher, looking for all the world like a giant sawed-off pump shotgun. "Well, yahoo," I said as the engineers gave me the weapon. "Where can we go to shoot this?"

Firing weapons at China Lake was not much of a problem. A

number of the engineers and myself just loaded up a pickup truck with several different pieces of hardware and a couple of cases of 40mm ammunition as well as some other calibers, and we moved out into the desert. A half mile or so out in the desert, we just unloaded the truck and had some fun.

Though the engineers at China Lake obviously knew their business, the guys weren't shooters like we had in the Teams. The men at China Lake didn't understand just how accurate you could be with an M79 without using the sights. Experience with the weapon gave you enough accuracy to drop a 40mm grenade within a couple of yards of any target you wanted, out to several hundred yards from your firing position. The 40mm pump action had exactly the same firing characteristics as the M79, and I proceeded to show the engineers just how we did things in the Teams.

That 40mm pump action could put out four grenades as fast as you could operate the action. I liked the weapon so much that, if it wasn't for its size, weight, and ammunition, I might have carried one on point. Though I did give the tri-barrel a good wringing out—I even have a picture of myself at China Lake with the weapon—I wasn't nearly as impressed with it as with the 40mm pump action. "Don't worry about hitting the target exactly," I told the engineers. "We'll just blow the whole bunch of them away with this son of a bitch."

Though the 40mm pump action was nice, it did have some drawbacks too. The tri-barrel could operate with the 40mm buckshot round we were now using in the Teams, but the pump action couldn't feed the shorter round through its action. The pump action was also a big, heavy bitch when loaded up, but the firepower it gave more than made up for its weight. Though it was a little fragile for dragging around in the jungle, I was sure that the 40mm pump action would get all the care and maintenance it needed from the guys in the Teams.

The only real question I had for the engineers about the 40mm pump action was "When can we have a couple of these?"

"All right," the head engineer said later, "if you like it, all you have to do is send us a request stating what you want and we'll get the launchers to you."

Returning to Team Two later, I brought back all the data I had on the launchers along with my own recommendations. A message was fired back to China Lake ASAP asking for several of the 40mm pump actions for trials in Vietnam. The only problem with our getting the launchers as fast as we wanted them was that China Lake had only one.

I had been told while out at China Lake that the unit had a guy who lived in some shack out in the desert and was one hell of a machinist. That man had made the first 40mm pump-action launcher completely by hand, apparently only from machinist's sketches. Later I learned that it had taken more time to take the first launcher apart, measure it, and make a set of production drawings than it had for that machinist to make up the original weapon. The production pump action was slightly different from the one I had fired at China Lake, but the few improvements only made the weapon better.

Only a very few of the pump-action grenade launchers were ever made, and, to the best of my knowledge, all of those went to the SEALs. Since that time, the weapon has long been out of the SEAL inventory, and most of the guys in the Teams today have never heard of a 40mm pump action. We have one down at the UDT-SEAL Museum now, serial number 3, on public display. When some of the young lions saw the 40mm pump action on display, we took it out and shot it once; they still want it in the Teams today. Firepower is something the Teams are always on the lookout for, both then and now.

Though all of the 40mm launchers we had were great chunks of firepower, they all suffered from having large, heavy ammunition. The 40mm high-explosive round is about the size of a frozen orange juice can and weighs about half a pound. High-explosive 40mm rounds came packaged six to a cloth bandoleer. The shorter 40mm buckshot rounds came packaged in the same size bandoleers but were packed nose-to-nose, with twelve to a bandoleer.

On the average operation, a SEAL armed with an M79, an XM148, or even a 40mm pump action carried only a couple of bandoleers of 40mm HE (high explosive), with maybe a couple of buckshot rounds in a shirt pocket. Along with the buckshot rounds, a SEAL would have one or two 40mm flare rounds along as well.

While walking point with the XM148, I carried only a single bandoleer of 40mm HE rounds. On one operation going in on a possible POW camp, Mikey Boynton was armed with an M79, and he carried at least four bandoleers of HE and a bandoleer of buckshot rounds. That, along with his CAR-15, four hundred rounds of ammo for it, a pistol, a knife, and a good handful of fragmentation grenades made a nasty load of killing to carry around. When different kinds of ammunition vests became available to the Teams later in the Vietnam War, it was common for a SEAL armed with a 40mm launcher to carry thirty-six 40mm rounds on an operation.

The 40mm high-explosive fragmentation round was the most common 40mm round used in the Teams. New rounds for the 40mm were being developed constantly during the Vietnam War; some were good ideas and others didn't last very long. Of all the HE rounds available, we used the M406 HE round the most. The earlier M381 HE round was exactly the same as the M406 except for the kind of fuze it used.

To arm itself, the M406 round has to travel between fourteen and twenty-eight meters from the muzzle of the weapon before it will detonate on impact. This distance keeps a grenadier from blowing himself to hell, like I almost did when I fired an XM148 into the ground right in front of me. The M381 round has to travel only about three meters before it's armed. This round was way too dangerous to use in the jungle, even for the SEALs. With a three-meter arming range and a five-meter fragmentation radius, the M381 round could hit just a twig or branch and nail both the firer and probably a couple of his teammates as well.

Even the M406 round had its dangers. As I remember, it was at Fort Bragg in 1968 that there was an accident with an M79. While a soldier was firing his 40mm on the range, the round detonated in the barrel of the weapon just as it was fired.

Such an accident would take out the firer and anybody else who was nearby. Later investigation determined the cause to be a crack in the base of the HE projectile when the round was made. Such a crack let the hot propellant gases force their way into the projectile and detonate the explosive. An accident like that was a rare thing, and the first I had ever heard of. To prevent such a thing from ever happening again, all the 40mm HE rounds would have to be radiographed (X-rayed) after they were assembled.

Now, the fuze of the 40mm HE round is a complicated and expensive little bugger to produce, and the bean counters in Washington were always looking for savings in production costs. The leaders in D.C. were told by the bean counters that this X-raying would be very expensive and that the accident might happen only once in a couple of hundred thousand rounds. After it was suggested that these same leaders go out to a range and fire a couple of hundred rounds from an M79 to see what they thought of it, it was decided to use X-rays as part of the inspection process for 40mm rounds.

This wasn't the only time some self-important desk jockey stuck his nose in where he didn't have any business. When we first arrived in Vietnam, a close-in defense round was wanted for our M79s and XM148s. Since the 40mm HE round couldn't be used with fifteen meters without being too dangerous to the firer, something like a 40mm buckshot round was needed for the sudden face-to-face encounters we had in the Delta.

Several different buckshot rounds, and even a fléchette round, had been developed for the 40mm by the time Second Platoon arrived in Vietnam in 1967. But when we tried to get our hands on some of the new ammunition, the powers that be in Saigon wouldn't release the new rounds.

According to Saigon, the new 40mm rounds had only a fifty-yard range and were unsuitable for our operations. But we wanted the damned things just for close-in work and already had the HE round for distances. Besides, it was rare for us even to see a target at more than thirty meters, unless we were shooting across open water or a rice paddy. We finally got the new rounds, but only after some argument.

R. A. Tolison and Bob Gallagher scrounged up some star cluster flare rounds for our M79s during our first tour. These were handy rounds that prevented us from having to carry pop-flares for signaling while on patrol. Later in the war, we started receiving the special 40mm rounds, such as the buckshot and flare shells, as part of our normal ammunition allowance. But during that first tour, it was sometimes pure hell to try to get anything that the unqualified desk jockeys in Saigon or Washington thought would be excess to our needs.

We had trained for years in the Teams for what we were now doing in Vietnam, and we were still learning what it took to operate effectively. But most of the people making the decisions about what we would need had never even been in a combat zone, let alone had a round fired at them in anger. That was the kind of situation that made it such a pleasure to work with the guys at China Lake, Frankford Arsenal, White Oak, and places like that. The men in those places just wanted to get what we needed to us as quickly as possible, and with as little bureaucratic bullshit as possible.

CHAPTER 14

The Stoner

T HERE IS PROBABLY NO WEAPON that is more closely connected with the SEALs in Vietnam than the Stoner light machine gun. Though we were not the first unit to be issued the Stoner—the Marines had it as early as 1966—the SEALs used the weapon in combat from the first day we had one until the last SEALs left Vietnam.

The Stoner we used was a full-automatic weapon that fired the same round as the M16 rifle but carried its ammunition in a metal disintegrating-link belt. With an average rate of fire of about 850 rounds per minute cyclic, the Stoner packed "boo-coo" firepower in a small package. Used from 1967 onward almost exclusively by the SEALs in Vietnam, the Stoner became something of a SEAL trademark, one that Charlie quickly learned to respect.

Eugene Stoner, the same man who designed the M16 rifle and most of its family of weapons, came up with the Stoner 63 in the early 1960s. Wanting to make weapons training easier and to simplify stocking spare parts, he designed the 63 to use a single receiver that could be assembled as a carbine, rifle, magazine-fed light machine gun, belt-fed light machine gun, medium machine gun, or fixed machine gun, depending on which parts you attached. In the Teams, we were interested only in the belt-fed light-machine-gun version of the Stoner 63, but the Marine Corps had been interested in the entire 63 weapon system for some time.

In the early 1960s, the Marine Corps tested the Stoner 63 weapons system. The Marines liked the fact that it was available as a 5.56mm-caliber belt-fed machine gun. By 1966, they had ordered over a thousand Stoner 63s, mostly in the rifle configuration but with the parts needed to assemble a number of carbines and machine guns. Combat testing in Vietnam resulted in a number of changes being made in the Stoner for the Marines, and in March 1966 the modified Stoner 63A became available.

Politics being what it was, the Marines lost most of their Stoners in 1967. The Army Material Command just didn't like the Stoner and wasn't about to let the Marines have a different weapon from the Army; it didn't matter if the gun was better than the M16 or not. In 1967, the Marines had to turn in all of their Stoners, even though the weapons had been found "suitable for Marine Corps use without further testing."

In January 1967, the Navy ordered eight Stoner 63 light machine guns for testing by the SEAL Teams in Vietnam. Second Platoon from Team Two was already in Vietnam when the new Stoners arrived. Our introduction to the Stoner began when our first weapon was shipped to us in February, while we were still at Can Tho.

Second and Third Platoons each received one of the two Stoners that arrived from Team Two. The weapons we received were the early Stoner 63 model with a long barrel, black wooden foregrip, and black plastic butt stock.

Ammunition wasn't much of a problem since the Stoner fired the same round as the M16, but we needed to use linked belts with our weapons. Ready-linked ammunition was available, but only in limited amounts. What came with our Stoner in the way of ammunition was a container of loose links. The Stoner man carried an empty sandbag to try to recover the links whenever he could. Most of the time, stopping to collect loose fired Stoner links was anything but easy, especially when someone was shooting at you, and most of the guys didn't even try. But we did recover the occasional handful of links and had a fair supply of new ones. After a mission, a bunch of us would sit around the ready room, having a beer, swapping stories, and relinking ammunition by hand.

Ammunition belts could be carried in a plastic box bandoleer that held 150 rounds and hung down from a bracket on the left side of the weapon. The only real problem with the side-mounted belt box was that it was in exactly the right position to get hit by your right knee as you walked along. The ammunition boxes became a real pain in the ass early on. Only four boxes came loaded with belts in an ammunition can and we didn't receive very much in the way of preloaded ammunition belts in the first place. So the boxes were something you had to hang on to whenever you could.

Modified standard ammunition pouches were able to carry a full 150-round plastic belt box, and a Stoner man could attach as many pouches to his harness as he wanted. A number of the guys took to carrying extra Stoner belts across their shoulders like bandoleers worn by the revolutionaries in old Mexico. I found that exposed belts carried Pancho Villa style tended to pick up jungle crud and get all crappy, possibly causing a jam when you needed all your firepower the most. I also thought the crossed belts made a nice target for Charlie to aim at.

All in all, we liked the Stoners for the additional firepower they gave a squad. But the weapon was temperamental—especially the first Stoner 63s we received. You had to keep the Stoner clean and take good care of it if you wanted to depend on it. Some of the guys in the Teams didn't like the Stoner because of the amount of care you had to give it. Other operators liked the lightweight little machine gun so much that it was their primary weapon. These guys lavished care on the gun and would carry a Stoner whenever they could.

Bob Gallagher was one of the best weapons men in the Teams, but he had his troubles with the Stoner soon after we received our first one back in 1967. While on a night op on April 11 with Ronnie Roger and Joe Camp, Gallagher was the one who took the hit from the Stoner and not one of the enemy. When one of the guys attempted to unjam the squad's Stoner, the weapon malfunctioned and ran wild, firing about six rounds uncontrollably. Gallagher took a bullet right through the ring finger of his right hand.

So much for the operation. The accident took place at about 2210 hours, and by 2240 hours, the three-man team had extracted. Though the accident was unfortunate, Gallagher wasn't hurt too badly. He still had his finger, though an infection set in and he was told to take it easy for a while until his finger healed. The high-velocity 5.56mm bullet had gone right through the bone, and the doctors had to put in a metal pin to allow the finger to heal properly. By April 30, Gallagher was cleared to operate, not that he hadn't already gone out with us since he was hit. He did take some time off from operating and put it to good use. Since he was due to take his E-8 exam soon, he spent some of his spare time studying for it.

The use of the Stoner did cause some problems inside the Teams. There were "weapons experts" who never saw much action but did nothing except badmouth the Stoner every chance they got. On the other hand, there were men in the Teams who were real hunters and had nothing but good things to say about the Stoner. Any weapon, and it doesn't seem to matter how simple it is, can screw up. The more complex a weapon is, the more problems it will have, and the more bugs they need to work out of it before it's perfected. The Stoner wasn't the best weapon the SEALs have ever used, but it was the best thing available during most of the Vietnam War, and we put it to some hard use.

There are some SEAL veterans now who talk as if they were experts on the Stoner and how the Teams used it in Vietnam. When I hear these people talk about the "balance" of the Stoner, and how it could not be effectively used without a stock on it, I wonder just what the hell they think they're talking about. How do you balance the weight of 150 rounds of ammunition being fired from the belt drum with just a ten-ounce stock? For me, a stock on the average weapon in Vietnam was just something more to be carrying around. If you had to shoulder your weapon in order to aim at a target, you shouldn't have been shooting at it.

Personally, I know of operators in Vietnam who carried a CAR-15 most of the time and never extended the stock except in training. Our average engagement range was about fifteen to twenty-five meters, and often a hell of a lot closer than that. A heavy initial base of fire was what we wanted in the SEALs. The Teams were not the kind of unit to lie down on a paddy dike and have every man shoulder his weapon and pick targets.

Obviously, there are people who will argue with me, but my

favorite configuration of the Stoner was the short-barreled version with a 150-round drum attached and the stock removed. This gave me a loaded weapon that weighed only sixteen pounds and was a fraction under twenty-seven inches long. Slung around my neck on a piece of line, my Stoner would hang ready for use just in front of me and was very well balanced indeed.

For all that we liked about it, the Stoner had some very real problems. But the folks at Cadillac Gage in Warren, Michigan, who made the Stoner, as well as the engineers at China Lake, were more than willing to listen to our suggestions and make the changes we felt were needed. When Second Platoon came back from Vietnam in May 1967, we had a list of suggestions and lessons learned from our experiences in Vietnam. One of the lines read, "Use of the Stoner LMG (light machine gun) is not recommended until the drum magazine becomes available." In May 1967, the Navy asked for a delivery date for thirty-six new Stoners from Cadillac Gage, each to have a 150-round belt drum.

We started to receive the new model 63A Stoners later in 1967 and they were a big hit with most of the SEALs in Vietnam. The new drum went underneath the weapon and fed in a belt from the left-hand side. The drum made it easy to move and even run while still using the Stoner but was fairly slow to reload. A number of different drums and feed directions were tried in combat. A 250-round belt drum was made by China Lake but was really too big and made the Stoner clumsy to handle. Right- and left-hand feeds were tested, along with drums that would feed into them. But the Stoner I most commonly used in Vietnam was a 63A fitted with a drum and a left-hand feed.

Most Stoner men who used the drum would save the belt that was loaded in the drum for use during movement or while breaking contact. When set up for an ambush or observing from a set location, you could load a loose belt into the Stoner. If you had to move, it was easy to load the end of the belt quickly from the drum by snapping it on whatever belt was already feeding into the receiver.

For the types of operations we conducted in Vietnam, the Stoner fit very well into our arsenal. Stoner men were normally highly disciplined and they took care of their weapons constantly. One of the reasons behind the need for discipline was that you didn't always want a Stoner man to shoot. There were times when only one or two targets might be in sight, and you didn't know who else might be in the area. The last thing you wanted to do in a situation like that was let your Stoner man hose down the area. Nothing else in Vietnam sounded like a Stoner, and once that weapon was fired, everybody knew the SEALs were in town. If there was a large force of VC anywhere around, the sound of a Stoner going off could bring them running.

The SEALs were not the first men to use the Stoner in Vietnam, but we sure made a success out of the ones we had. One time down in Can Tho, a Marine colonel came down to the river to see a SEAL squad that was just coming in from an operation. The colonel just wanted to meet the SEALs, but in the Teams we never give a sucker an even break, especially not a Marine.

As each man of the patrol came off the boat, he spoke to the colonel, telling the officer what his job was, what he was armed with, and where he was in the patrol. When it was his turn, the Stoner man just looked at the colonel with a big grin on his face. "Sir," the SEAL said, "I'm the Stoner man and this is a Stoner light machine gun. The Marines don't think this weapon is any good, but I want to tell you that the SEALs love it." The colonel didn't know what to say or do, so he just moved on.

Whatever politics made the Marines turn in their Stoners was a mistake, in my opinion. In the SEALs, we knew that the Marines and the Army had been testing the Stoner long before we ever saw one, but they turned it down, whereas we couldn't get enough of them. The Navy even officially adopted the Stoner as the Mark 23 Mod 0 machine gun. Originally, the Mark 23 was the Stoner 63A model. But when the improved Stoner 63A1 became available, it was adopted under the Mark 23 nomenclature.

In 1968, I helped run the Training Platoon when Gallagher was away from the Creek. When a platoon went through predeployment training for Vietnam, most of the weapons training went on at Camp Pickett. The Stoner became a big part of training. The weapon had proved itself well for us in Vietnam and everyone became familiar with it in predeployment training. The Stoner was good, but it was only as good as the man who operated it.

During one of our debriefing sessions after an op in Vietnam, two of the guys pointed out that even a Stoner couldn't give you the edge sometimes. The op was a body snatch down in the Song Ong Doc area. When we hit the target hooch, the VC just fled out the back of the building. The two Stoner men swore they had him in their sights, but he got away without a mark on him. You could see the tracers being fired as the two Stoners converged on this running VC. The red streaks closed on the man, and passed right by without any reaction, other than maybe making him run a little faster. And the tracers were only loaded one for every four rounds of ball ammunition. That meant that for every red streak you could see go by this VC, there were four other bullets that you couldn't see.

If I remember correctly, the two Stoner men were Duke Leonard and Chuck Fellers, two of the best Stoner men I knew. But sometimes it didn't matter how good a man was, or how great the Stoner could be; it wasn't that VC's time, and he just got away clean.

But there were also some serious accidents involving Stoners in addition to what happened to Bob Gallagher. The worst Stoner incident in Vietnam had bad results for the SEALs. Team One had transferred Mike Platoon from the Rung Sat down into the Mekong Delta. Mike Platoon was going out on an operation when one of the Stoners on board the insertion boat opened fire.

Apparently, the vibration of the boat's engines caused the takedown pin holding the trigger housing on the receiver of the Stoner to vibrate out of position. When the pin fell out, the trigger housing moved enough to release the cocked bolt, firing the weapon uncontrollably. First-Class Boatswain's Mate Walter Pope was killed by the runaway Stoner and at least one other SEAL, Frank Toms, was severely wounded.

Exactly how the accident happened was never known. Probably no one on board the boat saw what happened when the Stoner started firing. But the results of the accident were soon felt throughout the SEAL Teams.

One of the results was that the Navy would no longer purchase more Stoners or even spare parts for the weapons we had. The word was put out to all the SEALs to be real careful with our remaining Stoners due to what had happened. The pin that had fallen out and caused the accident was modified so that it now took a special effort to remove it when cleaning the weapon. But the reputation of the Stoner really took a beating from that accident.

Up in I Corps's area, a Stoner was recovered from a VC weapons cache in January 1969. That was probably the only Stoner the VC ever had, and was one that had been lost in a river down in IV Corps's area. U.S. Army Captain Mark Gwinn, Jr., laid claim to the weapon, which had been held by the VC for about a year, according to a prisoner. The Stoner was pretty badly rusted up from having been underwater for much of the year, but when Captain Gwinn test-fired the weapon within ten minutes of recovering it, it worked fine. Apparently, there were about seventy rounds of ammunition in the drum of the Stoner when it was lost and these rounds still worked, a tribute to both the ammo and the Stoner.

Captain Gwinn scrounged a spare barrel, some parts, and links from some SEALs he knew, and used the recovered Stoner for several months before we heard about the gun. According to Captain Gwinn, he put about twelve thousand rounds through the weapon while he had it, even nailing two VC at a range of just over six hundred meters. Apparently, he liked the Stoner as much as or even more than we did in the Teams, and was trying to talk some of the higher-ups in the Army Special Forces into adopting it. It wasn't long before we heard about the gun in Little Creek and it turned out to be a Team Two weapon. Captain Gwinn was told to turn the weapon over to us, and our long-lost Stoner finally made it back to Team Two.

When we received the Stoner at Little Creek, the weapon was still fairly screwed up. Parts were rusted and it was obvious it had not been taken care of while the VC had it, in spite of what Captain

Gwinn had tried to do in the way of repairing the gun. After spraying the weapon with WD-40, we took it to the range and it fired fine, no problems. Probably the only reason the VC hadn't used it was that they couldn't get any linked 5.56mm ammunition. Our Stoner men were still picking up their links whenever they had the chance.

In 1970, it was more than links that we wanted for our Stoners. The Team was short of OPTAR ("Operating Target," our general operating budget) money at the time, so we couldn't just buy what we wanted from Cadillac Gage. Because of the accidents that had happened with the Stoner, especially the Team One incident in 1968 that killed a SEAL, the government had suspended any further purchase of Stoners and parts.

Cadillac Gage, the manufacturer of the Stoner, knew about the recovered weapon in its headquarters near Detroit. Captain Gwinn had been sending Caddy Gage letters asking for parts in order to get the weapon in better shape. The fact that this weapon was still operating at all was a good selling point for the system and the maker wanted the piece back. The company offered us two brand-new weapons for our old one. Now we were in a good position, and we tried bargaining for three weapons in the short-barreled version, and some spare barrels. I think the bargaining finally finished at two guns and several spare barrels for our recovered weapon.

A good deal for us, but now we had to turn over our Stoner to Cadillac Gage in Detroit. There was civil unrest all over the country and Detroit wasn't spared. Hijacking airliners was also becoming something of a hobby among the country's nut cases at the time. All in all, this was not the best time or place to fly into with a weapon like a Stoner. But I was assigned to hand-carry the weapon to Detroit, and I always carry out my orders. Going along with me on the trip were Roy Dean Matthews and Robert (R. J.) Thomas, who was just a second class at the time. While we were at the company, the three of us were also going to attend the Stoner Armorers' School.

I got orders listing me as a federal courier for automatic weapons and it was off to the airport with me, Matthews, and Thomas. The Stoner was all wrapped up in paper and didn't look like a weapon as I carried it. And that package never left my hands. At the ticket counter I even asked for a carry-on luggage tag for my machine gun. The girl behind the counter just giggled a bit and handed me a tag.

The group of us waited for our flight in the lounge, drinking a few beers. Two guys in suits came over to speak to me while we were waiting.

"Excuse me, Chief Watson?" one of the suits said.

"Yeah," I answered, "that's me."

"Is that what we think it is, in that bag?"

"Yup."

"Would you mind coming with us?"

"Nope," and off we went to a small closed room.

Standing in the room with one of my teammates, I was a lot more relaxed than these two suits, even though they had Security written all over them. "Would you mind if we unwrapped it?" they asked me.

"Nope."

When they got all the paper and padding off the weapon, one of the men exclaimed, "It looks like a Mattel toy rather than a weapon."

"Some toy," I answered. "It fires linked 5.56mm ammunition from a disintegrating belt at a rate of eight hundred fifty rounds per minute, with a muzzle velocity of thirty-two hundred feet per second. It can empty its hundred-fifty-round drum magazine in a little over ten seconds. All of this from a weapon with an all-up weight of sixteen point seven pounds loaded. Like I said, some toy."

"Do you mind if we are the ones who rewrap it?"

"No." There wasn't any reason for me to be disagreeable. We had already told them that we didn't have any ammunition with us.

But the situation was a lot different on the plane. Calling me forward from where we had been sitting in the back, the pilot flat refused to fly the plane with that Stoner in the passenger compartment. My career would have been over if anything happened to that weapon and I wasn't about to let it out of my sight. After a short standoff in the cockpit, the pilot came up with an agreeable solution. We flew on to Detroit with the weapon secured in a forward compartment that was accessible only through the cockpit of the plane. When we landed, nobody went near that compartment until I was able to retrieve my weapon.

In Detroit, we picked up a car from the government motor pool and moved on to our hotel. We had a reservation at one of the big-name hotels in downtown Detroit, advance per diem, a car—the whole nine yards. This trip was first class and we were going to be in Detroit for about a week.

When we went up to the hotel check-in counter, I still had my Stoner right with me, all wrapped up in paper and padding. The three of us were in civilian clothes, so the guy doing the check-in didn't think anything in particular about us. "Do you have a safe that I can put my machine gun in?" I asked.

The guy just looked at me and laughed, "Put your machine gun under your bed."

Okay, I thought, *I told you.* By this time we were getting a little tired of the machine gun joke anyway. But it turned out the hotel had a little surprise for us. When we were getting ready to go up to our rooms, the man who had checked us in noticed on our orders that we were all Navy personnel. "Hey," the check-in manager asked, "you guys are sailors, aren't you?"

"Yeah," I answered tentatively.

"Have you got your uniforms with you?"

"Yeah."

"Well, I'll tell you guys something," he said in a quiet voice. "We've got a cosmetologists' convention here in Detroit right now. You can see that there are women all over the place, can't you? You go up to your room and just walk back down in uniform. If you don't get picked up before you get back here, there's something wrong with you guys."

A proper SEAL always works with whatever intelligence he can gather on a target area. "Thanks," I said to the check-in manager, and we all went up to our rooms and changed clothes. R. J. Thomas wanted to run off someplace by himself and this didn't matter much to me. Though he proved himself one hell of an operator—he was later awarded the Navy Cross for an operation he had done the year before—he was into the youth culture of the 1960s. That "hippie shit" was nothing Roy Matthews or I wanted anything to do with. We were both "men-o'-warsmen" who had been brought up in the Roy Boehm school, so all we wanted was a beer, some food, and good female company.

While R.J. went off on his own, Roy and I were looking forward to a pretty good time. We had put on our uniforms and didn't look too bad, even by our standards. By this time, I had a couple of tours to Nam behind me, and Roy I think had about the same. This gave us a fair selection of ribbons on our uniforms as well as our new Tridents, the Navy Special Warfare insignia. In Detroit, there weren't one hell of a lot of sailors to give us competition anyway.

Going down to the bar, we sat down with a couple of drinks and checked out the action. Right behind us a couple of ladies sat down at a little two-seat table and started eating dinner. These ladies were having what I guess was the house special, a real big steak with all the trimmings.

Roy had a style that evening that even I was in awe of. After running off at the mouth for a little bit, he got up, took a chair from one of the other tables, and sat down at the ladies' table. "Hi, girls," Roy said. "How are you today?" And he then proceeded to start eating their dinners!

"Me and the chief here are from Norfolk," Roy said. "Are you girls interested in getting laid?"

Aw shit! We're going to jail, I thought. But Roy hadn't gotten smacked yet. In fact, the two ladies were eating the whole thing up, though not quite as fast as he was clearing away their dinners. These were two pretty good-looking ladies, and I was interested to say the least. Not showing any partiality, Roy was eating from both the ladies' plates, though not quite at the same time.

The three of them got done eating, and I mentioned something about getting a bite to eat myself. "But I'm not hungry, Chief," Roy said.

"No, I guess you're not," I answered.

Roy and the ladies got up from their little table and joined me at the bar. When the bartender came up to us, he could see what was going on and asked, "Would you fellows like to buy the ladies a drink?"

"Yeah," Roy said, "but if we don't get laid, we want to get our money back. We don't want to just piss money away."

Roy was what you might call forward in his dealings with the ladies. But whatever it was, apparently it was working. At least the ladies were still with us and not storming off in a huff. As a matter of fact, they were giggling and commenting on how cute they thought Roy was.

One thing led to another and up to their room we went. By about six o'clock the next morning, I was in for a little surprise. I woke up with someone nudging me awake. "Hey, Jim," she said softly, "are you awake?"

"What?" I grumbled back.

What the lady wanted was considerably different from what I thought it might be. Instead of a morning edition, she said, "I think you better go back to your own room."

"What's the matter?" I asked.

"It's getting light outside."

"So?" I said. "Is there some problem here in Detroit with house detectives or something?"

"No," she answered, "but you were drinking pretty heavily last night when you and your friend picked us up."

Now all the alarm bells were going off for me. If these ladies wanted us out of there before it was light enough to see, just what were they? If she was admitting she was ugly before I could even see her, just what the hell did she look like? I was still too young to take my vows and join the chaplain corps.

"Roy," I called over to the other bed.

"What, Chief?" Roy answered.

"The ladies want us to get out of here."

"Fuck 'em, we don't have to get to Caddy Gage till what time?"

We did leave the ladies' room. But the problem wasn't exactly along the same lines as what I had thought. The lady I was with had been wearing a wig the night before and she just didn't want me to see her with her real hair all mussed up. We talked to them and they told us they were both beauticians and were in town for the convention. Apparently, they didn't live too far away and had a friend who owned a bowling alley in Pontiac, north of Detroit, where they hung out a lot. The ladies told us the location of the bowling alley and then we went our separate ways.

R.J. had gotten back to the hotel on his own steam, so the three of us went on over to Cadillac Gage in Warren. The people at Cadillac Gage couldn't have been happier with their weapon. Taking the Stoner down to their range, the engineers fired a few rounds through the weapon and were enthusiastic about its still working.

After touring the plant and seeing how the Stoner was made, we sat down to the maintenance course Cadillac Gage offered on the Stoner. What we wanted was kind of an abbreviated version of the official course. Actually, we just told them to give us the manuals and show us the new tricks that weren't in the books yet. We were on liberty and didn't want to spend all our time at Caddy Gage.

The one thing that impressed the engineers the most wasn't the condition of the Stoner they received, or even our opinion of the weapon as a whole. What they couldn't believe was that we had hand-carried the Stoner to Detroit on board a civilian aircraft. What they weren't going to do was give me some new Stoners to take back with me. "Well, you aren't going to get this weapon until I get the two new ones," I said empathically.

"We cannot issue you these weapons," the company rep told me.

"Whoa, buddy," I said. "You just give me that other weapon back."

"No," he said, "you aren't getting it back."

"Aha," I said in a less than friendly voice, "you want to play fuck-around hoss, you picked the wrong person."

"No, you just don't understand," the rep went on. "With the situation here in Detroit and the laws the way they are, we can't just give you a weapon. We will ship the weapons through channels to Little Creek."

"Okay," I said, "if that's the way it has to be, you're going to ship the sons of bitches while we're here. If they don't go out, we aren't leaving."

But there really wasn't any trouble. The folks at Caddy Gage just had their hands tied by all the red tape they had to follow. They took us down to their shipping department and we saw the weapons that had been promised to us start on their way. After that, the engineers showed us some of the other toys Caddy Gage was making—all sorts of little bitty tanks and armored cars. Neat stuff, some items built for police work and others for straight offensive military operations.

But for all that they showed us, I wasn't going to spend all of my time in Detroit at Caddy Gage. We had a government motor pool car and we were going out to get something to eat. R.J. wanted to go someplace he had heard about, so we gave him a ride. This was not the kind of thing I wanted to do, so after some slight argument—which R.J., being the junior man, lost right away—Roy and I went back to the hotel.

After we got back to the room, Roy came up with a suggestion as to what we might do to pass the time. "Let's go up the road," he said, "and see if we can't find that bowling alley the ladies were talking about."

"Do you really think we should?" I asked, a little taken aback.

"Hey, that one I had was a piece of work. One of us ought to get laid at least."

So off we went to Pontiac. We even found the bowling alley without a lot of trouble—except for the fact that it was getting dark, and starting to snow, and we'd had a few drinks before we left. The roads get pretty slick in Michigan during the winter. I managed to skid out only once. We bounced over the curb but didn't do any real damage to anything. Besides, we found what we had been looking for, and the girls were even there, not that they were thrilled to see us.

Things worked out all right though. Roy did pretty well, but I was more or less stood up. We just took it easy and generally had a good time. But this is one SEAL who doesn't want to visit Detroit again in February. No wonder those people try to go down to Florida during the cold months. But Cadillac Gage was in Michigan and that was the company that built the Stoners for us.

There is only a tiny handful of Stoners left in the Navy and most of those are in museums. We have several on public display down at the UDT-SEAL Museum in Fort Pierce, Florida. It does an old frog good to see the look in the young lions' faces when I hand them one of the museum's weapons. For all the bad things that could be said about the Stoner, when it came right down to it, the weapon was what we needed, when we needed it. There isn't much more that you can ask for.

CHAPTER 15

Boobytraps—Theirs and Ours

T HE SCARIEST THING to run into in the jungle wasn't Charlie or some mythical snake whose bite would kill you within one step. The nastiest thing was the boobytrap. A boobytrap is an inanimate object, simple or complex, and its whole reason for being is to maim or kill the person who is unlucky enough to bother it.

For the most part, Charlie's boobytraps were designed to maim rather than kill. A wounded man takes several other fighting men out of action to take care of him, and Charlie knew this rule well. And an area that had boobytraps in it, or was just suspected of having them, would slow a patrol down considerably.

A boobytrap can be nothing more than a sharp piece of bamboo sticking up in a pathway. Or it can be as complex as a network of command (electrically) detonated mines strewn along the sides and in the trees of a canal. The VC built all kinds of boobytraps and had their own ways of marking their locations.

The sharpened piece of bamboo, or punji stake, was very simple and easy to make from the stuff growing all around you in the jungle. Its availability was what helped make the damned thing so popular. If you've never handled one, you would be amazed at how sharp a cut piece of bamboo can be. The stuff can have an edge like a piece of broken glass. Even if a punji stake wasn't stepped on directly, an angled one could cut right through the top of a boot and nail you in the ankle.

Sometimes, punji stakes were dipped in excrement or some other rotting material to effectively poison them. I never ran into one, but in the jungle, such a thing could give you a wound that would fester and become infected quickly.

Just the punji stake, a little piece of bamboo, was nasty enough. But Charlie had much more sophisticated things just lying in wait in the jungle. Trip wires could be connected to a grenade, a bamboo whip with punji stakes on it, or even the firing device of an explosive mine.

And some of the mines the VC had were big. A water mine that nailed me in Nha Be during my second tour weighed several hundred pounds. The VC would take explosives out of American dud artillery shells and aircraft bombs and build whatever they wanted. Steaming the explosive out of a dud bomb is not exactly the Oriental way to a long life, but no one could ever say that Charlie didn't have guts.

Sometimes, the VC would just use a piece of ordnance the way it was as a boobytrap. A five-hundred-pound aircraft bomb buried under a roadbed, with an improvised pressure fuze in the nose, could easily destroy an M113 armored personnel carrier (APC) and seriously damage a full battle tank. Any GI who happened to trip such a device didn't have to worry about being maimed; he would just disappear into a bloody mist. A lot of GIs kept their dog tags tied to their boot laces just in case they were killed by this boobytrap, or any other kind of explosion. Funny thing was, if you found a piece of a guy who had been killed, it was often just a boot. That didn't happen to me or anyone I know—it was just part of the scuttlebutt that travels around a war zone.

My personal experiences with boobytraps started well before I ever traveled to Vietnam. Early in February 1965, I was one of the first SEALs from Team Two to go to the U.S. Army's Ranger School. It was not exactly one of my favorite training sessions. As a matter of fact, I recommended that the Team not make the school part of the standard SEAL training curriculum. But there was one thing that Ranger School did for me that I never forgot: It taught me about boobytraps big time.

During Ranger training, you're almost always on a patrol of one kind or another. Physically, the training was an ass-kicker. UDTR was much harder, but I wore out three pairs of boots while at Ranger School.

The instructors at Ranger School acted the part of the aggressor much of the time while we students were on patrols. Part of the instructors' role as the enemy involved boobytraps along our patrol routes. The boobytraps were designed to simulate the real thing. When triggered, they made a flash-bang, whistle, or bright flare, without really hurting you. But there was no question in your mind that you had screwed up big time. The trip wires the instructors laid out didn't hurt, but you couldn't ignore the fact that if the things had been real, you'd have been either dead or maimed.

The Ranger instructors nailed me with many a trip wire. And there was one Ranger lesson that I never forgot: When you got near an objective and decided to go balls-to-the-wall and attack, that was when you found out the place was wired.

There was this dangerous feeling when you had gotten close to the target—and I mean within fifty meters or so—that you had avoided all the dangerous obstacles. Sometimes you had already gone through an area of boobytraps and you figured the rest of the way was clear. *Okay, we've got the upper hand,* you thought. *Let's get this over with in a hurry.* And then you hauled ass to the target. That was the lesson that was brought home at Ranger School: You just didn't do it. The detonation of simulators drove that particular lesson home solidly.

The three times I did predeployment training for Vietnam, I don't remember ever tripping a boobytrap. Not even during our first training in 1966, where we were all learning what was needed to survive in Vietnam, did I ever set off a trip wire. That is a major part of a point man's duties, to detect boobytraps before the main body of the patrol reaches them.

At Camp A. P. Hill, Virginia; Camp Pickett; and Union Camp, North Carolina, I would take patrols right through areas that had been wired up by our instructors. The lessons of Ranger School stayed with me, making me that much more cautious; what trip wires I came across, I always detected before it was too late.

Once things started in Vietnam, it was too late to consider going back. The boobytraps over there weren't simulators. If you hit a wire in the jungle, you were a dead man, or pretty well maimed.

Out of the nine SEALs from Team Two who were killed in Vietnam, three were taken out by boobytraps. Joseph A. Albrecht and Lieutenant Frederick E. Trani were both killed by enemy boobytraps within six weeks of each other in 1968. Eugene Fraley was killed by a malfunctioning SEAL boobytrap he was preparing in January 1968. Of the thirty-five SEALs from Team One who were lost in Vietnam, four were killed by boobytraps, with an additional four SEALs killed by a possibly boobytrapped mortar round. Even UDT 13 lost three men in Vietnam, and two of those were lost to mines. Bob Gallagher, the Eagle, wasn't immune to enemy boobytraps. Even with his EOD (Explosive Ordnance Disposal) training, Bob is missing some fingers today because of enemy boobytraps.

None of the men who followed me in Vietnam were ever injured or killed by an enemy boobytrap while I led the patrol. My experiences in Ranger School and elsewhere had taught me just how careful to be when crossing enemy territory, and how much caution was too much. One of the things I never did while on point was wear gloves of any kind. The slightest pressure against your skin could be the warning that would save you and your teammates.

I paid a lot of attention to the way I walked while on point. The last thing I wanted to do was miss a trap and have it nail the third guy down the line in our patrol. Lifting your feet carefully and being aware of how things felt as you moved your leg and put your foot down could give you all the warning you needed to find a boobytrap. Another thing I did was hold a small stick, more of a twig really, out in front of me when I moved through close areas. If the stick brushed against something that didn't feel right, I would reach out to check it. The funny thing was, I never did find a trip wire in all my time in Vietnam.

The technique with the stick was one I had been taught prior to going over to Vietnam. It had worked well for me in training and worked just as well in Vietnam. With all of the modern technology they have in the Teams today, I wonder if this simple trick has been passed down. Sometimes you forget the old techniques when learning about all the new bells and whistles. A hostage situation is one

I could see taking place today where there would be a possibility of encountering boobytraps. Doors and windows are a prime location for a trip wire or another kind of fuze. The answer to this sort of thing is one we learned in Vietnam: Don't go in the front door. If you suspect an entrance is boobytrapped, find another way in, even if you have to make it yourself.

Later on I learned that Mikey Boynton had found a trip wire during his first operation incountry. They don't come much bigger or badder than Mikey, but he was close to loading his drawers when he realized the wire he was pushing on with his chest might not be a clothesline. Mikey got through his boobytrap, and I survived mine.

Though I was injured by a water mine at Nha Be, it was the result of an active choice rather than just tripping over the damned thing. The EOD men who had accompanied me on the operation where the mine was recovered wanted to take the thing back to the base for study. After all, that's the way EOD learns about new enemy devices, by taking them apart and seeing what makes them tick, sometimes literally. Not exactly the job I most want in the world. The one time I was involved with such an operation, the charge went off. All of the EOD men were killed and I was very severely injured. I healed, though, and was able to return to Vietnam for my third tour.

It was during my third tour that I tripped a boobytrap—actually, "fell into it" would be more accurate. The operation was a body snatch and Chuck Fellers and Duke Leonard were backing me up. Along with Chuck and Duke, I had a number of men from Father Hoa's bunch. (Father Hoa—pronounced Wha—was a Chinese Catholic priest who had put together an amazing group of anti-Communist fighters, many of them ex-VC or even ex-NVA.) The operation fell to shit fast. I had just killed our target when he came to his hooch's door with a weapon in his hand and I'd taken the man's family out in the same blast. Before I had time to react to this, we started taking fire from all sides. I pulled my men together and we left the area, running along a paddy dike and taking random fire from the tree lines around us. It was while running along the dike that it happened—I stepped in a punji pit.

It didn't take long to hit the bottom, but not much time is needed to feel your own heart stop. Before I could fully realize what was happening, I had hit the bottom of the four-foot-deep pit. No stakes. Whoever had dug the pit hadn't lined the bottom of it with punji stakes. Not having time to think about the situation, I scrambled out of the hole and continued on. The situation was a hairy one, and if it hadn't been for the bravery and skill of the Seawolf crews, I don't think we would have gotten out as unscathed as we did.

Though I wasn't a very superstitious or religious man at the time, it seemed that my falling into the punji pit and coming out again was more than just luck. Somebody was watching out for my dumb ass that day. And I heard the lesson loud and clear: "You fucked up. Better remember this—you might not be around the next time!" No problem; if anything I was even more cautious after that. But I never let practical caution get in the way of the mission that had to be performed. Worrying too much about things like booby-traps can screw your mind over and keep you from operating at all. A balance has to be reached between caution and bravery; training and listening to the lessons already learned can help you reach this necessary balance.

One of the biggest lessons I learned about boobytraps was to never go in the easy way. The easy way is where they will be waiting for you with either an ambush or boobytraps, or even both.

The lesson of never take the easy way was driven home for me in no uncertain terms during my first tour in Vietnam. To this day I don't know whether Rick Marcinko was acting on a hunch or if he had hard intel, bit Rick wanted us to patrol Ilo Ilo island.

Ilo Ilo was a small, maybe half mile by quarter mile, chunk of almost dry mud sticking up out of the mouth of the My Tho River. From the upriver end to nearly the center of the island was a small canal, maybe six feet wide and only a few feet deep at most. Rick said he knew of a VC medical center on Ilo Ilo and that we were going to take it out. The central canal just looked like the easiest way in, too easy in fact. What we did was crawl through the several hundred yards of mud flat on the downriver side of the island in order to begin our patrol.

Eventually, after a very long, hot, and exhausting day, we found a cache of VC medical supplies and then located a bunch of the VC themselves. In the ambush we initiated, we nailed five of the six VC. One of them got away. It always seemed that in an ambush, you managed to miss one.

It was on the way out that I was made a believer in the axiom "Never take the easy way." All through the jungle canopy over the canal were strewn command-detonated grenades and fragmentation mines. Lines were leading from the pull rings of many of the grenades back to the *boheo* (covered sleeping platform) where we had ambushed the VC. As we slowly moved along the canal to leave Ilo Ilo, it was obvious what would have happened to us if we had come in by the front door.

Even though we had VC coming up behind us, we still took care to watch for trip wires on our way out. Upon reaching the main river, we found that the tide was out, just like it had been on our insertion at the other end of the island. We had to crawl through several hundred yards of mud again before we could reach the Mike boat waiting for us just at the water's edge. We reached the Mike boat without major incident—unless you consider the 81mm HE round fired from the Mike boat, which skipped along the mud's surface between Bob Gallagher and myself, an incident. But the lesson learned at Ilo Ilo island always stayed with us and was passed along to other platoons coming to Vietnam.

The lessons about boobytraps we learned in Vietnam worked two ways. It wasn't very long after we started operating that we were planting boobytraps of our own against Charlie and his northern cousins. Because of the nature of the Vietnam War, many innocent civilians were around, so we were particularly careful about what we planted and where.

The first major target we had for our own fiendish devices was to attack Charlie's supply base. Larger units than ours were trying to cut off the flow of supplies coming from North Vietnam to the VC in the South. The Ho Chi Minh Trail in Laos and Cambodia was not the sort of target the SEALs were suited to attack. And the Navy forces of Operation Market Garden were choking off the flow of supplies traveling to the VC by way of the sea. For us, it was the supply caches already in place in the Delta region that were a primary target.

During our first tour in 1967, we didn't have much available to us in the way of boobytraps. I believe it was Bob Gallagher who had some very special ammunition made up for us to leave behind when we investigated supply caches. We would bring back AK-47 ammunition—7.62×39mm or 7.62 intermediate, it was called then—from some of the supply caches we found. Bob had a local unit, probably an EOD unit, break down the ammunition, pull the bullet, and dump out the powder. The empty cartridge would then be filled with powdered Composition B explosive and the bullet reinserted.

The finished product was indistinguishable from a regular round of ammunition. Somebody, not me, tried one of our doctored rounds in an AK-47 that was set up for remote firing. Though I never saw the weapon myself, the word was that it had been blown all to hell from the explosive-filled round. There was no question that any VC who fired a weapon loaded with one of our rounds was going to be a casualty.

The boobytrapped ammunition was left behind when we located a cache or had a firefight with the VC. We had loaded magazines for AK-47s that held a few of our little nasties along with regular ammunition. Of course, not all of the rounds in an ammunition cache had to be doctored. If only a few rounds were left around strategically, they had an effect all out of proportion to their numbers.

With weapons blowing up, the word got out around the VC camps that there was something wrong with their supplies. Men were reluctant to fire a weapon that they thought might kill them with the next shot. It was a long time before the supply caches were restocked with matériel from the North.

The results of the AK-47 ammunition were so good that other types of ammunition were doctored. Chinese and Soviet 82mm mortar rounds were boobytrapped to explode when they were fired. The fuze was modified so that it appeared okay, but as soon as the round hit the bottom of the mortar tube, *boom*.

One platoon left some doctored mortar rounds behind when it located a VC mortar emplacement. Returning to the emplacement some time later, all the platoon found was a destroyed mortar with the muzzle peeled back like a banana. Blood was all over the mortar pit, but there were no bodies in sight. The next VC mortar team in that area was probably a little clausty about firing its weapon.

By 1968, the folks at the Naval Special Warfare Projects center at China Lake began supplying us with factory-made boobytraps. The China Lake people had taken over the manufacture of booby-trapped ammunition and sent us over whole sealed boxes of the stuff. Several calibers were used, including 7.62×39mm and 7.62×54mmR, known to us then as 7.62 intermediate and 7.62mm long. The boxes the ammunition came packed in were original foreign packaging, with all of the seals and markings intact.

The new ammunition was so good that we couldn't tell the difference between it and the regular, safe rounds. Even though paperwork, very classified paperwork, was filed on every ammunition dump that was "salted," we very quickly got to the point where we didn't trust enemy ammunition we picked up in the field for our own use. If the stuff didn't come out of a box that we knew the origin of, we just didn't shoot it. And if we didn't trust the ammunition, I wonder just how Charlie felt about his supplies.

In a firefight, if a weapon was needed, you didn't hesitate to pick up an AK and fire it. But there was no doubt that everyone was getting just a little clausty about using an enemy weapon. The boobytraps put out by the VC were bad enough; it would be a real bitch if you got nailed by your own trick.

China Lake was putting out a good deal more in the way of boobytraps than just the ammunition. There were six or eight different devices that they made for us by mid-1968 using simple, everyday items. The only difference was, they were deadly. Different kinds of fuzes were installed inside these objects to set them off if they were operated, messed with, or just moved. These items could be left behind in enemy territory, looking like they had just been dropped or fallen out of someone's pack. They very quickly put a dent in the VC's resupplying themselves through battlefield pickups.

Many of these items are still classified even today. But one of them deserves particular attention. There was a flashlight that could be filled with high explosive by the user before it was put out into the field. The flashlight had a battery and an electrical fuze that could be tested and then armed. When it was tested, a small light went on. When it had been armed, there was a thirty-second delay before the fuze was live, and then any movement of the boobytrap was enough to set it off.

Eugene Fraley was real big into boobytraps and knew what they could do. He had built himself a small sandbag enclosure where he could assemble and test the boobytraps before taking them out into the field. The enclosure was set up so that Gene could put his hands through two holes and manipulate the device he was working on. If something went wrong and the charge blew, he would have lost his hands, but you can live without your hands.

In January 1968, Gene was incountry operating as a member of Seventh Platoon. Seventh had been operating in Vietnam since October the year before and had already suffered a casualty from a VC boobytrap. Bob Gallagher had been injured but was back with his platoon within a few weeks.

Gene Fraley wasn't as lucky. On January 21, 1968, he was preparing one of the China Lake boobytrap flashlights for use on that evening's op. Apparently the device tested properly, and Gene took the flashlight out of the sandbag enclosure where he had assembled it. No one is sure of what happened next. Gene probably pushed the arming switch too far after he tested the circuit. When he moved the flashlight out of the enclosure, the safety timer on the fuze was already running. As soon as the fuze armed, thirty seconds after the switch was moved, the flashlight detonated.

Gene was holding the flashlight when it went off and probably never felt a thing. The wound to his head was massive and instantly fatal.

The boobytrap fuze used in the flashlight was immediately suspended for use, and it was a number of years before the higher-ups once again allowed the SEALs to use them. Boobytraps are dangerous by their very nature, but the Navy pays the SEALs to work with danger.

Boobytraps have not gotten any simpler today. In fact, they have become even more complex with the increase in available technology. Electronic fuzes, which were the size of a flashlight battery in the 1960s, can be smaller than a pencil eraser today. What the Teams use today is very classified, and for a good reason. But without a doubt, there is nothing more feared in combat than the explosive device or deadly trap that might claim you at any time. That was what helped make the life of a point man so interesting. Yeah, right!

CHAPTER 16

SEALs, Snakes, Sharks, and Other Critters

I N BOTH THE SEALS AND THE UDTS, we spent one hell of a lot of time in the water. From that first three-hundred-yard swim in training to the twice-weekly ocean swims, the leg muscles needed to drive our large, stiff swim fins were kept in shape. In the SEALs, we did a lot of underwater work, including night sneak attacks and qualifying dives to keep our skills sharp and maintain our 5326 SEAL NEC (Navy enlisted code). In the UDTs, even more time was spent in the water due to their mission profile, which was primarily water oriented.

Personally, I never particularly liked diving. I did what was needed to perform my job, but I never did develop the love for being underwater that some of my teammates had.

The same cover that allows the SEALs and UDTs to use the water to hide our activities keeps the people on the surface from seeing just what else might be moving around in the deep. There have been sea stories about monsters in the deep since the first cave-man climbed aboard a log and paddled along. Sailors have long talked about giant squid, sea serpents, killer whales (not just the pretty ones in the water shows), and ravaging packs of sharks. More than a few of the stories have some basis in fact. There are some big critters under the waves, and we haven't spotted more than a fraction of them.

Shark stories really began making the rounds of the public after the movie *Jaws* hit the screen in 1975. That was after I had retired from the Teams, so the movie didn't mean much to me. It didn't mean a great deal to SEALs or UDT men in general. Though the public was reporting sharks everywhere, and that they were eating people like peanuts, shark attacks just didn't happen much. Your chances of getting hit by lightning are much greater than the chance of being eaten, or even bitten, by a shark.

For all the time I spent in the water, and that was much less than some operators did, I never had an encounter with a shark that was worth raising a hair over. There hasn't been a history of shark attacks in the Teams, from World War II to the present day. There really isn't even much of a history of shark attacks in the Navy as a whole, though there certainly have been some tight moments for downed pilots and shipwreck survivors.

There was one time when a shark didn't leave a UDT man alone, even though he was leaving it alone. He wasn't on duty at the time, preventing it from being counted as an "official" loss.

It happened in St. Thomas in the Virgin Islands in 1962. That was the year the SEALs were commissioned and we were too busy getting ready to operate to be in St. Thomas for our usual training. However, UDT 21 was down there conducting winter refresher training, dive qualifications, and general water work. This was always a good time in the Teams. You were down in a beautiful, warm, sunny area, while back at the Creek winter was still blowing in from the North Atlantic.

In spite of all the work that was normally done while down at St. Thomas, a good frog was always able to find some time off. Lieutenant Gibson was enjoying a day off with a young lady, of which there were many on the island, as it was also the height of the tourist season. Frogs and tourist women got along better than you would believe. Being a frogman just seemed to draw in women like flies to honey.

Gibson and his lady were enjoying themselves just swimming in the waters of Magens Bay. That bay was not one of our training areas; it was actually one of the popular tourist spots. While his date was on the beach, resting in the sun, Gibson was swimming out a ways from shore. That was when the shark attacked.

We are told in training that if a shark comes in toward you, you can usually fend the animal off by striking it in the nose as hard as you can. Most divers, civilian and military, who have had a rare encounter with a curious or incoming shark will tell you that just hitting the creature will drive it away ninety-nine times out of a hundred. This may have been what Gibson remembered, only his time was that one odd chance.

The shark's first bite took off Gibson's left hand, high up on the wrist. A bite like that is what tells me that Gibson was probably trying to hit the shark on the snout. Whatever it was that happened, Gibson sure as hell knew he was in trouble. His shouting and yelling drew the attention of his date on the beach, and that lady did something that would be hard for even a SEAL to do: She went into the water to help Gibson get back to shore.

Several years ago, at the UDT-SEAL Museum in Fort Pierce, Florida, I finally met the woman who had tried to get Gibson out of the water that day. She told me that she didn't know why she'd done it, except that she wanted to try to help bring him in.

When she got to Gibson, he was still alive but slipping into shock. The first thing she noticed was that his hand was missing. In spite of his terrible wound, Gibson was still trying to make it to shore. While they were struggling along in he water, the shark hit Gibson again, this time biting off one of his legs.

Never abandoning Gibson in spite of the obvious danger to herself, the woman towed him in to the beach, but it was far too late. With several of the major arteries in his leg and arm severed, he bled to death, probably well before he ever felt land again.

Though the attack took place while Gibson was off duty, the Team reacted quickly to the loss of one of its own. By the next day, Scott Slaughter was organizing a shark hunt and most of UDT 21 was involved. Slaughter was one of the most experienced men in the Teams when it came to sharks, especially killing one. Scott had developed the bang-stick for use underwater against dangerous marine life such as sharks.

The shark has a fairly primitive, though very effective, design. The animals are tough, and catching one is easier than killing it. A shark's skin is tough and they can take a tremendous amount of damage before dying. A caught shark, whether on land or in a boat, can still bite anything that comes near it, sometimes hours after it has been taken out of the water.

To take out a shark quickly, Scott Slaughter developed the bang-stick, kind of an underwater warhead for a spear. A bang-stick holds a cartridge, often a shotgun shell, inside a short barrel that can be screwed down on a spear shaft. With its safety turned off, the bang-stick will fire its cartridge when the muzzle end is driven into a target. When the target is a shark, hitting one anyplace around the head will usually blow a good-sized portion of the head clean off. Even a tough critter like a large shark can't take that kind of punishment, and a good bang-stick hit will kill one almost instantly.

With Slaughter leading the way, the men searched Magens Bay for the shark that had hit Gibson. Using nets and chumming the water (throwing out bait scraps and blood), they drew in a shark and nailed that sucker. There wasn't any question that they had gotten the right animal. When the shark was cut open, Gibson's hand and leg were still inside it, identifiable by the watch on Gibson's wrist.

As I remember, it was a good-sized, maybe eight feet or so, black-tipped shark, not an easygoing critter but not known to be one of the real man-killers such as the great white. In fact, the attack was so unusual that a professor of marine biology from one of the eastern universities came down to St. Thomas to examine the shark. After his examination, the scientist said that there was something wrong with the shark, that it was sick, and that this was what had led to the animal's making its attack on Gibson.

Out of the fifty-year history of the UDTs and the SEALs, that shark attack against Gibson was the only one ever recorded. That should underscore the rarity of an actual attack by a shark against a swimmer. Sharks were encountered every now and then, however, usually in the warmer waters of the Caribbean.

The one shark encounter I had that stands out in my memory like Gibson's attack didn't take place while I was on a Team swim. I was lobster hunting with Gene Tinnin down in St. Thomas back in early 1961 while I was taking UDT diver training. The Team was down in the islands doing water qualifications and training. Gene and I were doing some underwater swimming, trying to pick up some langoustes, the big spiny lobsters they had down there. We went along the bottom, keeping an eye out for langoustes as we passed over coral heads. When I reached out and touched one coral head, pulling myself along, it turned out what I had grabbed wasn't coral.

Darting out from beneath my hand was a good-sized sand shark. Those rough-skinned sharks can rest on the bottom, resembling nothing more than a long rock or coral head. Though sand sharks really can't hurt you easily, when that one took off, my young frogman heartbeat sped up just a bit. I'm not scared of a shark, but I am mighty respectful of them, and that one animal did get my blood moving a little faster. As for Gene, I think he was laughing too hard, while trying not to drown at the same time, to have much concern for me.

Though the shark menace is very overrated, there are more than a few other things you have to be concerned about underwater. Again, it happened more often on sport swims than during actual training. When you're out langouste hunting, if you don't pay attention to what you're doing, you could meet a moray eel under less than ideal circumstances.

A moray, though edible and, I am told, quite tasty, is nothing to mess with on a chance encounter. Reaching over six feet in length, with a thick, muscular body, a moray has a mouthful of needle-sharp teeth and is not known for letting go once it has a grip on you. But unless you stick your hand right in front of the eel and threaten it, that critter doesn't want to bother with you.

There is an occasion where you might stick your hand in the wrong place easily, and that's while lobster hunting. Big spiny lobsters live in holes and crevices in the reef, backing in so their long antennae stick out of the hole. The spiny lobster—what we called langouste—is really a pretty creature, with a tan, red, and brown body with white and black markings. And for all of their good looks, langoustes are even better eating. The spiny lobsters have no real claws like their cold-water relatives and can be easily caught by a skin diver just swimming down from the surface.

But for all of their relative harmlessness, the langoustes tend to have rowdy roommates. When you came up to a langouste sticking its long antennae out of a hole, you had to pay attention to the situation. If one of the lobster's antennae was sticking out to the side, pointing at you, or if one was pointing up and the other down, there was a good chance that lobster was sharing his hole with a moray eel. Sticking your hand into that lobster's hole would be asking for trouble. Leave it alone and move on to the next one.

The spiny sea urchin couldn't attack you if it wanted to. The little black ball moves around the coral slowly, eating whatever it is sea urchins eat. But the nasty little devil is the underwater world's answer to the porcupine. Bristling with brittle barbed spines several inches long, a sea urchin moves about like an animated pin cushion, which is exactly how you feel if you ever run into one.

It was while I was going through UDTR training down in Puerto Rico that I had my first, and last, encounter with a sea urchin. Heinz and I were on a sneaky-pete type of op when we were supposed to reconnoiter a beach area from a rubber boat. As part of the boat crew, Heinz, who was my swim buddy, and I were acting as the recon swim pair and were the first in to the beach.

Heinz and I went into the water and swam up to the beach. The water turned shallow, with a large number of rocks and coral heads about, as we approached dry land. When the water was about knee-deep, I figured we would take our fins off so we could move through the water more easily. Our fins at the time were Voit Duck-feet, very stiff, hard-rubber slip-ons that were over a foot and a half long. Not the kind of thing that makes walking through the water easy or quiet.

Moving over to what was either a rock or a coral head just awash in the water, I sat down to take off my fins. As I was developing and polishing my skills as a UDT man, one of the Navy's best, I did not expect to sit down right on top of a spiny sea urchin.

Sea urchin spines are stiff but brittle. Once they break off under your skin, there isn't any way of just pulling them out. The damned things are stiff enough to go right through a coral shoe, but crumble if you try to get a grip on them. My rather painful lesson gave me a red and sore ass for the rest of the night and for some time to come. The body will get rid of urchin spines, but the process takes a while and is not something I recommend to anyone.

From that point on, I learned to watch out for more than just a suspected enemy on shore. The seas have all sorts of little ways of reminding you that you're just a visitor at best, big bad frogman or not. It did seem that everyone in the Teams managed to encounter a sea urchin at one time or another, either while undergoing basic training or while down at St. Thomas. The lesson is a painful one and not something a person will soon forget. But it is at least one of the less dangerous ways of learning how to look out for yourself in the water.

Sea urchin spines are nasty, but not really dangerous or poisonous. Other creatures moving about in the ocean are just as unaggressive as the sea urchin, only they're one hell of a lot more dangerous. Jellyfish are particularly nasty, and you find them just about anywhere there is salt water.

It was in Chesapeake Bay that I met jellyfish that would just tear your ass up when on a swim. Down in St. Thomas and Puerto Rico, they didn't seem to be much of a problem; at least I didn't meet any when I swam there. But when swimming off Little Creek in Chesapeake Bay, you could run into whole swarms of jellyfish.

Jellyfish are anything but threatening-looking beasts. The almost translucent body of a jellyfish can be blue, green, pink, red, brown, or even a clear white, and just floats along in the current. But where the danger really lies is in the stinging tentacles that hang below the body.

Some jellyfish, like the Portuguese man-of-war or the sea wasp, have serious venom in their sting. And it's not like a land insect or snake that will sting or bite you only once or just a few times. The tentacles of a jellyfish are covered with thousands of stinging cells that will each inject a small portion of venom. Some jellyfish stings only raise a painful red welt along where the tentacle brushed. Others inject a poison that can paralyze or kill a man within ten minutes of contact.

The underwater encounter I dreaded the most was to run into a jellyfish at night. It seemed to happen on underwater rather than surface swims, and the worst contact would be when you hit a jellyfish with your head. A full wet suit protected your body and a hood covered your head, but the tentacles of a jellyfish would wrap around your face mask, stinging every exposed skin surface—your lips, cheeks, and forehead—until you pulled them off.

The tentacles of a jellyfish trail behind the critter as it floats along, like long deadly threads. Jellyfish can have tentacles thirty or forty feet long and use them to kill the small fish that the organism feeds on. Dangling jellyfish tentacles were, I think, one of the reasons that the design of the TRASS swimmer delivery vehicle (SDV) was changed from an open cockpit to an enclosed one. Passing through a swarm of jellyfish tentacles would cause serious damage to the men inside an open-cockpit SDV long before the rather slow vehicle could be turned or brought to a stop. The new enclosed boats protected the passengers and helped keep a mission going forward.

Personally, I never had a run-in with a jellyfish. But I did swim in water where you could see them. Those may have been among the times when someone greater than myself was looking out for me.

Not all underwater encounters have such serious results. There are dolphins that swim in Chesapeake Bay; you can see them jumping out of the water just a few dozen yards from shore. But the waters of the Chesapeake are dark and muddy. Though I am sure there were dolphins nearby when we were on a swim off Little Creek, and even watching us in their own way, I personally never met one in the wild.

Teammates on the west coast have had chance encounters with whales while on swims in the Pacific. Meeting a critter underwater the size of a small bus would have a sobering effect on the ego of a

SEAL. An SDV probably looks like a small, crippled cousin to a whale near Coronado.

It doesn't really matter what you run into underwater; chances are it will leave you alone if you don't bother it. And the best way of ignoring something is to just concentrate on your mission and getting the job done.

With a majority of their operations on (relatively) dry land, a whole new field of possible run-ins with nature faced the SEALs. When I went down to Panama and attended the Army Jungle School there, I was introduced to a wide number of critters that normally a boy who grew up in New Jersey would rarely get a chance to see up close and personal. Though I never met any of the nastier occupants of the Central American jungle, I'm certain that I heard at least a few of them among all of the sounds a jungle makes.

In Virginia, there are more than a few breeds of poisonous snakes. Though most of the people living in the state never encounter a poisonous snake throughout their entire lives, the SEALs tended to train in areas that were a little wilder than Virginia Beach, even on a Saturday night.

During Team Two's development of predeployment training for Vietnam, a number of different training sites were examined. Sites in Virginia and North Carolina were checked for possible use. They were all wild, undeveloped pieces of countryside where you could run into all kinds of wildlife.

During my time at Union Camp in North Carolina, and Camps Pickett and A. P. Hill in Virginia, I spent a lot of time in the woods and swamps. During my training, I didn't encounter much more than deer and Bob Gallagher's training problems. The deer we ate, and the training we completed to the Eagle's satisfaction.

Later during Team Two's commitment to Vietnam, training was conducted in the Great Dismal Swamp, which begins only about twenty miles or so southeast of Little Creek. The huge, marshy area of the swamp was perfect for conducting predeployment training and was very convenient to the Team's headquarters.

During at least one training session I've heard of, Rick Marcinko taught his charges one hell of a lesson in the difficulties in maintaining silence while on patrol. While taking his men along a stream during the day, Rick stopped every now and then to pop one of the many water moccasins that infested the area with a handgun. A water moccasin, also known as a cottonmouth, is a large, aggressive, thick-bodied, territorial reptile with a nasty disposition and a pair of poison fangs to back it up with.

After watching Rick blow away a number of these snakes during the afternoon, those men would have to patrol through the same area that night. The stress of a combat zone could be pretty well duplicated by having to walk through an area filled with poisonous snakes. And all during a patrol, you stayed silent, even if you felt something slither across your feet.

I never had to deal with Rick's idea of pleasant walking company, but snakes of all kinds were common throughout parts of Vietnam. From the three-foot-long krait to the monster Burmese python, you could find reptiles everywhere in the jungles and swamps of Southeast Asia. The kraits didn't look like much, but they carried some of the deadliest poison of any snake in Vietnam. And the pythons could get above thirty feet long and weigh more than a fully grown man.

For all of the snakes in Southeast Asia, I was never that concerned about them. If you leave the snakes alone, much like the sharks, they tend to leave you alone. Just walking along, even carefully walking while on point, will put out enough vibrations to let any snake around know that you are coming. Unless you have it backed into a corner, a snake will prefer to run. Even the big snakes with the bad reputations, such as the eighteen-foot-long king cobra, will leave an area when given half a chance. Dumb as it is, a snake knows it can't eat you and is usually more scared than you are.

Of course, just because I wasn't worried about running into one didn't mean I didn't have a healthy respect for all those snakes in Vietnam. In some areas, the Viet Cong would even make booby-traps out of tied-down snakes. In tunnel complexes, which I thankfully stayed out of, the VC would tie a snake to the ceiling, pissed off and ready to bite anyone that came near. The idea of running into something like that in the dark is enough to give a SEAL nightmares.

But for the most part, we had no trouble with wild snakes. During my first tour of duty, Second Platoon even kept a small python, only ten or so feet long, as kind of a mascot. The guys fed the snake a chicken every week, and that snake just wanted to lie quietly in the sun most every chance it got.

Of course there were other reptiles in Vietnam that you had to keep an eye out for. Since the SEALs operated in the water so much, we had the best chance of meeting a crocodile on a one-to-one basis. There were saltwater crocs near the oceans and those things can reach a length of twenty-five feet or more. That's not a lizard, it's more of a dinosaur, and a meat-eater to boot.

In fact, saltwater crocs have a reputation of being man-eaters if given the chance. Of course the really big crocodiles were more than just rare; they were damn near legends. One of the twenty-five-footers was killed in the Philippines in the early 1990s and it made international news.

Much more common in Southeast Asia is the smaller Siamese crocodile. The little crocodiles, only six to eight feet long on the average, could hardly do more than, say, rip an arm or leg off, or maybe drag you into the water to drown. At least they couldn't swallow you whole, like those huge saltwater monsters.

Occasionally, a SEAL waiting quietly at an ambush would spot a croc moving in the water. A croc moves along with just its nostrils and eyes above water; the rest of the animal's body is awash. It looks like nothing more than a floating log or other piece of flotsam; at least that's what the one I met looked like.

It was during my first tour in Vietnam while waiting at an ambush site one night. The squad was sitting at the ambush site, silently waiting our target to make an appearance—only something else was making a target of us, and it wasn't the VC. A soft *swish-swish* sounded out from the water. Not even really a splashing and certainly not the noise a sampan makes. And right in front of us, it moved through the water.

At the time it looked as big as the battleship *New Jersey*, but it was probably only about six or seven feet long in reality. Only a few inches of the eyes were sticking out of the water. None of us did anything and the lizard just moved on quietly. It probably just didn't want to mess with a bunch of SEALs anyway.

But crocs weren't much of a concern in Vietnam. I've heard that some guys in Team One actually ended up having to shoot one during an op. But in Team Two, we never gave them much thought.

What was a problem in the waters of Vietnam was the leeches, thousands of them. A single leech really can't do you much harm itself, other than giving you the willies when you first spot it. But the bloodsucking devils can leave you open for infections that, in the hot, humid environment of Vietnam, are nothing to laugh at. In some areas hardly any leeches were reported, and in other spots they were thick and heavy. And leeches weren't found just in the water; in the jungles of Vietnam, leeches would hang from moist vegetation and drop onto you as you passed by.

It seemed the west coast guys up in the Rung Sat had the worst of the leech problem. Those guys even took to wearing nylon pantyhose while on ops in known leech areas. The pantyhose would help prevent the leeches from getting a grip on you, especially in the crotch area. And when an op was over, what leeches did manage to get a grip would come loose as soon as you pulled the pantyhose off.

If the idea worked, more power to the guys in SEAL Team One. But they did let themselves in for a good deal of ribbing from those of us in Team Two. "Oh, you're a west coast pantyhose wearer" was a line that I might have let slip more than once in my lifetime. But if you weren't in the Teams, your lifetime might grow short rapidly if you were to say the same thing to a west coast SEAL.

The guys from Team One swore by their pantyhose and had their wives send them pairs in the mail from home. I also understand that the pantyhose were hot suckers to wear in that humid environment over there. My personal experience with pantyhose is limited to those worn by the opposite sex. In fact, I never did have any trouble with leeches in Vietnam or Cambodia.

It must have been that blend of alcohol and nicotine I kept in my bloodstream that kept the insects off me for the most part. An adult lifetime of carefully balancing cigarettes and beer sure paid off. Now, of course, when I go up to Michigan, I get eaten alive by mosquitoes. So much for trying to quit smoking.

But insects of all kinds were a major problem almost all over Vietnam. In August 1967, some SEALs from Team One were setting up an ambush site when one of their number had a run-in with one of the local inhabitants. A SEAL named Hertenstein was bitten by a spider while settling into his hide for the ambush. Within minutes, the SEAL was swelling up and having a hard time seeing and breathing. Quick action on the part of his teammates got Hertenstein to a medical unit that was able to give him the treatment he needed.

Team Two SEALs were not immune to meeting up with unfriendly Vietnamese natives that weren't VC. In May 1969, after I had been wounded in January and evacuated back to the States, Lieutenant James Thames led a squad from Sixth Platoon on a canal ambush. The ambush was a dry hole and the extraction was a real nightmare.

The deep mud you find in Vietnam just wouldn't let the SEALs move off the canal bank to meet the extraction boat. Finally, the LCM that was picking up the squad threw a line over to shore and towed the men off the muddy beach. While the squad was washing its clothes off in the Long Tau shipping channel, Lieutenant Thames had the bad luck to make personal contact with a Communist jellyfish. Badly stung, Thames had a severe allergic reaction and had to be medevaced to the Third Field Hospital. Recovering quickly, he was back with Sixth Platoon just a few days after his encounter.

For myself, my meeting with the Vietnamese insect kingdom had less spectacular results, but was a lesson I wasn't going to forget either. It was relatively early during my first tour in Vietnam. I was operating as the point man for Bravo Squad of Second Platoon under Rick Marcinko, who was an ensign at that time. All of the training we had taken back in the States had made us very good at our jobs, taking the war to the enemy. But nothing substitutes for the experience you gather as you operate in the field.

On this one operation, we were being supported by Seawolf helicopters on call for the first time. After inserting by PBR, we patrolled along a number of paddy dikes to check out a village that was supposed to have a number of VCI (Viet Cong Infrastructure) officers and cadres living in it. After setting up our security perimeter, we checked out the village. Searching the hooches, we found little more than women and children and a large quantity of food and general gear. The amount of materials indicated that the village was used by the VC, only the targets we wanted weren't there at the time—or so we thought.

As we moved out from the village, we were ambushed by the men we had been looking for. While we had searched the village, the VC had been waiting outside our perimeter, preparing to ambush us.

The ambush didn't go well for the VC. We were able to bust through their killing zone before they had a chance to set it up properly. While we ran from the ambush, the Seawolves came in and demonstrated the skill and bravery that made them such an asset to the SEALs throughout the Vietnam War. We headed toward the river for extraction, with the Seawolves covering our trail. Still, the situation was a hot one for us, and it became even hotter for me.

Moving along still on point, I pushed a low hanging tree branch aside while keeping an eye out for possible boobytraps or another ambush. As I ducked under the tree branch, I was ambushed by an enemy I wasn't looking for.

There was a nest of stinging red ants on the branch I ducked under. When I pushed through the vegetation, hundreds of the ants fell on me and slipped down my neck and under my shirt.

There are cultures in this world that use stinging ants as a torture, and I can tell you that must be some mighty bad interrogation. Those ants slipped down my back, stinging and biting all the way. The ants weren't poisonous and wouldn't have caused me any real damage, but I took care of the possibility of damage myself.

While I had been running along, I had been carrying my XM-148/CAR-15 with my fingers on both triggers and the safeties off. We were in the middle of a firefight and I thought I would need the weapons at any moment. When the ants started stinging me, I clenched my hands and fired both weapons.

The roar of the CAR-15 going off was bad, but as the point man, I didn't have anybody in front of me who could be hit accidentally. What I did have to worry about was the high-explosive grenade launched from the XM-148. The 40mm M384 HE round is a small charge of explosive wrapped with a coil of square wire, notched every quarter inch or so for fragmentation. As the grenade fired, my immediate thought was, *That 40mm has a five-meter killing radius!* The round smacked into the paddy dike not six feet from where I was standing.

However, the same engineers who had designed the 40mm grenade to be so lethal also put in a minimum safety distance within which the fuze will not arm. That was so idiots like me would have to work harder to blow themselves up.

Not having the grenade to worry about, I now concentrated on the little red torturers running up and down my back. The squad didn't know what had happened; they just saw me open fire into the dirt and start jumping about like a madman. "It's goddamn ants or something," I said. "They've gone down my back!"

Now, I love Bob Gallagher dearly, one of the reasons being the Eagle's ability to size up a situation calmly and see exactly what to do.

"Shit," he said, "jump into the canal and drown them."

After I followed Bob's advice, the ants stopped being much of a problem. Our other problem, the VC, caused the squad to follow me in jumping into the canal, giving the Seawolves an even more open field of fire. We pulled out of the area, the VC chasing us and the Seawolves covering us all of the way. Getting to the river, we extracted and finally had a chance to catch our breath.

As I said earlier, from that point on I started wearing a wide-brimmed floppy bush hat on operations. I also started keeping an eye out for more than just man-made boobytraps while on patrol.

Some of the guys during our first tour developed a fascination with the local wildlife—the critters, not just the ladies—early on. The first week in April 1967, R. A. Tolison bought a pet monkey while he was up in Saigon. The little beast was cute and was soon put to work as a traditional navy "deck ape" on board a Mike boat.

Just within a couple of days, another monkey, this time a pretty wild one, was caught and also put on board the Mike boat. No matter what you might see in the movies or on TV, monkeys make lousy pets. They're nasty and dirty, and can have real bad tempers. On the other hand, they can be funny as all hell and do the damnedest things trying to copy you.

One time, we all wondered what a drunk monkey might look like. After giving it a little scotch, we found out: It looks a lot like a sailor on shore leave after a long time at sea. A monkey with a hangover, on the other hand, looks like a chain saw waiting for you to grab hold of the blade. Only I think a chain saw might do less damage.

One of the monkeys—I think it was R.A.'s—we named Jocko, but I don't remember what the other one was named. It didn't matter much; the other monkey never left Vietnam. One day while we were working in the Ordnance shed, the area where we kept our special weapons and explosives, that monkey decided to try to act like a big bad combat man.

The little beast got hold of a fragmentation grenade and hightailed it into a nearby bunker. I don't know whether the monkey thought it was food or what, but one thing was for sure—none of us were going into that bunker.

Since there wasn't anything of importance in the bunker, we just stood around outside, drinking beer and waiting. Some of the guys made bets on how long we would have to wait and started a pool on time periods.

Then the inevitable happened: That monkey pulled the pin, grenade went off—THUD!—and the bunker shook a little and dust rose up from the sandbags. Scratch one monkey and time to clean out the bunker.

Jocko, on the other hand, ended up going back to the States with us and became something of a mascot back at Team Two. Frank Scollice would be seen tooling around Virginia Beach with Jocko on a leash, riding in the car with him. At the occasional stoplight, Jocko would jump up on the hood of the car and let everyone around know what he thought of being taken from Vietnam to Virginia.

CHAPTER 17

The Black Market

WHEN U.S. SOLDIERS began arriving in Vietnam in large numbers, they affected the local economy in a number of ways. Not the least of these was the fact that the average GI, sailors included, was paid a great deal more than his South Vietnamese counterpart. In general, the U.S. serviceman enjoyed a much higher standard of living than the average Vietnamese, North or South.

This situation aggravated something that has developed in every war zone since Cain chased Abel. What I'm talking about is the black market. A black market arises anytime there is a shortage of some desired commodity, and in a war zone there are all kinds of shortages. The fact that the average U.S. serviceman had a comparatively great deal of money to spend just caused the black market to grow larger and faster than it otherwise would have.

One thing that was in short supply on the black market in Vietnam was, surprisingly enough, money. "Hard currency," or plain old money, never seemed to be in a great enough supply in Vietnam. Vietnamese piasters were on the market, but nobody who was dealing in anything worthwhile wanted them. Deals were made in materials, even drugs, gold, and foreign currency. Greenbacks were wanted most of all, good old U.S. dollars, and the larger denomination the bill, the better.

Paying for stolen goods to sell on the black market with piasters just didn't get you anywhere very fast. "Importers"—read fences—needed to pay their own suppliers or other people with money they could spend. And eventually, if you followed the supply pipeline long enough, you often found an American at the end of it, and you better pay that greedy bastard in cash. This whole situation created a black market for money, at an exchange rate much better than any official trading.

The system worked something like this. If you had greenbacks to exchange, you had no trouble finding someone to help you make the contacts you needed. Small amounts were exchanged right on the street by people who would search you out. The U.S. serviceman on pass was constantly approached with offers to sell him services and products and to buy any money he might have.

If the official exchange rate was, say, 150 piasters to the dollar, for a U.S. $20 bill you could get 250P to the dollar on the black market. Bigger bills would get better rates. A $50 bill might get you 300 to 400P per dollar, and a $100 bill a better exchange rate yet. Even MPC (military pay certificates), which were also not supposed to be in the hands of the Vietnamese, were accepted on the black market and even exchanged like dollars, though not very readily and at a much lower rate.

When I was platoon chief for Sixth Platoon on my second tour, I had already had my experiences with the black market in Vietnam. One of the things I wanted my men to know was the dangers of trading with these people. Besides the obvious fact that you were dealing with a rough crowd and had no legal recourse if and when you were screwed, the VC were involved in the black market big time.

What I taught my men was that, if you became involved in such trading, all you did was help buy the bullet that killed you. My men listened, and I don't know of any who became involved in the black market. As I was the platoon chief, my men looked up to me for a different kind of leadership than they got from either the platoon officer or the assistant platoon officer. I like to think that I fulfilled their trust in me.

From what I understood, a number of U.S. personnel were involved in the black market in Vietnam. Many of these people had their families back in the States send them greenbacks in the mail. The exchange was made and piasters accepted. Then these same citizens deposited their piasters in a checking account at the Bank of America. When they went home, the piasters were exchanged, at the official rate, for U.S. funds. A clean scam and little or no proof available of illegal dealings.

Some aspects of the black market were dabbled in by the SEALs, even myself. Never was there any dealing, at least not in my platoons, and I don't believe even at Team Two, but there were practicalities to consider.

The PX got shipments of liquor only at certain times, and no matter how hard we tried, we couldn't get to a PX while the shelves were full. Either the PX was sold out, or you had used up the monthly allotment on your ration card. This was a serious situation, and to take care of the problem, we bought booze on the black market. But you better believe it pissed us off to do so.

Shortages weren't a problem, though. All you had to do was walk through downtown Saigon and there were the goods, being sold on the street. The American exchange might have run out of Jim Beam or whatever, but you could be sure that the little mama-san down in the market would have a bottle or two out on her blanket, table, or stall. So much for the security and fairness of the ration cards and PX system.

Sometimes, an op against whoever was helping to supply the market seemed like a good idea. But we were busy enough just dealing with Charlie and his northern cousins. Besides, the black markets were there before there were SEALs and they will be around long after we're gone.

CHAPTER 18

Personal Camouflage

O NE OF THE THINGS THAT WE LEARNED well before going to Vietnam was the value of camouflage. It was amazing the way you could blend into the background if you were properly camouflaged and just stayed still. Movement draws the eye quicker than anything. But if there isn't any recognizable pattern or outline for the eyes to settle on, an observer just looks right past you.

Camouflage was also what earned the SEALs their nickname in Vietnam, "the men with green faces." When the SEALs first began operating in Vietnam, the VC had no idea just who we were. The Army always moved in large groups, there were no Marines in the Delta, and the Navy stayed on boats in the rivers. We didn't operate like any of them. All Charlie did know was that there was a new player on the field, a player who operated in the same way that Charlie did himself.

The VC started to pass around a description of green-faced devils that appeared from out of the night. And when the devils disappeared, either somebody was missing or there were just bodies lying around. Rarely were there any witnesses and often there hadn't been a sound. The Vietnamese called us either "the men with green faces" or sometimes "the devils with green faces." Either way, our camouflage had become our trademark in the Delta of Vietnam.

There never was any kind of standard pattern to our face camouflage in the Teams—at least I'm certain there wasn't on the east coast. Things may have been different in Coronado with Team One. What standard there was consisted of the basic rule of lightening the shaded areas, such as the eyes, and darkening the highlights like the cheeks, nose, and forehead. Patterns were supposed to be irregular and cut across facial features. In this way, the face would be broken up, would be less recognizable, and would blend in more with the jungle.

Camouflaged faces were something of a game for us at first—who could be the ugliest, scariest, or funniest? Besides being good for a laugh, the camo game had a good side effect, and that was scaring the hell out of the VC. Though I don't have any photos of myself all cammied up, I do have one of R. A. Tolison coming off an op during our first tour. With his tiger-stripe fatigues, floppy bush hat, and cammied face, R.A. looks like a stepped-on toad that has been left out in the sun to get ripe.

On the serious side, face and skin camouflage was important. Not only did you have to break up the features of the face, but the oils in the skin shone and reflected light. This might not seem like much just looking at people during the day, but at night it really made a hell of a difference. The oils in a person's sweat would make the face gleam and stand out with only a little light shining.

Though you might not expect it to be the case, black men have even more trouble with camouflaging their faces. Dark skin tends to break up the features well enough, but perspiration makes a black man's face gleam like a mirror in the dark. So even Bill Goines, the only black man in Team Two at the beginning, cammied up right along with the rest of us in Vietnam.

The camouflage face paint sticks the Army had available weren't exactly the best thing for the job, but during our first tour in 1967, they were all that was available. The Army camouflage face stick comes in a small metal can, three quarters of an inch in diameter and maybe half the length of a cigar tube, with caps at both ends. Inside the tube is a double-ended stick, officially light green on one end and loam on the other. The colors really were just green and olive drab.

The paint sticks were a bitch to use: They were hard, and you could never get the paint to come off the stick well. Ultimately, we used the trick of putting bug juice (insect repellent) on the ends of the sticks to make them spread better. But after doing that, you could smell the insect repellent. And anybody who tells you that the jungle odors mask smell just hasn't been there. The smell of insect repellent carried pretty far. The VC claimed to be able to smell American beef-eater GIs just by their sweat. I wonder how much of that claim can be laid on bug juice's door.

Besides its consistency problems, the Army camo stick irritated the hell out of your skin if you used it for a long time. And the SEALs cammied up for every operation. You would carry a camo stick with you on long ops to put on more camo as sweating and brushing against objects wore the stuff off. All in all, paint sticks were not one of the high points of the Vietnam War.

By 1968, a cosmetics company came to the relief of the SEALs in Vietnam. The Elizabeth Arden company had been approached by the folks in the Naval Special Warfare Projects office at China Lake. After being told our complaints about the issue camouflage face paints, Elizabeth Arden's people quickly came up with a superior replacement. The new cosmetic camouflage paint came in half-ounce and one-ounce squeeze tubes like toothpaste tubes. The colors were light green and loam; later black was added.

The Arden stuff was great and was at a premium in Vietnam. The makeup went on easily, didn't wash off from your sweat quite as fast, and was not irritating if you wore it a long time. The manufacturer had even put a nonsmelly insect repellent in the mix. You still had to touch up the stuff in the field after an extended op, but the small tubes fit into your pocket easily enough.

Later in the war, a small compact-type container was available. I never used one, but I heard that the compact had several colors of makeup in it, as well as a small mirror. Just the thing to get ready for a date when you were going out dancing with Charlie. I'm not sure I would have wanted one of the compacts; I heard the guys who had them took a lot of razzing from their fellow SEALs.

Joking aside, the camouflage was serious enough. Before going out on an op, you usually cammied yourself up, but occasionally guys would cammy each other up to make sure they covered everything. The face, ears, and back of the neck were all painted. Even the hands were cammied up at first, but that camo didn't stay on very long.

It may have been Frank Moncrief who did it first, but a bunch of the guys started wearing black leather glove shells on ops. You couldn't feel your weapon or have good sensitivity with your fingers when wearing gloves. To remedy this, Frank and the other guys cut the fingers off their gloves at the first joint. You had just a covering for the back of your hand and part of your fingers, good enough camouflage and protection for the hands as well. I never wore the gloves; I always wanted all the touch I had in my hands in case of boobytraps and trip wires when I walked point.

The effectiveness of camouflage was amazing, and very difficult to believe on your first exposure to it. During World War I, the Navy tried a kind of camouflage paint for ships called dazzle pattern, developed by the British. The pattern was jagged lines of contrasting colors. Sitting next to a dock, a ship painted in dazzle pattern would stand out sharply. At sea, it would be very hard for something, such as a submarine, to target that same ship, because you couldn't see it clearly enough to calculate a good bearing or speed.

Though used again during World War II, dazzle pattern was eventually rendered obsolete by modern sensor systems. Besides, traditional Navy officers liked their ships to have a smart, neat look about them. Dazzle pattern, something like the SEALs themselves, was too out of the ordinary for general acceptance by the black-shoe Navy.

I really learned about camouflage while I was in Army Ranger School back in 1965. During the swamp phase down at Eglin Air Force Base in Florida, the importance of proper face and skin camouflage was first brought home. In one operation, we were going to go down onto the white sand beaches of the Gulf of Mexico. The instructor gave us some orders that were a little hard to swallow. "Now, look," he said, "you're probably not going to believe this. You've all been pretty heavy on camouflage all through Delanica [mountain phase] and while you were at Bragg. Now you're going to be on white sand. Think about that. For this, you want to wear white shirts."

"You have got to be shitting me" was my answer. "At night, you want us to wear white to blend in!"

It was hard to believe, but we followed orders. And the white shirts we wore did blend into the background of the beach. If a man was ten yards away from you, you couldn't see him. On the other hand, if a man was wearing regulation fatigues, dark olive-drab cloth, you could pick out his silhouette.

Though I am probably biased toward the Navy SEALs, the Army did teach me some good lessons in Ranger School, lessons that I was able to pass along once I got back to the Team. Even as a hard-headed SEAL, I was willing to learn from others' experience. When I was in France in 1966, my French swim buddy John gave me a set of tiger-stripe coveralls. It was still very classified information as to whether Team Two would be sending any SEALs to Vietnam. But the writing was on the wall for any experienced fighting man to see that the Vietnam War was expanding.

John was a French swimmer-commando and had experience in French Indochina, later Vietnam. He knew which camouflage worked the best in the jungles and grasses. He also admonished me to keep the coveralls in the same shape as when he gave them to me, no bullet holes.

Tiger stripes were one of the better camouflage patterns for us to wear in Vietnam. The jagged lines of light and dark in a tiger-stripe pattern blended in very well with the wavering shadows cast by tall grasses and reeds. At the very beginning of the Teams, Roy Boehm had purchased a bunch of camouflage coveralls to help us hide in the night. These coveralls were commercial patterns of mostly brown and tan splotches such as you would see a duck hunter wear. All of those early outfits were pretty well used up by the time Team Two was sending platoons to Vietnam.

For the most part, in Vietnam we wore whatever issue camouflage uniforms were available. A number of the guys, myself included, would wear blue jeans on operations for their increased protection in the brush. Even though blue isn't the most common color in the jungle, there wasn't much of any problem with the pants showing up and giving someone away. You didn't stay clean long enough while on an op for the blue to stand out anyway.

Today, many of the Teams wear black uniforms and web gear for most of their operations. Though tiger stripes are rare, you can still see the occasional old-timer in the Teams with a tiger-stripe uniform on a training op. New camouflage uniforms specific for an operating area are available for today's SEALs. White coveralls for northern ops, tan camo for the desert, and different green and brown patterns for jungle or forest areas are issued. And many of the uniforms are treated to keep the body's infrared signature at a low level because of all the sensors on the battlefield today. A long step from the Levi's, black pajama top, and floppy bush hat I wore in Vietnam.

CHAPTER 19

Heavy Weapons and Firepower

W E DIDN'T MUCH USE heavy weapons in the Teams during the Vietnam War. Firepower was something we were concerned with primarily in terms of volume of fire. A SEAL squad, or even a platoon, wasn't large enough to perform any kind of holding action, especially against a larger force. When we made contact, we wanted to put out an overwhelming quantity of fire in a very short time, preferably without reloading.

Actions like the above would often stun an enemy force, holding it in place long enough for us to get the hell out of there. "He who fights and runs away lives to fight another day" was a saying closely followed by the Teams in Vietnam.

When Team Two first deployed direct-action platoons to Vietnam in 1967, we were still developing our basic idea of firepower. A good example of this was the weapons we mounted on the STABs at Team Two. Prior to our deployment, a number of different weapons were tried out aboard the STABs. We even tested the M20 3.5-inch rocket launcher (bazooka) to see if it would be a valuable addition to the STABs.

The bazooka was just too large and unwieldy for convenient use, and the ammunition too limited in its effects, for the weapon to be worth our taking along. But the idea of having a heavy weapon on board the STABs stayed with us. If it was on board, we wouldn't have to man-carry it, a major argument against our using heavy weapons.

When we arrived in Vietnam in 1967, the primary weapons aboard the STABs were .50-caliber M2 and 7.62mm M60 machine guns. Field experience quickly taught us that the .50s, though very powerful, had ammunition that was just too bulky for the number of rounds available on board the relatively small STABs. The .50s were dismounted and the space filled in with M60s.

The 7.62mm M60s could have 800 rounds of ammunition stored in the same space that was taken up by only 210 rounds of linked .50-caliber ammo. This gave the STABs a much greater organic unit of fire. We could put out more effective rounds for a longer time than we had before. But our volume of fire, the number of effective rounds that could be put out in a short time, was still something we wanted to increase.

Later in the war, the 7.62mm minigun showed up in the Teams. The little six-barreled GE minigun could put out a whopping six thousand rounds per minute—that's one hundred rounds per second—when firing at its maximum rate. When mounted in a gun tub with a useful amount of ammunition, such as was put into the Mike boat, the minigun was a major firepower multiplier. But the ammunition and power supply requirements of the minigun just made it impractical to put it aboard the STABs. Besides, we didn't have the damned thing available to us during my first tour.

What we did have available was several extra .50-caliber machine guns. One weapon we wanted was a 90mm recoilless rifle. Though the Teams did have 57mm M18 recoilless rifles available, they were a World War II design and much larger and heavier than they had to be by the mid-1960s. The M67 90mm recoilless rifle was a later design and weighed five pounds less than an M18 57mm, while at the same time firing a shell almost twice as large.

What we wanted the 90mm for was primarily to use the M590 canister—commonly called beehive—rounds that were available for it. The M590 canister round turned the M67 into a giant shoulder-fired shotgun, launching 2,400 finned steel fléchettes out to a maximum range of three hundred meters. Though the 57mm had the T25E5 canister round available for it, that rather anemic round carried only between 150 and 175 steel slugs that it could throw out to over fifty meters. In a choice between the two, there wasn't much choice at all.

The thing was, the M67 was an Army weapon and not available

in Navy stores. This was not a problem for Rick Marcinko's Merry Marauders. It seemed that a local Army armored cavalry outfit had a shortage of .50-caliber machine guns. The Army captain in charge of these APCs (armored personnel carriers) in the Delta just couldn't get enough .50 calibers to outfit his vehicles to his satisfaction. But the captain did have an M67 recoilless rifle that he wasn't using. Very quickly, the Army captain was the proud owner of a brace of .50s and we had our recoilless rifle.

Ammunition wasn't really much of a problem; we stole it from the Army in Dong Tam. Since we wanted only the beehive round, we could get what we needed without too much trouble. Actually, "stole" is too strong a word; "traded for" or, better yet "cumshawed for" is a more accurate description. "Cumshaw" is a good Navy term that basically means shrewd trading. Of course in the case of the ammunition, the trading tended to be a one-way deal; we got something but the Army didn't.

The 90mm worked pretty well for us, though we didn't use it very often. When we got in a world of shit or wandered into an ambush, it was just the thing to convince Charlie we were too much to mess with.

Some good came to others because of our little cannon as well. Some of the PBR guys we were operating with kept getting sniped at from a particular point in the river near Toy Son. We had an operation going on that particular night, and so weren't available to help the PBR guys take out the sniper. Instead, we loaned them the 90mm recoilless and some ammo, and showed them how to operate it.

Bob Gallagher laid out a simple plan for the PBR sailors to follow that was likely to get them good results. "Take this life jacket," Bog told the guys, "and attach a one-cell survival light [a small flashlight] up on the collar where it can be seen from shore. Tow the jacket behind the PBR on a good length of rope and make sure the jacket floats with the light on the upper side.

"Keep one or two of your guys on watch, armed with M16s loaded with just tracers. When they see a muzzle flash from the sniper firing at the life jacket, they can point out the spot with their tracers. Be sure they fire on semiautomatic only: nice, steady, single shots spaced out evenly. With the M16 guys laying in on the sniper's flash with the tracers, you can aim at the spot with the 90 and let him have it."

The plan worked without a hitch. The next day the PBR guys gave us back our 90mm and said that they had opened fire on the sniper and never heard a shot in return.

Not hearing any return fire was good, but that could have been due just to firing the 90mm recoilless. I swear, that weapon had to be the loudest thing I ever heard that you could shoot from your shoulder. With the backblast tearing out from the rear of the damned thing and the buzz saw of fléchettes going out the front, it was dangerous from both ends.

We didn't use the 90mm for very long. For me, it was just during that first tour, and it was a very large and heavy weapon for use by the SEALs. But while we had it, it did a good job. Today the Teams are still using the same idea in a new weapon. The Carl Gustav 84mm recoilless rifle is found in the Teams' armories and is an even smaller, lighter chunk of firepower.

CHAPTER 20

Artillery,
the Really Big Gun

F OR ALL OF THE ABILITY of the SEALs in combat, we were not
supermen. What made things work for us more often than not
was the fire support we actually received during an operation. Air
support is a whole subject in itself. We had mostly helicopter gunships at our disposal, but fixed-wing craft were also around and
occasionally used to good advantage. Other fire support came from
heavy artillery of one kind or another. During a mission briefing,
we would be told what kind of artillery was available for us, where
it was located, and how to contact it.

Funny thing was, of all the different kinds of artillery units available to us throughout the Vietnam War, it was naval gunfire support that was the most accurate. Having been aboard large Navy
craft at sea and having seen the complicated procedures they went
through in order to direct and fire the guns, I had a hard time understanding how a ship could be more accurate than land-based
batteries.

Firing from a ship, you had to contend with the ship's moving
forward, rolling from side to side, and possibly pitching fore and
aft; with crosswinds, if any; and with a target that was far over the
horizon. In an actual naval battle, your target was also moving.
With land-based artillery, you still had the same problems of wind
and distance, but at least your gun was standing still when you fired
it. That didn't seem to matter, however; naval gunfire support was
just more accurate and by far the preferred backup for a SEAL
mission.

U.S. Army artillery was okay. It was certainly better to have those 105- and 155-millimeter guns covering your backside than just leaving your ass out in the breeze. It was ARVN artillery that was a bit dicey to use sometimes. Those guys just seemed not to be able to read a map, let alone accurately drop fire anywhere near your position. There were times the ARVN artillery units seemed to be working more for the NVA than our side. Personally, I never used ARVN arty support, but when your back is to the wall, you'll call in anybody who could help.

The one time I did run into direct problems with artillery support, it was an American unit that was causing the problem. It was during my second tour in Vietnam with Sixth Platoon near Long An. We had just finished a body snatch operation and were on our way out of the AO. Things were going well; we only had about two or three klicks to go and we would be able to meet up with the Mike boat for our extraction. All of a sudden, I heard the very distinct *thoop* sound of an M79 firing.

The only guy in our patrol who was armed with a 40mm M79 was Doc (Larry Johnston), our corpsman. Out of habit, I always placed the corpsman on rear security, so Doc was at the far end of the patrol. Calling a halt, I moved back to Doc's position to find out just what he had been shooting at. There had been no danger signal sent up the line and something just wasn't right.

Reaching Doc's position, I asked him, "What are you shooting at?"

Doc's reply was "I ain't shooting!"

"You heard that 40mm go off, didn't you?" I asked.

"Yeah."

"Did you hear the round detonate? Because I didn't."

"Nope."

"And you didn't shoot?"

"Nope."

At this time something came up to distract me from the problem of the ghost 40mm. Overhead, we suddenly started to hear the freight train sound of 155mm artillery rounds traveling through the air. After being out in the field long enough, you were able to distin-

guish the different calibers of artillery rounds going overhead by
the sound that they made. This was a sound I was very familiar
with. Only this time I wasn't the one calling in the fire.

Being downrange of somebody else's fire mission was not where
I wanted to be. Suddenly, our mission wasn't going as well as it had
been just a few moments before. Getting on the radio, I called back
to the local TOC (Tactical Operations Center), which coordinated
local fire support. Our radio procedure wasn't the most formal in
the world, and this was one of the occasions where simplicity over-
rode the need for technique.

"Knock off the shit" was my simple message to the TOC.

"What do you mean, Whiskey Sour?" was the puzzled response.

"I mean knock off the artillery," I said. "It's going out right
over our heads!"

"Hold on, Whiskey Sour. We'll contact the firebase." And the
TOC put me on hold.

Nice position to be in, inside enemy territory with friendly gunfire going overhead. And somewhere there was a ghost M79 to be
concerned about. And I hate being put on hold.

"Whiskey Sour," called the TOC after a couple of ice ages had
passed, "they're not shooting."

"What!" I answered, starting to get pissed. "Don't tell me
they're not shooting, because if Charlie has got 155s I'm getting the
hell out of here and going home!"

In spite of the shells going overhead, we continued to move out
to our extraction point. The artillery didn't strike anywhere near
us, but it was still a bad situation. We never did find out what had
caused the sound that stopped the patrol. What I did find out the
next morning didn't exactly fill me with confidence in our military
brothers in the Army.

Arriving at the TOC and the artillery units near Long An, I
found out that they had indeed been firing the night before. But
they knew it couldn't have been their arty I had heard; the target
they'd been shooting at wasn't anywhere near us. Only thing was,
somebody had misread the map coordinates. So, it turned out, they

had bombarded our area by mistake. Shit happens, and we were lucky to get away clean at times.

The best SEAL story concerning artillery that I heard involved Harry Humphries during his PRU adviser tour in 1968 or 1969. As I said before, our radiotelephone procedures would sometimes take a backseat to expediency when we felt the situation demanded it.

During one of the refresher courses at Gunfire Support School, which we always took prior to a deployment, one Marine major always closed his air support session with the same advice. "All right, gentlemen," he would say, "you have now learned all the proper procedures, nomenclature, targeting, and effects. All that is well and good, but remember, if you get in trouble out there, we speak English. So do you. Just tell us what you see and where it is. We'll take it from there. You don't have to ask for 'one round white phosphorus' or 'fuze super-quick.' We know what we have and what it does better than you do. Just tell us what the target is and where you see it. We'll take care of it."

The artillery people didn't exactly like that advice the one time I knew of someone really following it. Harry Humphries was a PRU adviser operating out of Can Tho. One night Harry and his people began getting into it hot and heavy with a bunch of VC. Having walked into a hornets' nest, Harry did the best thing he could. He called in fire.

The target was enemy troops in the open. What was available was Army artillery, 105s and 155s. Apparently, Harry had a grandstand view of what the artillery was doing to the target, not something that happened every day. The results got Harry a little excited.

Calling in on the radio, Harry said, "Sock it to 'em, sock it to 'em. Do it! Do it!" as the artillery poured in on his target. After quite a bit of fire, and the elimination of the enemy threat, Harry called back, "Okay, that's enough! That's enough!"

When Harry got back to the base, an Army officer came up to him. The man just got right into Harry's face. "Where did you get your gunfire support training?" the officer demanded. "Don't you know how to call in a fire mission?"

"What are you talking about?" Harry asked, completely unruffled.

"What's this comment, 'That's enough'? It should have been 'End of fire mission.' "

"No," Harry answered, "just like I said. You got them all; that's enough." And with that, Harry walked away.

It wasn't often that you could really see what artillery was doing to a target, but that big gun at the other end of your radio was sure a comforting thought while you were in the field. We did have smaller fire support available to us on occasion, and we did see this stuff hit the target.

Besides all of the small arms, 40mms, and machine guns aboard a Mike boat, there was also a 106mm recoilless rifle carried on the overhead. The 106 fires a walloping big shell for such a small piece of artillery, and the backblast coming out the other end makes one hell of a noise as well. We used both high-explosive and fléchette rounds with the 106. It was great when taking out a bunker at range with HE or clearing an area with a storm of fléchette "needles."

What wasn't popular about the 106 was the fact that it stood out in the open on top of the Mike boat. It might have packed a big punch, but nobody wanted to get out from under the armored sides of the Mike's hull and service the gun during a firefight.

Other "artillery" was also available on the Mike boat for our use. In an open area at the bow of the boat was an 81mm Mark 2 direct-fire mortar. Developed at the Navy Gun Factory in Washington, D.C., the 81mm Mark 2 could act as a standard muzzle-loading mortar and fire all the standard Army mortar rounds. When operated like a standard mortar, the Mark 2 was aimed at a target and the round to be fired was dropped into the muzzle. As soon as the round struck the bottom of the barrel, it hit a firing pin and was launched in a high arc to a target that could be out of sight behind a hill, building, or obstacle.

What made the Mark 2 especially neat was the fact that it could be fired as a trigger-operated, direct-fire weapon. In this mode, it could be aimed directly at a target and fired by pulling a trigger, just like a regular firearm. The direct-fire system was what I most liked about the Mark 2, and it could really put a hurt on a target. The nine-pound M362 HE round could blast apart a VC bunker with a single good hit.

Though I never personally used one, early in the Vietnam War, the Navy even came out with a fléchette round for the Mark 2 mortar. The 81mm Mark 120 Mod O antipersonnel round could be used only in the Mark 2 mortar and then only in the direct-fire mode. Carrying twelve hundred steel fléchettes that were released soon after leaving the weapon's muzzle, the Mark 120 round would turn the Mark 2 mortar into a 3-inch shotgun with a maximum range of 183 meters.

Though the 81mm was normally very accurate when fired, I still have a vivid recollection of the one on the Mike boat giving my squad fire support during our first tour in Vietnam. While struggling through a wide tidal flat of deep mud, Bravo Squad of Second Platoon was trying to extract from a bunch of very pissed-off VC we had found on Ilo Ilo island. Waiting just a few hundred yards away was the Mike boat, putting out covering fire over our heads to the VC they could see onshore.

In spite of the situation, the sight of an 81mm HE round skipping along the water and the mud caused me to pause and stare. Right between Bob Gallagher and myself dashed the deadly bomb, touching the surface every so often just like a flat stone skipped across a pond. The mortar shell continued on its way until it finally detonated against the shore of Ilo Ilo. The 81mm Mark 2 might be accurate, but that's cutting things just a little too close.

Still, Bob and I thought the idea of a mortar on a small boat was pretty neat. Some higher-ups in Ordnance must have thought the same thing, because later on during the Vietnam War, they designed a small, direct-fire 60mm mortar called the Mark 4. The Mark 4 could be mounted on a .50-caliber pintle such as those used on the back of a PBR. But during my first tour in 1967, the Mark 4 wasn't available yet; or if it was, nobody told us, because we would have wanted one.

The regular Army M19 60mm mortar was something that Bob and I wanted to try out in one of our STABs. The M19 was a regular muzzle-loaded mortar that could be drop-fired or fired with a trigger. Though it couldn't be direct-fired like the Mark 2 81mm, the M19 could put out a nice little three-pound M49 HE round to a respectable distance. Since the fiberglass hull of the STAB couldn't stand up to the direct recoil of a 60mm mortar, we came up with an adaptation for the boat. What Bob had me do was build a wooden box big enough to hold the baseplate of the mortar. Inside the box, we placed several layers of cut-down Navy mattress.

Instead of using the bipod of the M19, we hand-held the tube of the mortar and used Kentucky windage to help aim it. "Hey, look over there," Bob would call out as he saw the round hit. "Bring it up a little bit." Moving the tube slightly according to Bob's direction, I'd drop in another round and fire it downrange.

In general the system worked pretty well and had its uses in the field. An improvement Bob wanted to try was tying a string to the muzzle of the mortar with ranging knots tied into it. By holding the proper knot against the top of the box, we could have brought the mortar on target much faster. We had fun with the system but never did go very far with it. But that little mortar was fire support Bravo Squad could take with us on our travels in Indian territory whenever we used the STAB.

CHAPTER 21

Prisoners, Interrogations, and Father Hoa

N OT ALL OF THE SEAL OPERATIONS I was on in Vietnam were exciting shoot-'em-ups where your adrenaline was pumping and afterward you wondered where the time had gone. The average operation involved a lot of waiting quietly for your target to show up. Sometimes you could be on a site where you knew a particular target was going to show up at a pretty specific time. But more often, you worked on less detailed intel, came in early to a target site, and waited one hell of a long time.

During my third tour in Vietnam, I was working as the platoon chief for Sixth Platoon, which was probably the most successful individual SEAL platoon of the entire war. No small part of our platoon's success was due to our leadership. Lieutenant Louis Boink, now Captain Boink, was our platoon leader, and they don't come much sharper than Lou. Nicknamed the Marlboro Man by Fast Eddie Leasure, Lou Boink could sit down and practically stare a VC prisoner into telling everything he knew. Solid, hard, and stable as hell, Lou was like the prototype image of what a SEAL officer should be.

On one operation I was sitting along a canal bank, just waiting for the target to show up. Maybe three yards from me was Lou Boink. Squatting there in the mud, I could see Lou very clearly. He had his weapon in his left hand and had his right index finger in the mud, just swirling it in circles.

Has the boss lost it? I thought to myself as I watched. Just what the hell was he doing? Crawling over to where Lou was, I crept up close to him and, putting my mouth close to his ear, whispered, "Boss, are you all right?"

"Yeah," he answered very quietly.

"What are you doing?"

"Playing in the mud."

"Playing in the mud?" I asked with more than a little question in my voice.

"Yeah," Lou went on, "I'm sitting here just thinking."

"What are you thinking about?"

"Here I am," Lou answered, "with all of my education and everything, an officer in the United States Navy. And I'm playing in the mud waiting for some asshole to walk in front of me so that I can shoot him and go home."

It was everything that I could do to keep from busting out laughing right there in the middle of a free-fire zone. You have to know Lou to understand the humor in this, but the irony of the situation was really something. Lou was a very educated man and a real leader in the SEALs, and here we were, squatting in he mud, waiting to do what man has been doing to his fellowman since we started to walk the earth.

Ninety percent of the success that Sixth Platoon enjoyed could be credited directly to Lou Boink's leadership and abilities. And in spite of what he said that time on the mud bank, just killing somebody was never the way Lou operated. The big thing for Sixth, and the SEALs as a whole, was to develop intelligence on the enemy. With proper intel, you could operate better, faster, and safer than by just going out to try to ring up a body count.

Lou knew how important it was for our platoon to start making the right connections with the right people in an intelligence network. Whether the people connected were in our own intelligence agency, Father Hoa, or whoever, all of them were valuable resources. Very soon after arriving incountry, Sixth Platoon started hitting bigger and better targets. When we hit, we hit big time, and much of that success was due to prior planning and preparation.

We were so successful that back home people started questioning our results. Even Bob Gallagher, who knew I was operating as Sixth's platoon chief, questioned our results. "They just can't be getting district- and province-level prisoners all of the time" was something Bob was heard to say.

In reality, we had developed our intel sources to the point that it wasn't worth the risk to go after just a local village-level VC unless we knew he would lead us to better targets. That wasn't to say that we hit our targets all the time. Sixth Platoon had its share of dry holes where we came up empty. That operation where I saw Lou doodling in the mud turned out to be an empty op. And there wasn't anything you could do about a dry hole; you just got pissed off and tried a little harder the next time.

Ambushes could come up empty more often than other ops. Sometimes the timing wasn't quite right or the target just went another way. But a body snatch tended to be successful more often. And capturing a target was what we preferred. Questioning a prisoner could lead to greater targets further up the line. The best you could do with a body was gather up any papers it might have on it and just chalk up the body count.

Intel might say that a certain group of people would be coming down a given canal at a given time. And with information like that, the most you could usually do was set up an ambush and take out the target. A dead man couldn't tell you as much as a live one, and captures during an ambush were more difficult than a planned snatch. But taking out a high-level VC leader could still disrupt their operations badly.

Because of the VC cell system, the overall Viet Cong organization was a hard nut to crack. The VC used three-person cells where each man could tell you about only the two other men in his group. Only one man in a cell, usually the oldest veteran, knew one man in another cell, and that was how they moved the information along. Each cell was attached to a three-cell squad and three squads formed a VC platoon. This organization minimized damage from a man taken prisoner. By the time you managed to work your way along through the cell structure—and failing to capture a prisoner

alive could break the line at any point—word had gotten out that
a cell had been broken and the whole structure would be collapsed
by the VC themselves.

The best targets, and the ones we actively looked for, were VC
security or intelligence types. A security chief was one of the best
prisoners you could take, because that son of a bitch knew how the
whole province was put together. He would be one smart cookie
and could tell you about local POW camps, who the tax people
were, when they operated, where the caches were—a real gold mine
of information. But at the same time, the kind of man the VC made
a security chief would be a hard-core Communist and a very difficult man to crack, if you could crack him at all.

Interrogating somebody is an art, just like being a SEAL is an
art and not just the result of training. And SEALs are not trained
as interrogators; that was a lesson I learned real fast in Vietnam.
To the best of my knowledge, no SEAL was trained as an interrogator. We picked up little tricks on our own as we operated in Vietnam. Sometimes we could get a low-ranking VC to break just by
telling him who it was that was holding him prisoner. Other times,
we might question a prisoner over a day or so, and then bring in
the dog.

It wasn't that we let one of our scout dogs attack a VC prisoner—we didn't have to. The average Vietnamese saw a dog only
as a noisy guard and maybe something for the pot. Big German
shepherd scout dogs like we had just weren't seen in Southeast Asia.
And we had one dog, Rinnie, that just loved to tear the clothes off
a prisoner. Never attacked the guy, just tore his clothes off. Just
seeing a big, snarling dog being aimed at him was enough to make
the average Vietnamese babble like a tape recorder set on the wrong
speed. But you could never tell what would break a prisoner; that
was where the art came in.

In 1969, while I was in the hospital back in the States, one of
the SEAL platoons captured a very high ranking VC Infrastructure
leader, and this prisoner was a woman. I believe it was Fast Eddie
Leasure who ended up taking her prisoner, and she was a real hell-
cat. Apparently, during the capture, this woman tore Fast Eddie up

some, ripped his web gear right off him. He ended up winning some kind of medal for the action; it may have been just for managing to hang on to this woman and not just kill her out of hand.

But this VC broad was really tough, much tougher than even the average high-ranking VCI member. Fast Eddie and the guys really wrung her out, but she just wouldn't talk. The SEALs doing the questioning were far from gentle with a prisoner, but they wouldn't torture a person either, regardless of what some people might believe today. The guys didn't manhandle the woman or rape her or any of that shit you hear today, usually from fake SEALs who were never in the action in the first place.

Before turning the prisoner over to the higher-up intelligence people, Fast Eddie had an idea; he had the guys tie the woman up against the wall of the little hooch where they were questioning her. After securing her to the wall, they took off her clothes—and that was all it took. "Give me my clothes back," she said, "and I'll tell you what you want to know." For all of her hardness, the woman was modest.

And I learned that there were some people who just would not be broken—at least not by us amateur interrogators. When I captured a Red Chinese general in Cambodia, we had to keep the old general and his younger aide secured well apart from each other. Separation helps prevent the prisoners from cooking up a story between them and it keeps them from supporting one another mentally. The young aide broke very soon, after just some questioning. But the old general wasn't ever going to break if he could possibly help it. A Marine lieutenant and I worked on that old man for seventy-two hours, and he never gave even the slightest indication that he would answer our questions.

One of the things I learned while at Escape and Evasion School at the Marine base at Pickle Meadows, California, was that anyone could be broken by a professional who had all the time he needed and who knew exactly what he was doing. Different things would break different people. For some, it's isolation; you keep them separated from anyone else and just let the mind work on itself. For others, like the VCI woman, it's modesty, or humiliation, or pain.

For myself, I don't think I would last very long under a professional interrogator; I don't like pain. But that Red Chinese general was, I think, one of the rare ones who would die before you could break them.

The interrogation techniques we did use in the Teams in Vietnam were all basically psychological. We sure as hell didn't have the time, training, or mind-set for the physical kind of shit you are always seeing in the movies. Mostly what we did was question the prisoners, normally through an interpreter, and we would do our best to scare the truth out of them.

I was on a parakeet operation during my third tour when we were after a prisoner whom I had high hopes for. The target was a VC province security chief and I wanted this guy big time. On this parakeet, Little John Porter was with me as a Stoner man, as well as six of Father Hoa's people and the agent. The agent knew where the target was and could identify him, so he was acting as our point man in the aircraft. John almost always went with me on this kind of op when we were working with indigenous troops. With his Stoner, which he loved dearly, John would act as the main firepower for the team. He really was a bodyguard for his chief, an idea I wasn't able to argue with.

We came down on the target like a dropping bomb, bailing out of the chopper when it pulled up just a few feet above the ground. As soon as we were out, the slick lifted. That bird was our ride home and we didn't want to leave it exposed on the ground.

The gunships were circling overhead like two pairs of hunting hawks over a nervous rabbit patch. I had Sweetheart, my customized pistol-grip 12-gage, at the ready as John, the agent, and I ran up near the front door of the target hooch. Father Hoa's men had made quick work of waxing the security chief's three bodyguards staying in another hooch.

The security chief ran up to the door of his hooch to see what all the commotion was about. As soon as we saw him, we snatched him up and secured him. Using the radio I was carrying, I called in our pickup bird for the ride home.

Wham, bam, we're outa here, a classic parakeet op. Within minutes of arriving at the target site, we had our man and were on our way back home. That's what I liked about parakeets: no long walk in the mud and an early beer call.

Fūks, who was our interpreter, and I were sitting in the door of the helicopter with the prisoner between us. I don't think the man had ever been flying before, let alone flying without even a door between him and a real long drop. His eyes were so big they looked like just one huge eyeball in the center of his forehead.

It was very obvious that this Jap—a term that the SEALs picked up from their UDT forebears—did not like flying. I was going to use that fact to my advantage. I was much bigger than our prisoner and, with Fūks's help, we had made certain he knew that the green faces had his little ass. I grabbed the prisoner's neck and pushed his head between his knees so he was looking straight down to the ground. With his hands tied behind his back, the man was absolutely helpless. He knew I could throw him out of the chopper in a heartbeat.

We had known that the prisoner was security chief before the op even started. Besides knowing most of the people in all of the province's VC cells, security types also knew about work assignments, operational data, and which areas needed special security and when—areas like POW camps. POW camp rescue operations were so important to the U.S. military that they had already established a procedure to follow in case we developed intelligence on one. The operations were to be code-named Bright Light.

We knew that there were four prison camps in our AO but didn't know which would be active at any one time. The VC ran the POWs through the camps on a very random basis, and which camps were active was high-security information. There just weren't enough assets available to hit all the camps simultaneously. We needed to know which camp would be active and when it would have American POWs in it. And I had my hands on the man who could tell me.

Holding this man bent over, looking out the open door, gave him the chance to look straight down through two thousand feet of eternity. Far below us, he could see the jungle floor rushing past.

Now I personally have never known of a SEAL actually throwing a prisoner out of a helo. After all, if you did, how could you ever question him again? But we did cultivate some of the stories that were told of us inside the VC camps, and teaching a prisoner to fly was one of these.

Fūks was working closely with me and was the best interpreter we had ever had. He would translate exactly what I said with the proper emphasis and feeling. There was no question in the prisoner's mind what his position was and what I wanted.

"You son of a bitch," I growled, "you are airborne," and I pushed his head out even further. All the time I kept a rock-solid grip on the prisoner's neck. "Fūks, you tell him now, if he doesn't say where that prison camp is, he's gonna meet Buddha in about ten heartbeats."

Translating what I had said into Vietnamese, Fūks had the prisoner convinced he was about to learn to fly without wings. It took only a couple of pushes out the door, with me holding the prisoner's neck and shaking him like a terrier with a rat, before he broke. Sobbing and screeching, the VC said he would tell us whatever we wanted to know, but only when the helicopter was back on the ground!

Smart gook, I thought when Fūks relayed what he had said. I told Fūks to tell the prisoner, "Yeah, okay, but you better remember one thing: This son of a bitch can go back up as quickly as it went down!" So back we went to Hy Yen.

After we had landed, I told the pilot to hang around for a few minutes. I shouldn't have even bothered; we sat right there in the chopper and interrogated our prisoner. He talked like a physicked woodpecker. The prisoner answered all our questions and more. He even told us he would lead us into the POW camp, though that would mean another helicopter ride, something he was less than keen on.

It was already two o'clock in the afternoon and, to my knowledge, no one had gone out on a Bright Light operation yet, but I put together an operation by the next morning. This prisoner told us which camp would have the prisoners in it and how many of them there were. According to him, we could expect about twenty-five to thirty VN (Vietnamese) prisoners and, possibly, three Americans!

The Bright Light op that I put together never did get out any of the prisoners that we hoped for. In fact, the lead helicopter, which I was riding in, was shot down and the whole operation scrubbed just before the insertion was to take place. But the idea of taking a POW camp and possibly rescuing American prisoners was always worth almost any risk we had to take. And the whole operation started by my breaking that security chief prisoner by hanging him out of the helicopter. I wasn't about to drop a prisoner—that kind of murder would be pretty hard to live with for the rest of your life—but there were always stories about somewhere that a prisoner had been tossed out of a bird, and the VC heard the rumors just like we did.

There were people who could interrogate a prisoner much better than we could in the Teams. And because of the chain of command and the way we worked, we usually ended up turning over our higher-ranking prisoners to these people. After all, they could wring the intel out of the prisoners, and we wanted the intel for our operations. But we didn't have to like those people.

There was an NVA POW whom I turned over to one of these organizations, and it was not a Navy outfit. I made a lot of Brownie points for turning in the prisoner, and you had to play that political game sometimes over there. At the time I was working as an adviser with part of the Phoenix Program, but I still wished I had been able to give the prisoner to my own people back in the platoon. Besides not liking how some of the intelligence types operated in Vietnam, I knew that the intel from the prisoners often didn't come back to the platoons so that we could operate on it.

But the information that might have come from that NVA prisoner would have had a taint on it that would be hard to live with. We were never tried for war crimes in Vietnam—only the "losers" get tried—but some of the things that did happen during that war were criminal. There were so many stories about shit going on, and so many of them were obviously fake to those of us in the know, that it was easy for the few real stories to get lost in the shuffle. I witnessed what was being done to that NVA prisoner only for a few minutes, but if I had been that man, I would have been talking so much they would have a hard time shutting me up.

Of course, Vietnam was a different kind of war, and we weren't really fighting for our own country. We were helping another people defend their country. And what those people did on occasion was not how we operated back in the States. You can't use the same yardstick we did in World War II against the Germans to measure what was right for the South Vietnamese people to do in defense of their homeland against the Communists.

Father Hoa's interrogations were among the roughest things I ever saw. And sometimes you had to see them. If you got an invitation to one of Father Hoa's interrogations, that was a mark of real respect and honor from him, and you had damn well better go. I think it was also a chance for Father Hoa to see if his American allies would measure up to his way of thinking and if they had the stomach to do what was needed to get the job done.

Most of what I saw during Father Hoa's interrogations isn't something I can describe very easily. The only part I can really talk about is the first one I went to. Father Hoa had only indigenous people working for him, the normal Southeast Asian types who didn't even normally wear shoes, just sandals mostly. During this one interrogation, one of Father Hoa's people came over to me and pointed at my heavy jungle boots.

The man motioned to me to take my boots off. I couldn't see what the man wanted, but I wasn't going to insult him, so I took my boots off. What the man wanted wasn't some kind of Oriental ritual about removing your footwear inside a particular place. No, what the man did was slip my big boots over his own feet so that he could kick the prisoner better without hurting his own toes.

There were other tricks Father Hoa's people would use in wringing out a prisoner who they thought knew something important. This could mean the survival of Father Hoa's whole village, so there weren't any rules or Geneva Conventions to these people. A field phone uses a magneto that can put out a real jolt of electricity. And these interrogators knew how to hook a person up to this apparatus without causing much permanent damage.

A short time ago, I was asked to be an adviser for the TV program *Thunder in Paradise*. During one of the shows where the action was taking place in Vietnam, the main character was supposed to be a SEAL who was being tortured by the North Vietnamese. When they hooked the man up to the fake electrical wires, I told the staff to put his feet in a tub of water. When they asked me why, I said it would make a better connection for the electricity to go through his legs. The studio people and actors just did what I suggested, and they never did ask how I'd come to learn something like that.

But the people I saw using such techniques in Vietnam were not any of our people. And by "our people," I mean any Americans at all, not just SEALs. The people who were working for Father Hoa were all ex-NVA or ex-VC. These operators were doing their thing to their old comrades under Uncle Ho. The techniques I saw them using had been learned from the NVA and other Communists. Father Hoa's people were now turning these same techniques against their teachers.

Father Hoa's operators could be absolutely amazing. The best point man I ever followed was one of Father Hoa's people, an ex-NVA company commander. And Father Hoa's intel network was incredible, better by far than anything the Americans ever had operating in Vietnam. As far as unconventional warfare went, Father Hoa knew more than the American Joint Chiefs of Staff, or the Special Forces, or even the SEALs ever thought of knowing. And he built up all of this himself, learning a lot more than the priesthood ever taught him.

Father Hoa must have been highly respected by the governments of both South Vietnam and the United States for some time, even before the war in Vietnam heated up after 1965. One indicator of this regard was shown in a test done in Vietnam in 1962.

In December 1961, a request was approved by the secretary of defense for the purchase of a thousand AR-15 rifles, ammunition, and spares for testing in Southeast Asia. The testing agency was the

Research and Development Field Unit of the Advanced Research Projects Agency. The rifles were to be sent to selected Vietnamese units that were seeing a lot of combat at the time. The test would let our government see how the AR-15 operated against the Viet Cong in a combat environment without risking any of our own troops.

Out of the eight ARVN units to receive the AR-15s—and these units included VN Rangers, VN Marines, and VN Special Forces and Airborne units—ten of the AR-15s and ten thousand rounds of ammunition were sent to Father Hoa and his people. That was years before the U.S. military was able to get its hands on any AR-15s, and within a month or two of even the SEALs' getting the new weapon (and we went out and bought ours).

That story did surprise me a little when I first heard it, but it is a proven fact. The first few stories I heard about Father Hoa and his people I just shrugged off as embellishments from some intel types. But after working with the man, nothing would really surprise me about Father Hoa.

The fact is that I've learned more about Father Hoa and the scope of his operations in the last five years than I learned in six months of operating with the man on almost a daily basis. One thing that I was very glad to hear recently was that Father Hoa got out of South Vietnam when the government collapsed in 1975. Somewhere in Europe, I hope there is an Oriental by that name, who should be in his eighties by now, still kicking around. Orientals can live a very long time and Father Hoa is one man I'd give just about anything to hear from again someday. To this day I hold a world of respect for that Chinese Catholic priest and what he accomplished. I would just like to be able to shake his hand and tell him that I'm glad that he got out of there.

Father Hoa thought very highly of the green faces, and we respected him. He could probably still teach the SEALs something about fighting an unconventional war. He sure as hell taught me a lot.

CHAPTER 22

Twilight Cruise

E VERY CAREER NAVY MAN ends up finally taking his last assign- ment, his twilight cruise, as we called it. For me, the Teams changed quite a bit after my third tour in Vietnam. With the ending of the SEALs' commitment to action platoons in Vietnam, the Teams moved from an active war footing to more of a training orientation. The second decade of the SEALs in the 1970s was going to be a lot different from their first ten years in the 1960s.

With the training aspect increasing, and the possibility of action getting very small, the makeup of the Teams changed. The action-oriented operators, like myself and Bob Gallagher, seemed to have less of a place in the new Teams. Emphasis now was going to guys who had more in the way of education rather than hands-on experi- ence. The trouble was, I had seen that a lack of real-world experi- ence couldn't be made up by any amount of formal education.

Back when we were first starting to operate in Vietnam, increas- ing our firepower and support was the way to go. During the first half of 1967, the Teams still were looking at body counts as a way of measuring the SEALs' effectiveness in combat. Bob was always looking for ways to increase the firepower at the direct command of the SEAL platoons. When we couldn't carry a bigger gun, Bob looked at making a bigger gun available for our direct support. This was part of the idea that had him work on mounting an M40A1 106mm recoilless rifle on the overhead of the Mike boat.

When we first operated with the Mike boat in Vietnam, Bob became involved with the modifications to the boat that were sug- gested by our experience in combat. When the Mike boat, a modi- fied 56-foot Mark 6 landing craft, first began operating in Vietnam in 1966, the troop well was partially covered with a soft cloth sun-shade. Bob wanted to put a hard deck over the troop well to allow a helicopter to land if a medevac was needed, as well as to protect the men on board from a mortar attack.

The hard overhead cover would detonate a mortar round on impact, preventing most of the explosion and fragmentation from getting into the well deck where the crew and any SEALs on board would be. With the hard deck installed, there would be also room to put a heavy weapon, but the deck wouldn't be strong enough to accept any heavy recoil. Bob thought that a big recoilless rifle would do the job, since it didn't have any recoil and the back blast would be able to go out over the side because there weren't any walls around the overhead topside.

Bob scrounged up a standard tripod-mounted 106mm recoilless rifle, and he and the boat support people just secured the weapon topside by lashing it down to the deck. While Bob was setting up the weapon, some Navy commander from the base there at My Tho came down to where everybody was working on the Mike boat to see what was going on. This officer went up to Bob and told him that he couldn't put a weapon as big as the 106 on the Mike boat, that the weapon would tear the boat up when it was fired.

Bob looked at the commander and asked him if he was wonder-ing about the back blast from the 106. "No," the commander an-swered, "that deck can never absorb the recoil from a weapon that big when you fire it."

"Sir," Bob asked, "don't you know what the word 'recoilless' means? If you were man enough to hold this, you could fire it from your shoulder."

To me, that was just another example of how an education can result in an educated idiot. I've seen more and more often in my life that the majority of people who have very high level educations don't have enough common sense and street learning to pour piss from a boot even if the directions are written on the heel. If all you ever learned was "the book," when something comes up that's new, you don't know how to handle it.

And this didn't happen just in the Teams. Back before I was

even in UDT, when I was on board the USS *Gwin* and striking for quartermaster, we had an incident that shows my point. The *Gwin* was halfway across the Atlantic Ocean when the lookout reported a buoy in sight. In the middle of the Atlantic, there's nothing to anchor a buoy to, let alone mark with one. The ship's navigation officer called out, "You better look again. There's no buoys out here; there's none shown on the chart."

Just because something wasn't on the chart, it couldn't be there? All it turned out to be was a buoy that had broken loose from somewhere and drifted out to sea. But because it wasn't on his sheet of paper, that officer insisted the lookout must be wrong.

It's known by most people around me that I'm down on officers in general. Most of the time, my feelings are due to the officer in question confusing real life with book learning. It seems that there are some people who just lose their common sense when they get an education. Either that, or it slips away when they receive that piece of paper that declares them "an officer and a gentleman."

When I came back from my third tour in Vietnam, it was the fall of 1970. With my experience in the field, it was natural for me to be put in the slot of training chief for the Training Platoon. Though Vietnam was winding down, Tenth Platoon was still going to be deployed. Tenth Platoon left for Vietnam in December 1970, relieving Seventh Platoon at Vi Thanh, and was the last direct-action platoon from SEAL Team Two to be sent to Southeast Asia.

Since I had arrived back from Vietnam several weeks before Sixth Platoon returned, I was a chief without a platoon or a specific job to do. Lieutenant Commander Bill Salisbury was the XO at Team Two at the time and he just said, "All right, that's it, you're Training Platoon chief," and the assignment was mine. Bob Gallagher and I had switched being Training Platoon chief between us for a number of years, and Bob was deployed in Vietnam when I got back off my third tour. The slot was a good one and I took my job at the Training Platoon seriously.

Bob and I had set up a number of training sites during the early days, such as Camp Pickett and the SEAL base at Camp A. P. Hill. I was very familiar with what had to be done and how to do it, so operating as the Training Platoon chief wasn't a hard job to slip into. Like so many times before, I was fortunate to have a good cadre of petty officers working underneath me, and I could mostly spend my afternoons in the chiefs' club. The work was taken care of and, unless we were out in the field at Picket or A. P. Hill, training ran smoothly without my having to be there.

A new warrant officer arrived in Team Two, fresh in from the west coast, and, as with so many new officers, the Team didn't know what to do with him right away. As things worked out, he was assigned as the new training officer and I was working directly beneath him. The new warrant officer had come to Team Two with a good combat record as a real hunter over at Team One. He had a number of tours in Vietnam and the Silver Star among his decorations, so it was obvious that he had been doing something right over on the west coast. The thing was, I had noticed over the years that if an officer and an enlisted man did exactly the same thing, the officer would get the Silver Star where the enlisted man would normally get the Bronze Star. This wasn't anything special to the Teams; decorations according to rank were a time-honored tradition in the Navy.

Things should have been all right, this man being a hunter and all, but there was something else in his background that caused more than a little friction between the two of us. The new guy was a devoutly religious man, always carrying a Bible around with him, not exactly the kind of guy you would expect to find in the SEAL Teams. Right away he didn't like my attitude, my drinking, or my mouth.

Sometimes, when we trained out at Union Camp, we would bring our older kids, and sometimes even our wives, out to take part in the training. It would add to the realism of a problem when you had to train nonmilitary people in a particular skill or guerrilla activity. It was my having my eldest boy, Jim, out at camp during one of our exercises that caused the biggest problem between myself and the new training officer.

We were sitting around the campfire one night, just drinking a few beers and telling some stories. The kids who were with us wanted to know what it was like in Vietnam and we all were telling what we could. My son was sitting at the fireside, listening just like the other boys, while some good stories were being shared. The warrant officer pulled me aside and let me know that he thought it was wrong for me to let my son hear some of the salty stories that were going around. At the time, I think Jim was about fourteen or maybe a little younger.

I told that man that how I raised my family was my business. How he wanted to raise his own kids was his own concern, but I was raising my boy in the real world. That didn't sit very well, but there was nothing he could do, so I just went back to the fireside.

Not long after this, evaluation time came up and recommendations for promotion to E-8 needed to be turned in to the Navy. As my present platoon leader, the training officer was responsible for my evaluation and recommendation. What he did was write up a recommendation that I be promoted to E-8, and then turn around and write up the accompanying evaluation 180 degrees the other way. Where all of the numbers said that I was ready to be promoted and would be an asset to the Navy as a senior chief, his written comments said something very different.

In the write-up, he spoke of my combat experience and how he could tell from reading my record that I was a hell of a fighter, a hell of a SEAL, and that I had the awards and decorations to prove it. Then he went on to say that I wouldn't fit in the peacetime Teams or even the peacetime Navy!

These statements were more than a little contradictory with each other. I came right out and asked him what the hell he was trying to do. You had to read and sign your own evaluations before they could become part of your official record, and there was no way I was going to sign this thing. Then I went on to accuse him of not having any balls himself.

"What do you mean?" he asked.

"If you're not going to recommend me for E-8," I answered, "at least have the balls to come right out and say it. Don't just hide it here in the comments and try to slip it through. If you don't want me to make the rank, just don't recommend me. Don't be an asshole and recommend me, and then cut me down on the same sheet."

The officer went on to explain what he thought. "I've seen your record," he said, "and I've heard everybody talk about you. You're a hunter and a fighter and all of that. But you are just not going to fit in with the peacetime Teams. Your drinking and this—"

That was where I cut him off. "Whoa, padre," I said, "the one has nothing to do with the other. If I drink or not while I'm on my own time does not matter at all. It has never affected my military performance. You show me where, at any time, I have been negligent in my duties—whether it's reports, training schedules, or anything else."

And he couldn't do it. I might be a hell-raiser, but I have always put the Team first. A long time ago, I learned the Frogman Rule: If you can't party and get the work done the next day, you don't party.

It was about three or four o'clock in the afternoon when all of this went down. "All right," I said, "I'm going to the skipper [the XO]."

"You can't go to the XO without my permission," he blurted out.

"Well," I said, "I'm going. If you want to be there, you better be hot on my ass."

Without much more argument, I was on my way to the XO's office. The warrant officer went in with me and had a chance to tell his side of the story. Of course, I said my part about what was going on first. The XO just looked at what the training officer had written and told him that he had better rewrite his comments before he went home that night. Later that year, I did make senior chief.

What that man had done was a real mistake in the Teams: He let his personal feelings interfere with his military job. I had known a lot of other men in the Teams who had been very strong in their own personal convictions as to how to act or raise a family, but they never allowed their own beliefs to affect how they did their job. Gene Tinnin and Dave Hyde were two men whom I never saw take a drink, and they were both God-fearing men who took their religion seriously. There were not many men like that in the Teams, but there was a certain percentage of them in the SEALs and the UDTs.

Gene Tinnin was a hunter who knew he was a SEAL and what that meant. Gene had volunteered for the job and did everything that was asked of him to the very best of his ability. And a better family man, or a more religious man, you would have a very hard time finding, when he was away from the Team. I cannot remember even have seen Gene Tinnin take a drink, or even swear, while at the Team. But when it came time to go out into the field, you were hard pressed to come up with even as good a man, let alone a better one. I was proud to be able to call Gene my friend, and was very fond of him, his family, and even his fat basset hound, Chigger.

Though Gene and Dave Hyde didn't drink, neither of them ever missed a party. Gene always had a Coke, Pepsi, or lemonade in his hand and was the designated driver for the rest of us who imbibed more than a little. Dave was the same way, and neither of them would even think of looking down at the rest of us, who led a considerably different life. "You live how you want to live, and I'll do the same" was the unwritten law of the Teams. At least that rule held true while you were also the kind of man who would stay to get the job done, no matter what.

Though my training officer was wrong in what he had done, he was right in one small part of what he had said. The peacetime Teams were going to be something different from wartime, and maybe there wasn't going to be as comfortable a place in them for men like me as I might like. New leaders were coming along who didn't know what it was like to get shot at. With the new officer's career track in Special Warfare, you had a new breed of officer who was going to be able to stay in the Teams for more than a two-year tour and still make rank.

There were still many good young officers coming into the ranks of the SEALs who would keep the legend alive. And the earlier officers who had made their bones in Vietnam were becoming high-ranking, influential men who were able to shape the new Teams

into something really impressive. But there was still that small percentage of officers who passed training and ignored experience.
"You do what I tell you because I'm an officer" was the rule that
these men followed. They didn't care what you knew or how you
learned it. They just cared about what was on your sleeve or shoulder. I wasn't ready for that kind of Team.

By 1971, I was real close to having my twenty years in the Navy.
I had never pulled a shore duty assignment and thought that maybe
it was now time to put in for one. Bob Gallagher and I had talked
about this sort of thing before we left for Vietnam for the last time.
We were both healing up in the hospital from our latest adventures
when we decided that there wasn't anything more we had to prove,
to ourselves or anyone else. We had put our time in and had the
scars to prove it. So, of course, we both went over for one more try
at combat, just to be sure that we weren't planning on quitting for
other reasons.

With my last tour in Vietnam, I had proved to myself that the
aggressive spirit that I'd had so long hadn't left me when I was
wounded. It was time for me to go on my twilight cruise, and I put
in my papers to leave the Teams.

In order to spend a little time near my old home, I put in for
recruiting duty in New Jersey. In part, what I planned was to prepare myself for civilian life. I knew that going directly from the
Teams into the civilian world would be a real bitch. I figured that
recruiting duty would give me a chance to work with civilians a
lot and change more gradually from a SEAL and Navy life into a
civilian one.

When I received the assignment, I next had to report to Bainbridge, Maryland, for a five- or six-week course of PN1 School,
basically learning how to fill out the recruiting papers without
allowing for even one mistake. Going up to the gate at Bainbridge,
I had to park my car and wait just a moment outside the main gate.

Bainbridge was where I had first taken training as a E-nothing
recruit back in 1955, right after first enlisting in the Navy. The gate
at Bainbridge hadn't changed in the eighteen years that I had been
gone. Up on the sign, the only thing that had been dropped was the

basic Recruit Training School. Standing at that gate, I thought to myself how, when I had left there a short lifetime ago, I never would have believed I would go back through that gate someday as a senior petty officer.

Returning to the car, the first place I went on base was the chiefs' club. There I felt immediately at home, or at least I did for a while. Standing around the bar, I swapped stories with some of the other chiefs, most of whom immediately noticed the Trident on my uniform. There have never been many SEALs in the Navy, and back then we were fairly rare.

But things had changed, as I quickly learned. Speaking up from the far end of the chiefs' club bar, a woman's voice said, "Watch your mouth down there, there's women here."

Looking at the end of the bar, I saw another group of chief petty officers, and two of them happened to be women. "I don't see any women here," I said in my usual sensitive manner. "All I see are chief petty officers in the United States Navy. If you can't stand hot grease, get the hell out of the kitchen. Chiefs are going to be chiefs and sailors are going to be sailors."

They just sat there with their mouths open. The women's movement was just starting to build up some speed back then and the Navy was one of the targets. But I was never one for politics and I just put those ladies in their place. They didn't want equality; they just wanted to change us to their way of acting. I hadn't stood for any political crap in the Teams, and I sure as hell was not going to go along with it now.

After graduating from training, I reported to the main recruiting station in New York City to check in. Even though my station was going to be in New Jersey, the main regional office was in New York. At the time I reported, I was still an E-7 and hadn't gotten the word that I had made E-8 yet. I caused a bit of a stir at the main office. There was a chief of the command who was in the personnel office reviewing my records. Since I had a chest full of ribbons at the time, along with my Trident, these guys wanted to see if all of that color on my chest really belonged to me.

It turned out there was a small problem with my records. When they turned to the page in my file that showed my decorations, I was informed that I was missing two ribbons. "Well," I commented, "sometimes you just can't keep up with them all."

That was when I was told that I would be going to Perth Amboy, New Jersey, and operating out of the recruiting office there. I had asked for Asbury Park, but there was an Airdale (aircraft carrier) chief working out of the office there and I didn't want to try to boot anybody out of his slot just for me.

I was told the man in charge of the Perth Amboy office hadn't shipped a minority enlistment from his area since he had arrived there. This was strange, since Perth Amboy was a major population center for blacks and Puerto Ricans. What I was told to do was go down and try to straighten the place out.

The next day, I put on my blues and walked into the recruiting office in Perth Amboy. The office was located in the post office building and I caused a stir as soon as I walked into the place. The Airdale chief who was there saw me in uniform and was just astonished. "You came here in uniform?" he asked.

"Yeah," I answered, more than a little puzzled. "I'm proud of my uniform."

Then the man went on to show me the locker in the office where he kept his uniform. What he would do was come into the office in civilian clothes and change into his uniform for the day's work. All he would do was stay in the office all day and wait for people to walk in. He never went out in uniform, never visited the local schools and gave talks, never even just went out into the street.

This recruiter was absolutely cowed by what he considered the public's feelings toward the military at the time. It was true that in the early 1970s, it wasn't like the end of World War II; Vietnam hadn't been a popular war with many of the young people who had to fight in it. But that was no reason to hide, especially when your job was to get people to enlist in the military in the first place.

After I asked the chief where the local hangout for the young people was, he told me and I just left the building. My briefing up in New York had included the orders to basically just boot that chief out of there, but I didn't feel the situation warranted such strong action on my part. What I did instead was just go down to the local pool hall in my uniform, pick up a stick, and start shooting some pool.

Walking down the main street, I turned to the bad side of town, where the pool halls and bars were heaviest, picked the dingiest one I could see, and went in. The place was full of the minorities that I had been told to concentrate on recruiting. I have always been a pretty good stickman, so I just ordered a beer, picked up a stick, and asked, "Can any of you guys here play pool?"

Most of the guys in the hall looked at me like I was crazy. Here I was, a white man, in uniform, in their part of town, and I wasn't acting afraid. What they did was take me up on my challenge to play pool, and I beat their asses. It wasn't two weeks later that I was putting minorities in the Navy. And that Airdale chief had left for other duties.

Much of what I had done as a recruiter I learned from Bob Gallagher as a PRU adviser in Vietnam. You can't just put yourself in a bottle and pull the cork in behind you. The Air Force does that a lot in the countries where it has bases, as I saw in Turkey, and keeping yourself separate doesn't do anything to develop trust among the local people. If you are going to work in a neighborhood, or any area, you have to mix with the people.

All in all, my tour as a recruiter turned out to be a good one, and I think some of those young men I helped get started on a Navy career have left the service only recently. Not everything in my life was going well at the time though. My wife, Big Red, had lost our son on delivery. The boy lived only a few moments after he was born. In addition to that, Big Red's mom was pretty sick and there were other family problems, so I ended up getting a transfer for humanitarian reasons to a communications station down in the Carolinas.

I was within a year of retiring and the slot was supposed to be an easy one where I just had a place to report in every day. When I showed up, an E-8 senior chief with all of my decorations, Trident, and general attitude, the CO knew exactly where to assign me. I became the master-at-arms for the base. There was some trouble at the time with some minority sailors. The Navy was cutting out any kind of segregation at all, and some of the younger men were walking all over their senior petty officers. That didn't last very long after I took over as master-at-arms. I had the authority to close off the base just by telling the civilian guards not to let anybody out of the gate. My powers were wide and I used them to good effect.

The base didn't have but maybe fifty sailors on it and the officer in charge was just a mustang lieutenant. But as far as that man was concerned, I was the answer to his prayers. Between what was on my chest, the fact that everyone there knew what the Trident meant, and just my size, I didn't have much trouble with those young sailors. It wasn't very long before that base was someplace I would be glad to receive an admiral, or even Rudy Boesch, without any problems at all.

That lieutenant and I got along just fine. It took me only about sixty days to change that little radio command around entirely. In fact, the lieutenant and I represented the command at the Navy Birthday Ball that year. The lieutenant was really surprised that I had a dinner dress uniform, but I had bought that back when I represented SEAL Team Two at Master Chief of the Navy Delbert Black's retirement.

Big Red accompanied me to the ball, just as she had come with me to Black's retirement. The Navy Birthday Ball wasn't quite as much fun for Big Red as Black's retirement had been up in Washington at the Pentagon. At the retirement party, some senior Navy officer's wife came up to Red and asked if she was my wife. "No, I'm just his date," Red answered.

Then the woman went on to ask how could I have so many medals on my chest. Since her husband was a captain stationed at the Pentagon and I was only a chief, all of my medals couldn't be real, could they?

Big Red had a good time with her answer, and she wasn't shy about using four-letter words when it suited her. "Yeah, they're real," she answered. "He doesn't sit behind a fucking desk."

Those were some good times my last year in the Navy. But all good times end, and it finally came time for me to retire for real.

I went up to the Navy operational base (NOB) in Norfolk about six weeks before I left the service. While I was being processed at the base, I was made a tug dispatcher to give me an assignment. The day I actually retired was a more than busy one.

My daughter Samantha had been born on August 20, 1974, and I was scheduled to retire on the twenty-eighth. Both Red and I were really concerned about the birth, especially after losing Joe, but the Navy came through and looked after Big Red like she was the last mother on earth.

What I wanted to do was tie in Sam's baptism with my retirement, which was scheduled for eight o'clock in the morning. I wanted to go straight from the retirement ceremonies to the chapel for Sam's baptism. From there, I would be going to the chiefs' club, which had been locked in for an afternoon with my teammates.

The only trouble was that I couldn't find one chaplain who was available on a Friday. It was ridiculous. The situation was a real mess, and to say that I was pissed when I walked into the chiefs' club at NOB Norfolk that afternoon would be an understatement. One of my fellow chiefs was in the club and saw what must have been a real expression on my face. "Hey, Jim," he said, "you should be smiling. You only have a week to go."

I told my friend about what was going on and why I was so pissed: I couldn't get a chaplain to work the next Friday. "You just come with me to my office," he said. "I have some calls to make."

Chiefs have a network of contacts throughout the Navy and most of the world. After my friend called an admiral he knew up in the Pentagon, some wheels started turning very fast. This admiral was in charge of all of the chaplains in the Navy. Before I left the club, chaplains were practically lined up to offer their services at the baptism.

At the retirement ceremony itself, things were actually pretty hard for me. Bob Gormly was the skipper of Team Two at the time. Rick Marcinko was the listed skipper, but my old friend Rick hadn't been able to report on board yet. Gormly had Rudy Boesch bring the whole of SEAL Team Two to my retirement ceremony. As a retiring enlisted man, I rated eight sideboys to line my walkway as

I left the Navy for the last time. Actually, my sideboys were a few more than eight people. In fact, it was most of SEAL Team Two that lined up for my departure.

There was a Navy commander there at the same time who was also retiring. He actually ended up asking if he could borrow a few sideboys for his own ceremony. I told him that I was only a retiring senior chief and that he would have to ask Master Chief Rudy Boesch about using some of our men. The poor confused commander did end up with his sideboys, but not quite as many as the twenty-five men I had on either side of the walkway as I left the Navy. As a bosun's mate, Rudy himself piped me off the deck, and that walk was one of the harder things that I have done in my life. That was it, my last day in the active Navy.

The party that afternoon in the chiefs' club was a memorable one. Big Red had told me to use my separation pay for my retirement party. And even though we divorced only a few years later, I will always respect her for that.

During the party, I gave Bill Goines my chief's hat. Bill was still a first class at the time, but there wasn't much question that he would be the next plankowner from Team Two to make chief. "Bill," I said when I gave him my hat, "you know how much I love you. You make sure to put another star alongside mine before you get out." Another star would mean Bill retired as an E-9, master chief.

The party went on all afternoon and well into the evening. Then it moved down to my place in North Carolina for the next few days. That retirement party was something I will never forget, and I have Big Red to thank in no small part for that. Bob Gormly and Rudy Boesch saw to it my retirement ceremony itself was also something I would never forget, and I haven't. The only regret I have is that part of me didn't leave the SEALs that day. I get around the young lions today and the adrenaline still gets pumping. Once you join the brotherhood of the Teams, you can never really leave completely.

Chief's Note

I would like to thank everyone who helped make my first book, *Point Man,* the success it was. Without the support of my wonderful wife, Linda, all my former teammates, and the SEALs of today, this second book might have never happened.

Many letters and phone calls have come to me as a result of *Point Man,* and I was amazed at the number of young men who wished for information and advice on how to become SEALs themselves. To all of the young people of our country, whether future SEALs or not, the very best advice I or anyone else can give is to stay in school and get a good education. The youths of today are the leaders of this great country tomorrow. Many of us who have gone before you have sacrificed greatly so that you could be free to make your own choices; make your choice a wise one and don't let our efforts go to waste.

I can be contacted via the UDT-SEAL Museum at 3300 North A1A, North Hutchinson Island, Fort Pierce, Florida 34949; phone number: (561) 595-5845. All are welcome to become members of the UDT-SEAL Museum Association to help protect and preserve the history written by the many men of the Underwater Demolition Teams and the SEALs.

God bless you, and thank you one and all.

—James D. Watson, QMCS, USN (Ret.)
Curator Emeritus
UDT-SEAL Museum

UDT-SEAL
MUSEUM

Located on the Site in Fort Pierce, Florida, Where the Navy Frogmen Originated

The UDT-SEAL Museum presents the story of U.S. Navy special warfare from the early days of Naval Combat Demolition Units and Scouts & Raiders to Underwater Demolition Teams—better known as frogmen—and today's SEALs. Outdoor and indoor exhibits illustrate the unique history of the men who fought in World War II, and those who followed them in Korea and Vietnam and, more recently, in Desert Storm, Panama, and Somalia.

The museum is operated by the UDT-SEAL Museum Association. For information about becoming a member of the association and helping preserve the weapons, equipment, artifacts, vehicles, and valor of the country's most secretive fighting men, write to the association in care of the museum, or call (561) 595-1570, or fax (561) 595-1576.

UDT-SEAL Museum
3300 North A1A
North Hutchinson Island
Fort Pierce, Florida 34949
(561) 462-3597